THE GREAT

American

ATTRACTION

THE GREAT
American
ATTRACTION

TWO BRITS DISCOVER THE
ROLLICKING WORLD
OF AMERICAN FESTIVALS

RICH SMITH

THREE RIVERS PRESS
NEW YORK

All rights reserved.
Published in the United States by Three Rivers Press,
an imprint of the Crown Publishing Group,
a division of Random House, Inc., New York.
www.crownpublishing.com

Three Rivers Press and the Tugboat design are registered
trademarks of Random House, Inc.

Library of Congress Cataloging-in-Publication Data

Smith, Rich.
    The great American attraction : two Brits discover the rollicking world
of American festivals / Rich Smith.—1st. ed.
        p. cm.
    1. Festivals—United States.   2. Festivals—United States—Humor.
3. Travel—Humor.   4. National characteristics, American—Humor.
5. Smith, Rich, 1981–   I. Title.
    GT4803.S55 2008
    394.26973—dc22   2008008847

ISBN 978-0-307-39545-0

Printed in the United States of America

DESIGN BY BARBARA STURMAN

10 9 8 7 6 5 4 3 2 1

First Edition

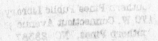

For Montgomery Brown,
my beloved hamster,
who oversaw the writing of this book

THE GREAT

American

ATTRACTION

Introduction

As I fell, following an attack by a Native American who had just leapt from his horse and pummeled me into the ground before sending a spear into my stomach, I knew that this latest trip to the States was to be far from the standard sightseeing tour experienced by other tourists. At least I had my candy. With this safely stored away, I was sure that I could keep my trousers on and leave the battlefield in one piece.

Perhaps I should explain, and inform you of my past experiences with America and why on earth I was lying in a field in central Montana after having been killed for the second time in two days.

In 2005 my accomplice Luke Bateman and I traveled 14,000 miles across America in an attempt to break obscure and outlandish laws. A frivolous crime spree, if you will. It was a thoroughly pleasurable experience, and ever since our arrival back in the U.K., I was yearning for any excuse to return.

The crime spree was a different type of road trip. In theory, although it was I who ultimately decided which direction we took, the location of the laws dictated where we would end up, who we would meet, and the very path our cross-country venture would follow. And I liked that. I enjoy small-town America, its people and history and peculiarities, and I like visiting communities in which the presence of a couple of Englishmen is something of interest.

In January of 2007, I happened to stumble across a video clip on a very well known video-sharing website documenting an event in Georgia known as the Redneck Games: hundreds of people in dungarees, yelling and screaming while jumping in pits of mud . . . it was enough to get my undivided attention. From then on, I scoured every festival and events guide on the Internet with a calendar, a map, and reams of scrap paper, and I began to make a note of my favorites.

With the crime spree, jotting a path was simple since I could turn up on any day of the week and break the law. However, actually doing so was far more difficult because, although I wanted to stay out for an entire year, I couldn't afford to. Festivals that were held outside of my budgeted two-month summer were out of the question (including, sadly, a bizarre-sounding fete called Mike the Headless Chicken Days). Also, most were staged over weekends and certain events over-lapped (the Mission Mountain Testicle Festival in Montana being one of the many casualties). Plus, although a rented car needed to be used at all times, reaching the far-flung locations would demand several domestic flights.

The only festival I decided to attend outside of the summer months was the World's Largest Machine Gun Shoot, in Louisville, Kentucky, which was to be held in April. It was an event that I had heard was simply a convention for gun enthusiasts and several Nazi sympathizers, and I realized that we simply could not miss it. Bateman and I decided to spend a few days there before returning to the U.K. and await the beginning of our major excursion in June.

A week before we were due to leave, Bateman sent me a text message. It simply read: "Don't think I can go." He had broken his ankle after agreeing to play rugby at the end of a heavy night's drinking. So I began a two-month campaign to have my flight money refunded due to his injury. A month later, Bateman pulled the plug on his entire involvement with the project, citing the fact that he wanted to spend the summer "getting a proper job." Isn't "professional sidekick" counted as a job these days?

Not wanting to travel alone, I enlisted the help of another friend, twenty-two-year-old Antony, who naturally jumped at the chance of embarking on a free two-month holiday. He was a perfect choice. He was funny, light-hearted, and, at that point, was the best kind of student at the University of Gloucestershire at Cheltenham University: one who had already failed (twice) and was simply enjoying the life of a couch surfer too much to return home to Cornwall.

Mercifully, there were no more surprises. Antony was about to embark on his first trip to America and I had finally been granted what I had wished for two years ago: my chance to return.

1. COWBOYS
AND INDIANS

*Dressed as a metrosexual gunslinger and a
heavily armed ticket collector, Antony and I join
Rick and Rod before battle at the reenactment
of Custer's Last Stand.*

have always found entering America to be a bizarre and oddly difficult experience. In 2005 I visited Niagara Falls, spent half an hour on the Canadian side of the river, and then spent an hour in a queue in order to return to the United States. Fifty cents and a quick flash of your passport will allow you safe passage into the U.S.'s northern neighbor; but an iris scan, fingerprinting, and a rigmarole of questions (including "Have you eaten anything while in Canada?") was required by Uncle Sam. Still, I was luckier than the woman and her baby I saw taken to an office adjacent to me and subjected to half an hour of shouting by an immigration officer. Goodness knows what she must have eaten.

It's because of past experiences like Niagara that the thought of entering the U.S. fills me with dread. And worst of all, the United States of America's entry procedure begins when you're 30,000 feet above sea level.

To enter, as long as you are a citizen of one of the twenty-seven eligible nations, you are expected to complete what is known as Form I-94W, Nonimmigrant Visa Waiver Arrival/Departure Form. This form, completed to the satisfaction of the terribly rude and sociopathic passport control officer, will allow you to spend ninety days in the Land of Opportunity. Along with your name, address, and nationality, the form's tenth section requests you to list the address at which you are staying—pretty impossible if you plan to trek from coast to coast in an impromptu style. It isn't even that easy to fabricate an American address, either: house numbering stateside can be anything from 1 to 50,000.

Still, the fun and desultory questioning doesn't begin until you realize there is more awaiting you on the form's reverse. This is where I really get perplexed.

"Do any of the following apply to you?" it begins, and then it lists a series of statements to which you simply tick the box marked "Yes" or "No."

Do I have a communicable disease or am I a drug addict? Nope. Mind you, how do British rock bands manage to sly their way past that one for world tours and America gigs?

Am I a criminal or have I spent five years in prison? No.

Have I ever been deported from the U.S. or previously removed from the United States? No.

Have I ever detained, retained, or withheld custody of a child from a U.S. citizen granted custody of the child? Well, let's have a think about that one. There was that time I withheld custody of a child back home, and that other time after a night out in Prague—neither of those instances involved a U.S. citizen, though, so that's a "No."

The form also includes the mother of all statements—one to which I'm sure the "Yes" box has never been ticked by anyone who has completed the form since its introduction in 1986. This one is so good I copied it onto my mobile phone word for word.

"C. Have you ever been or are you now involved in espionage or sabotage; or in terrorist activities; or in genocide; or between 1933 and 1945 were involved, in any way, in persecutions associated with Nazi Germany or its allies?"

Who in their right mind would even contemplate gracing ink to the "Yes" box? Even Rudolf Hess, who was still alive when the form was first completed, would have simply ridden his luck and hope he wasn't recognized.

The form then warns you that if you have answered "Yes" to any of the statements, you should contact the American Embassy before traveling to the United States since you may be refused admission. Of course, by now the plane is making its final descent into Newark International Airport, and it's just a little late to ask the pilot to turn around so you can convince the ambassador in London's Grosvenor Square that you have already served your time for crimes against humanity following the Nuremburg Trials.

Anyway, having been born in 1981 and been denied my chance of meeting anyone even loosely affiliated with Nazism by Bateman and his broken ankle, I made my way to passport control ready to face whatever impudent and graceless officer Newark airport had chosen to place on the day's rota.

"Hey, number fourteen, NOW!" he shouted. Antony and I shuffled ourselves toward his allotted booth before he really lost his temper.

"Been here before?" he asked sternly. I gathered he meant the U.S. and not booth 14.

"I have; Antony hasn't," I replied simply. The iris and finger scans followed, and he examined our passports meticulously, every so often looking back up at us in a way which suggested we had each replaced our official photo with a candid image of the two of us in bed with his wife.

Having finally passed security, Antony and I were free to leave the airport and catch a shuttle bus into New York City to begin our American adventure. Unfortunately, our first port of call was 2,000 miles west in the vast plains of Montana. The Manhattan skyline that appeared to glisten and shine below the cumbersome and dated wing of our plane as she descended onto American soil was to be as misleading as our collection of luggage at the carousel. While our fellow passengers departed through the terminal's automatic doors to hail a cab or collect a rented car, we made our way to the check-in desks and produced our documents once again in order to board a six-hour flight to Salt Lake City.

Ever since I first arrived there with Bateman in 2005, I've liked Salt Lake City. Sure, the Mormons may have ruined it slightly by deciding that all beer sold in the state should have an alcohol content of less than 3.2 percent. And yes, the Great Salt Lake smells of sulphur and is home to billions of flies that cling to the shoreline and move in massive swathes like the rippling effect of water whenever anything comes near. But, generally, Utah's largest city and capital is a pleasant place to be. The city stands at the foot of the spectacularly beautiful Wasatch Range, many of which are snow capped even when the thermometers have pushed the mercury past 100 (which happens often in the summer). Its downtown area is well laid out and unobtrusive—eight-lane inner-city roads mean that traffic jams are seldom seen.

Still, there was no time to hang around and survey the city's many architectural delights such as the Salt Lake Temple and the ultramodern public library, nor was there enough respite for a quick bathe in our motel's outdoor pool. Today was Tuesday and because flights there were expensive, we were left with an eight-hour drive through three states to Hardin, Montana. We were due at a dress rehearsal in two days' time. It would be the beginning of mine and Antony's acting careers.

The state of Montana has the nickname of Big Sky Country, which I'm sure has as much to do with the region's beautiful blue atmosphere as it does with the fact that there isn't anything of great interest on the ground. When you take into account that the state—the fourth largest in the Union—is three times the size of England but home to just a fiftieth of the population, it's little wonder why Montana appears to be totally deserted. Thankfully, the town of Hardin seemed open for business, and so Antony and I made our way to the chamber of commerce, where we were to learn more about the town's weekend extravaganza, Big Horn Days, and to see if we could become active cast members for the highlight of the weekend, the Custer's Last Stand Reenactment.

The Hardin chamber of commerce is situated in the town's old train depot and, although there were many displays and purchasable goods pertaining to the Battle of Little Bighorn in the front room, Antony and I headed straight for the back office to talk to the three elderly ladies who operated the chamber's business.

"Hello. Is it possible to speak to Dorothy or Betty?" I asked, thinking it was best to speak to one of the ladies with whom I had exchanged e-mails about the reenactment.

"I'm Betty and she's Dorothy," replied the lady closest to me. "How can I help you?"

"Um, we've exchanged e-mails . . ."

"Oh, yes," she replied, proving she was either very good at putting a name to a face, or that she didn't receive e-mails from the U.K. too often.

"Still possible for us to take part in the reenactment, is it?" I asked rather timidly. A look of worry shrouded Betty's face as she rose from her seat to fetch a large book from the shelf behind her desk.

In her e-mails, Betty had assured me that the show was always in need of fort soldiers, and that if we brought a navy jacket and a pair of navy trousers with a yellow stripe down the seam, we would be more than welcome to take part. I had both—albeit with some masking tape acting as the yellow stripe.

"Let's see. You could be a pioneer," suggested Betty as she

ran her finger down one of the book's pages. Antony and I quickly exchanged looks of disappointment.

Imagine, if you will, the situation in which I had found myself. I had driven from my home in Cornwall, England, to Gatwick Airport, flown to New York, waited three hours for a connection, caught another flight to Salt Lake City, and driven 600 miles to a small town in the middle of nowhere, just so an elderly woman could tell me that I could be a pioneer! Someone who dresses like a character from *Little House on the Prairie*, whose only action throughout the entire production was to simply walk from one side of the battlefield to the other! I realized I was going to have to be just a tad more insistent.

"Any chance we could be fort soldiers? You said that they are always needed. We've brought the navy jacket and trousers you asked for. I would have brought the gun, too, but they didn't sell them at the army surplus store where I bought the clothes, and I doubt I would have managed to smuggle it through customs anyway."

Betty looked up and slid her glasses from the tip up to the bridge of her nose. "Pioneer?"

Thankfully, Betty eventually submitted to our request and Antony and I were despatched with application forms, which we could complete in the town's main street on one of the tables on the sidewalk. At this point I turned to my new traveling partner and explained why I love "small-town America."

"Ant, isn't this wonderful? We are in a place with a population of just over three thousand; there is nothing but fields once you leave the town limit, and the closest settlement of any reasonable size is almost fifty miles away. We must be the only British people in the entire county."

It was a serious point on which to ponder, and made us both consider our role in the weekend's reenactment with

gravity. This, however, quickly diminished when we sat ourselves down with a cold drink to fill in the application, and
realized that the only other occupied table consisted of four
people, including an Englishman and his Scottish friend. We
were also dismayed to learn that without an American Social
Security number and no work visa, there was no way we
would be paid the $70 for our amateur dramatics.

After returning the forms (which had more disclaimers
and places to sign than my mortgage agreement) to Betty at
the chamber, and deflecting another of Betty's attempts to
encourage us to be pioneers, we decided that we would treat
ourselves and each purchase a kepi (a style of hat similar to
those worn by the French gendarmes) to complete our make-
shift, nineteenth-century regimental outfits.

Due to the popularity of Big Horn Days, Hardin's three
motels were booked solid for the three-day event. Antony
and I had found a room in Billings, Montana's largest city,
which was conveniently located just fifty miles west of Hardin along I-90. It was from here that Antony and I experienced our first decent night's sleep since leaving the U.K.

The next day, Antony and I found ourselves in Hardin a
couple of hours before the dress rehearsal was scheduled to
begin, and so we decided that it was a sensible idea to visit
the local museum to see if we could garner any more information about the battle. Before now, all I knew was that the
official name of the conflict was the Battle of Little Bighorn,
Custer's first name was George, it was probably the most famous Indian victory, and that Custer's men not only suffered
a humiliating defeat but were totally annihilated. I was pretty
sure that this common knowledge wouldn't mean much to our
fellow reenactors who presumably had years of background
on this, and would frown upon any faux pas made by two
bungling Englishmen who had attended the festivities sim-

ply for a holiday jolly. You'll be impressed with what we managed to discover in such a short amount of time.

What first struck me about the museum was the panoramic picture of the town taken in 1921 that adorned one of the building's walls. By simply exchanging the cars for their modern counterparts, the photo could easily pass as a picture taken now. Next, we learned that the museum's toilet is really nice—one of the most aesthetically pleasing places in which I have ever had the fortune to excrete. Similar to a bathroom you'd find in your grandmother's house, the room had the added bonuses of a moose head and Indian artifacts that you could study while business was being taken care of downstairs. Antony and I entered the museum hoping to learn more about the Battle of Little Bighorn and left the museum safe in the knowledge that the town hasn't changed greatly in the past eighty years, the toilet was lovely, and there has been a lack of facial hair on every single one of Hardin's previous twenty-four mayors (despite Montana's apparent dress code of denim dungarees, checkered shirt with oily baseball cap, and some sort of overgrown beard). That should impress the lads on the battlefield.

The site of the reenactment is five miles to the west of Hardin and fifteen miles directly northwest of where the actual battle took place, just outside the rather ridiculously named town of Crow Agency. A large, dated, and shabby-looking sign with the words CUSTER REENACTMENT SITE directed us from the main road onto a dirt track where traveling anything above ten miles an hour emitted huge clouds of dust from the rear tires of the car, shrouding anything behind us in a visually impenetrable plume of dirt, which seemed to take forever to settle. After 500 yards, the track reached the brow of a hill, the road became much firmer, giving way to grass, and the higher ground revealed something I was certainly not expecting. There, in the middle of a flat plain, among the rolling hills of Montana's Big Horn County, standing proudly before an assortment of corrals and camper vans, like some modern-day refugee camp, stood a grandstand large enough to accommodate thousands of people. I had expected people who had paid $16 to see the show to simply sit on a bank or jostle for position in an attempt to get a good view of the battlefield. But here were huge bleachers that stood perfectly positioned in front of the "stage" complete with fifty flags: one to represent each state in the union.

Once parked, Antony and I looked around for anyone who looked like they knew what two aspiring reenactors from England should be doing. Luckily, by the steps leading to the commentary box beneath the flag of Idaho, we found Dave Riley, the show's director, and Barbara Fickle, the Re-enactment Committee chairperson. (Before you start thinking that I have a brilliant and slightly disturbing knowledge of the state flags that allows me to identify Idaho's flag at a glance, I should point out that the state in question's ensign has the words *State of Idaho* emblazoned on it . . . twice).

"Excuse me, but we're fort soldiers," I said proudly. "Just wondering if you knew what we should be doing."

After informing us that we were still an hour early for the rehearsal, Dave introduced himself and Barbara, and talked us through our very complicated duties during each one of the weekend's four shows.

"Basically, you come out of the fort and die," remarked Dave bluntly, before Barbara added the killer line: "And you just lie there until the show ends and the national anthem is played."

Antony and I looked at each other, wiping sweat from our foreheads, imagining how hot life would be lying "dead" in the middle of a field in Montana's searing heat for the duration of the show. Antony then asked what both of us were thinking: "How long do we have to stay there for? The entire show?"

"Oh, no," Barbara replied. "You only come out of the fort at the very end for the final battle. You'll only be on the ground for about five or ten minutes."

So mine and Antony's basic duties as fort soldiers were to stand in the hot fort for almost an hour, hidden away from the audience, before falling to the hot ground and staying there for a bit.

Simple.

Dave made his way into the commentary box at this point, but Barbara stuck around long enough to give us her number one tip for reenactment debutants: "Bring bags of candy with you."

"Pardon?" I asked, not because *candy* is the silly American word for *sweets*, but because the advice just sounded so peculiar. "What do we need candy for?"

"For the Indian kids. When you die, they run across the field and try and get whatever they can from you. If you don't have candy, you could be in a bit of trouble. One guy lost his pants one year!"

"We are in the right place, aren't we?" asked Antony. "We haven't stepped into some sort of sordid, outdoor orgy, have we?"

With a lot of organizing to be getting on with, Barbara directed us to the best place in which to purchase candy before making her apologies and leaving us to assemble the tables where the reenactors would sit for lunch following the rehearsal. At one-thirty, an announcement thundered out of the site's public address system to inform us that the rehearsal was just fifteen minutes away, and if the actors weren't already in costume, now was the time to change and meet your respective stage manager. It wasn't difficult for us to locate our correct supervisor—since we were fort soldiers, we figured we should walk in the direction of the fort, a wooden structure made from thin tree trunks bound together, approximately 20 feet in height, with a 200-foot perimeter and two gigantic plywood gates.

The inside was pretty basic: a seating area, which appeared to have been constructed by me (or someone else of equally terrible construction abilities), a portaloo, and a large wooden desk, on which we were promised two water tanks would be placed for tomorrow's opening show. Other than that, the fort—which was only three-sided to allow the cavalry to easily take a break and drink when their presence was not required on the battlefield—was pretty spacious, probably because only a few soldiers had bothered to attend the rehearsal.

In all there were just five of us, and the first thing Antony and I noticed was that their perfectly itemized and historically accurate outfits put our half-assed efforts to shame. Our inept attempt at clothing ourselves didn't seem to bother our stage manager, Pat, however, who clipped his walkie-talkie onto the waistline of his trousers and came over to greet us.

"You two fort soldiers then?" he inquired.

"Apparently so," I replied, attempting to make a subtle apology for our attire. "What do you want us to do?"

"Well, Bob needs two people to open the gates . . ."

"We can do that," I answered quickly, sensing an instant promotion from fort soldiers to the more important-sounding "fort soldier/gate operative," or perhaps "defenders of the gate," maybe even "threshold protectorates." Yes, the title of *threshold protectorates* would fit Antony and me quite nicely.

Bob Port was a rather burly fellow who appeared to be in his early forties, with a gray biker-style mustache (where the hair continued down each side of his mouth) and a friendly and youthful face. He explained how to open the gates—a difficult procedure that involved removing the rope from around the handles and then pulling sharply toward the inside of the fort—before changing the conversation to something far more British. "Oh, man. I love your Britcoms. My wife and I watch them all the time." We assumed Bob would begin to list some of Britain's most recent finest . . . but we were to be disappointed.

"We love *'Allo 'Allo!*; *Waiting for God* and . . . what's that one where the guy lives off the land?"

"The Good Life!" I snapped in complete and utter shock.

"They're about twenty years old!" added Antony. "What about *Only Fools and Horses* and *The Office*?" Bob seemed puzzled.

"We like *Fawlty Towers* too," he added.

All was forgiven.

By now, the rehearsal was well under way, and because Antony and I had nothing to do besides open a gate and die, we remained talking to Bob until a voice from above our heads spoke to us. Looking down from a rickety-looking platform was a man whose outfit was exquisite. He was a rather dapper-looking fellow with what was starting to become the prerequisite reenactor mustache (this time of a thick, drooping handlebar and chin puff–style design). According to his business card—which he dropped from his 10-foot vantage point to land between a clump of long grass and a dead rabbit—his name was Rod Beattie and he was portraying the role of First Sergeant James Butler, the Last Man Standing at Custer's Last Stand.

"Those World War Two RAF jackets?" he asked.

"Um . . . yeah," I replied, not actually knowing what they were. "I think so anyway."

As it transpired, when he managed to navigate his way

down the ladder (two rungs were broken and not to be stepped on), Rod told us that he was an avid collector of military paraphernalia. He stood before us and studied our outfits, in the same way a headmaster would look disapprovingly at a pupil who had been made to stand outside his office. And he was right to do so, really. I was wearing Nike sneakers (circa 2005, not 1885), navy trousers that I had been given when I worked for a British tourist caravan park, and the navy jacket, which may have looked good on the previous owner but the sleeves of which came down to only a few inches above my wrist. Unfortunately, there wasn't much time for any formal introduction as our first command was issued by Pat.

"Open the doors!" he bellowed, as Custer's cavalry lined up in preparation for some sort of charge. A minute or so later the same call was made, and Antony and I welcomed both the cavalry who we had released just a minute before, and the "rescued" pioneers' wagons into the fort. As the dust settled and the horses made their way to the back of the enclosure, Rod shook our hands and made an incredibly friendly offer.

"If you want, I can kit you boys out properly," he suggested. "Just come to my camp."

"Which one's yours?" Antony replied.

"It's that one over there," he said, pointing in the general direction of five or six caravans and camper vehicles. "It has four flags, a tented area between the van and my outdoor kitchen, there's a giant buzzard on the sign—"

I interjected quickly. "We're not really gonna miss it are we, Rod?"

"No, I guess not."

The next act of the reenactment was the meeting of the peace treaty council. Here, representatives of both the Indians and the United States Army draft out and sign a deal in the very center of the battlefield before each faction returns to their respective camp. The treaty, in the show's timeframe at least, lasts about ten minutes before the two opposing sides exchange signatures and handshakes for spears and hand-to-hand combat in the show's finale.

"Wanna go down as part of the treaty party, you two?" asked Pat. You didn't have to ask us twice.

"Yeah, sure. We can handle that. What do we have to do?"

"Just stand there."

"Brilliant."

Out of the fort and into the direct sunlight and intolerable heat, military promotions with which we were being entrusted were arriving with increasing regularity. We began as badly dressed extras; now we were badly dressed "treaty party members/threshold protectorates." At this rate, one of us would be asked to play the role of Custer by Saturday.

Sadly, on a blisteringly hot day, the job of the U.S. treaty party was not an incredibly glamorous one. Antony, Pat, a few pioneers, and I stood in a straight line directly facing the actors portraying Red Cloud and Gen. Philip Sheridan, who led the negotiations for their respective sides. In the center of the battlefield, on the only bit of raised land, stood a small table. Beside it, a tribal translator gestured the words of the Indian leader while the actual speech was read out by a narrator in the commentary box for the audience. In reply, Sheridan would also move his hands as if explaining, and a different, clearer announcer would voice his words. The whole interaction is pretty effective and very well orchestrated, but for me, the best part of the scene was our retreating march back to the fort and the return to my shady position by the gate.

The final battle itself was more or less a nonstarter. The main aim of the rehearsal was to check that people would know where to be, and that both the sound system and narrators were in fine tune. Because it wasn't an official show, the cavalry units for both sides were nowhere near full strength, so Antony and I simply ran out of the fort when instructed and fell to the ground when everybody else did. As we made our way back to the fort and then in the direction of our free lunch, Bob and Rod assured us that the real show's battle would be a completely different experience altogether and that we should prepare ourselves for a "proper attack." But no worries; we were going to be fine—Barbara had told us where the best sweet shop was and I was planning on buying enough to feed the entire tribe.

After a standard but incredibly satisfying lunch of sloppy joes, some cookies, and a side of potato salad, Antony and I began talking to our new friends some more about their role as reenactors. It turned out that both Rod and Bob were a couple of Custer's Last Stand veterans—2007 saw Rod's ninth year at the reenactment and Bob's fourth. Rod lives 80 miles from Hardin and uses his annual holiday from work to make his yearly appearance at the show. Both loved taking part, and their involvement was something that obviously meant a lot.

I think it was because of our resonant voices that our English accents grabbed the attentions of a fellow reenactor—the only one without whom the show couldn't continue. Gen. George Armstrong Custer—or Mr. Rick Williams when not at events like this one—was an amateur reenactor who had begun his career in civil war reenactments in 1999, and because of his obvious resemblance to Custer, had found himself playing the role for the past four years. Like us, this year's show was his first in Hardin and his explanation as to why he decided to come all the way from his home in Ohio to take part sounded like an actor describing being asked to be in a film alongside his childhood hero.

"I've been doing this for a few years now, and you don't turn down an offer like this."

The meeting with Rick didn't last long—he was quickly whisked away to take part in interviews with newspapers, and to meet and greet fellow riders. Nevertheless, Rod invited him to his camp whenever he was available. Rod also asked Antony and I to join him for some postrehearsal refreshments.

Rod had described his camp perfectly. There was indeed a stuffed buzzard that sat atop a homemade wooden sign with the words *Camp Wishah-Kudah-WunWun* on the top plank, and COMPANY L MESS, 1ST SERGEANT JAMES BUTLER, and ORDERLY SERGEANT written beneath.

"Wishah-Kudah-WunWun?" I asked as Rod sat down to loosen his boots.

"Yeah," he chuckled. "I wish I coulda' won one." We looked blank. "It's just a joke."

As Rod stepped into his camper van to look for clothes that would befit two fort soldiers better than our sad ensembles, we were introduced to Rod's wife, June. She appeared to be in her fifties, with long brown hair that reached her lower back. Oddly, she looked more natural in her nineteenth-century pioneer outfit than her everyday attire.

"Here it is," shouted Rod as the door of his camper swung open, "my toy box."

A wooden crate was placed on the ground, and the cover, removed. It was like no toy box I had ever seen. In the place of colored building blocks and miniature cars were knives, holsters, belts, and bullet shells, which Rod had amassed over his years as a military enthusiast. And boy, he takes enthusiasm to a whole new level. At the age of fifty-four, he has a full-time job as an electrical supervisor, he and June run a secondhand collectibles and historical memorabilia store, and he is the founder and curator of a memorial museum. With the inclusion of his saddle (which he used before he retired as a member of the reenactment's cavalry), his complete outfit was worth over $3,000.

As Rod rummaged around for things he felt we required to make our costumes more fort soldier–y, he told us about his own military background. After serving for only seven years in the United States Army, Rod had risen to the rank of sergeant and his résumé read like G.I. Joe's. He was a paratrooper, a qualified armorer and survival expert, a jumpmaster, a gunner on the *Redeye Air Defense Missile*; had served within the divisions of the infantry, armory, and air cavalry units; and was a fully trained commando.

I know all this because Rod loves to talk. Mention any conflict, and Rod has a fact about it, or an anecdote, or, if you're really lucky, a detailed account of the combatants and the weapons used. It may sound boring, but listening to the human military encyclopedia was an absolute joy. He was a brilliant storyteller; children would hang on his every word.

In the two hours we spent at the camp, we learned about the battle of Rorke's Drift and that the Zulus never did commend the Brit's gallant defense of the outpost like the 1964 film starring Michael Caine would have you believe. We also discovered that Rod's father was a friend of Ernest Hemingway, and that one of the camp's flags—a star in the center of a white rectangle on a red background—meant that Rod and June had a son overseas in the U.S. military. Thankfully, the star was blue and not golden. Gold would have meant that his son had been killed while serving in Afghanistan.

At five o'clock, Antony and I decided we had outstayed our welcome and it was time we should be leaving. Rod and June didn't agree.

"We've been known to feed everyone on this site," shouted

June as she pottered away in the kitchen. "You're welcome back anytime."

"We have to get some candy anyway, Rod," we replied. "Better go now before the shop closes."

We made our good-byes and were again instructed to visit Fort Custer General Store, where we could not only buy some sweets but also buy the correct insignia for our $5 kepis.

Fort Custer General Store was like no other shop I had ever entered before and was a strange mix of souvenirs, tacky play items, and food essentials. To make the experience a little stranger, a small boy was following us around the store and hid behind the end of each aisle, staring at us unflinchingly.

At the checkout, we found the correct insignia for our hats and decided to buy some sweets from the large and plentiful supply. Forty or so different types were available ranging from the usual sours and liquorice to candies based on soft drinks like root beer and Dr Pepper.

"Don't get the root beer ones, mate—it just tastes like the stuff you get at the dentist," I warned Antony.

The sweets were served to us by Christian, the child who had been hiding from us. We opted for a selection of differing sweets, so the Indian children would definitely find something they liked and would hopefully allow us to keep both our trousers and our dignity.

"Why don't you ask them?" said the woman behind the counter to Christian after he had whispered something into her ear. "He wants to know where you're from," she asked us.

"England," we replied.

"He thought you were from Australia."

"Australia!" we exclaimed. By the way he looked at us we thought he may have believed us to have been from another planet.

We left the shop, and strangely enough, so did Christian,

picking up a motorized scooter from the shop next door to the store.

"I got this for my birthday," he explained.

"Um . . . that's nice," replied Antony. "You like it?"

"Yep."

"Right."

"Bit lazy, don't you think? You don't even have to use your feet," I added.

"Yep."

As Christian shot off back in the direction of the store, Antony and I made our escape by crossing the road and returning to our car. As we did, we could see Christian in the distance—by this time he had turned his scooter around, eager to get a last glimpse of the "aliens" and their "spaceship."

The following day, Antony and I arrived at Rodney's camp complete with two toy cap guns we had bought earlier in the day from Toys "R" Us in Billings, figuring Rod could supply us with small holsters for them. I approached him to ask if his "toy box" contained such helpful items, but asking a man like Rod for a holster for your pathetic toy gun is like joining a group of Hell's Angels and arriving for your initiation on a moped. Instead of making fun of our weaponry, Rod looked up at us and said something we definitely were not expecting.

"Who's the best arm wrestler?" he asked. Believing he was about to clear his camp table and get June to officiate, embarrassing me in front of Bob and Rick, who were only a few feet away and already in costume, I decided I would allow Antony to take up Rod's challenge.

Antony, however, was already pointing in my direction. "He is."

I geared up for my first-ever international arm wrestle.

But instead of clearing a space for the battle, Rod headed into his camper van and came out holding some sort of rifle.

"Rich, have you ever seen an 1866 Sharps Carbine Conversion?" he asked.

"I think we both know the answer to that, Rodney," I replied, thinking he was either referring to the rifle or constructing his sentences by selecting words from the dictionary entirely at random.

"It's quite heavy, so I figured the stronger of you guys should have it," said Rod. He handed me the rifle and a shoulder strap to which it was attached.

As well as the lending of the rifle, Rod had laid out entirely new outfits for Antony and I, and we were asked to enter Rod's camper van so we could change into our new apparel.

I shall now attempt to explain what we were wearing and use the appropriate names, followed by a standard explanation for those of you whose knowledge of historical military uniforms is not in the same league as Rod's. Accompanying my original sneakers and navy trousers were a model 1866 Conversion Sharps Carbine (a big rifle), a model 1855 Carbine sling (a belt to which the rifle was attached), a prairie belt (a belt in which rifle shells were kept), a kepi/forage with cavalry sabers and regimental number (my hat with correct insignia), and a bowie knife (a Crocodile Dundee "That's not a knife, *that's a knife*" kind of knife). Plus, Rod had provided me with a thick white shirt and a navy waist jacket. This made me glad I had the rifle. Without it, my costume made me look as if I were more likely to ask for your train ticket than defend a fort.

Antony's outfit had more of a Wild West feel to it and consisted of a model 1858 Remington Percussion Revolver (a gun), a model 1860 flap holster (a holster), a buckskin jacket with fringe (a coat with frilly bits on the pockets), a campaign hat (similar to a cowboy hat), and another bowie knife (Croc-odile Dundee special). Antony was also given a pair of boots that rounded off his outfit perfectly. Unfortunately, no such boots were available in my size.

As the five of us made our way to the fort for the begin-ning of the show, Bob explained that the director had decided to change the show's ending so the battle took place directly in front of the audience instead of several hundred yards away on the hillside. Also, the show's committee had managed to persuade a descendant of one of the real battle's Indian chiefs to open the show and speak on behalf of his people.

To be honest, when the Indian chief's descendant picked up the microphone and began to speak to the two-thousand-strong crowd, I wasn't sure if he was speaking English or some sort of a Native American dialect. To Antony and I, it sounded more like the drunken ramblings of a man at closing time.

And then we found out that, unfortunately, these were not the only changes that had been made.

Blasting out of the stand's speakers was a song I had never heard before, though it was originally released in 1984. Lee Greenwood's "God Bless the USA" is a bona fide song of patriotism, aimed at evoking the raw emotions of every proud American and kindling their passion in the virtues of the flag. And, in my opinion, it is complete and utter tripe. And it's not because it makes everyone who is in its audible proximity stand still from jingoism (as if the rules on musical statues had been reversed). It's the song's laughable lyrics. If you wish to find out how truly terrible the song indeed is, please make sure you obtain the single by some sort of illegal means—I wouldn't be able to sleep at night if I knew I was responsible for adding a single penny to one of Mr. Green-wood's royalty checks. It was with great dismay that Antony and I realized we were to be subjected to the song at least three more times as we were signed up for four shows.

Following the ear-wrenching "music," Bob released a fearsome shot from a cannon that stood outside the fort's gates—shocking the audience and scaring the hell out of Antony and me, not expecting it since it hadn't been used in rehearsal. After that, the show followed the same pattern as the rehearsal, except that Antony and I had been relieved of our treaty-party responsibilities. All the fort soldiers who hadn't bothered to turn up for the previous day's practice run were now present, and with Bob's wife, Jill, now alongside Rod in the lookout post, the fort was at full strength.

Soon the time came for the attack. Rod helped me load my rifle and then handed Antony five more blanks to store in his six-barrel revolver. In each show, the fort soldiers have two chances to use their firearms: once when Custer makes his initial charge to save the pioneers, and then during the final battle. As we opened the gates to allow Custer's cavalry unit through, I dropped to one knee and fired off a shot. Antony's gun simply clicked after he'd managed to find his revolver's only empty chamber.

When the cavalry returned, and the treaty scene had finished, Custer and his men made their way to the nearby hillside from where the final attack is launched. Pat informed us we had a matter of minutes until we, too, had to descend onto the field of battle, and Bob loaded his revolver and talked us through what he thought we should know.

"You ready?" he asked. "Be careful out there."

"I've got some candy. It's all good, Bob," I replied rather smugly.

"I'm not talking about the kids, I'm talking about the rattlesnakes."

"The what!?" Antony and I both replied in horror.

"Just remember they can strike a distance equal to a third of its length," added Rod.

"Thanks," I replied sarcastically. "But I'll be too busy running from them to worry about getting a ruler out to make sure I'm a safe distance away."

"Yeah, if these people think I'm going to be lying still whilst a snake is trying to bite me, they can piss off," added Antony.

Rod and Bob chuckled to themselves as if we were just making friendly prewar banter.

"Oh, and you'd better keep hold of that stuff. Those kids'll take anything," Rod warned.

"Get ready, people!" shouted Pat as we made our way to the side of the fort. "Custer's attacking!"

"Pat?" I asked. "What happens if no Indian actually kills me? Do I just walk around for a bit?"

"If no one kills you, you commit suicide."

Both Antony and I were nervous. In the center of the battlefield were dozens of horses who, from the blanks being fired, had created a whirling of dust and smoke. And it was into the melee of ferocious activity that we were expected to run.

"CHARGE!" bellowed Pat as he sprinted past me, falling to the ground just yards from the fort.

"I'm following you, Bob," I shouted as we darted across the plain and into the fray. After a jog of about a hundred yards, I aimed my rifle high into the sky, as I was advised, and released my one and only shot before coming to the realization that only Antony and I were the remaining soldiers who were yet to be killed. Just then, and totally unexpectedly, an Indian on horseback raised an axe above his head before wielding it toward me. He obviously missed on purpose, but I knew this was my time to "die." Having previously decided how I was going to act out my death, I slowly fell to my knees before slumping face first into the ground, making sure I landed atop Rod's rifle. Antony, however, didn't have the same luxury of choosing his own demise and was unceremoniously introduced to the soil by a dump tackle of which an NFL personality would have been proud.

When all army units had met their fate, the Indians gathered Custer's flag and returned to the center of the battlefield, where the announcers explained more of the story and the repercussions of the war. It was time for the Indian children to leave their camps and begin their pillage. All of the warnings I had been given about the ferocity and ruthlessness of the children's plunder was greatly exaggerated.

"Do you have any candy?" asked a young girl politely.

"Yes. You can have the whole bag if you want," I replied kindly, before realizing what a horrible and foolish mistake I had made.

I had two pockets on the front of my waist jacket in which I could have stored the sweets, or I could have even strapped the bags to the back of my belt or rifle strap. Instead, I was stupid enough to place them inside my right-trouser pocket— a place where it was surely morally and ethically wrong to invite a young girl's hand.

Although we had been instructed to stay perfectly still once we had been killed, I decided it was wise if I were to employ a bit of posthumous nerve twitching—the kind that loosens a bag of sweets from out of your pocket and onto the ground.

After the American national anthem was heard, all troops rose from the dead and the audience was allowed to walk onto the battlefield and converse with members of the cast. Rod was in his element, lapping up the attention—it's the part of the show you can tell he has waited a year for. Antony and I simply skulked around hoping no one would ask us anything and uncover our pitiful knowledge of everything we were wearing.

Luckily, no one wanted to speak with us, and ten minutes after the end of the performance, Ant and I made our return to Rod's camp, shortly followed by June and Bob. It was about half an hour before Rod and Rick joined the group.

"You love it don't you, Rodney?" asked Antony.

"I do indeed," he replied. "Absolutely love it."

After just one performance, it appeared as if Rick wasn't too ecstatic about his role as Custer. He had only fifteen minutes at our camp before he had to take part in newspaper and television interviews for the rest of the evening, before his appearance in Hardin's street parade the following day. Custer was a wanted man on and off the battlefield, and it seemed as if everyone wanted a piece of Rick. Rod wasn't too happy either. At the rehearsal, we were asked to remain "dead" during the national anthem, and resurrect after it had finished, and so today we had been lying down for the song's duration. Rod and many of the fellow reenactors were not in favor of such an act.

"I want to stand for the anthem," he declared. "I've had a word with Pat and he says they are going to play 'Taps' (a bugle song similar to the 'Last Call') tomorrow while we're dead, and then we rise for the anthem."

All in all, the show went very well and was ruined only by two helicopters, which passed overhead, ruining the authentic feel of nineteenth-century Montana. What was strange, however, was that in our mock battle, not a single Native American ended the performance on the ground pretending to be dead. Surely, that can't be right? I thought. To find out, Antony and I decided to witness the actual site of the battle, to discover just how accurate our reenactment was to what really took place in 1876. Rod and June told us that the battlefield was well worth a visit and were kind enough to invite us to come back to eat with them in the evening.

"The site is very good, Rich," stated Rod. "Best of all, I think it's free."

For $10, the public are allowed to explore the grounds of Little Bighorn Battlefield National Monument, and at over 750 acres, the area's vastness is overwhelming. Along the luscious and undulating hills, white marble markers signify where both soldiers and Indians fell on June 25, 1876. And they are peppered everywhere, impossible to count. Historical estimations put the battle's length at less than thirty minutes, in which time more than four hundred men lost their lives and two hundred more were wounded. On the brow of the hill where Custer and his men drew their final breaths, and where the concentration of markers is at its most dense, an obelisk commemorates the fallen soldiers. Only 500 yards away is Custer National Cemetery, home to the remains of almost five thousand people: not only the battle's 7th Cavalry unit but also the dead of more modern conflicts. Despite the cemetery's name, Gen. George Armstrong Custer's body is no longer present—it was reinterred and taken to be buried 1,500 miles west in New York.

The park's visitor center and museum contained many interesting facts about the battle as well as some rather strange exhibits, one of which contained a razor and a bar of soap once used by Custer. Other exhibits that caught my eye mentioned that many of the Indians actually used rifles in the battle (better ones than their adversaries); Custer and Crazy Horse were both aged thirty-six at the time of the Little Bighorn; and five months after their defeat, the American army won the rather interestingly named Dull Knife Fight. Before we made our way back to Hardin, I noticed a display that depicted what nations were represented in Custer's unit. Of the 793 enlisted men, 473 were born in America, 129 were Irish, and 127 were German. The remaining 64 were drawn from 14 other countries including the United Kingdom and 2 who were simply categorized as "at sea."

Back at Camp Rodney, June and her husband were busy preparing the evening's meal and we learned that the committee wasn't pleased with Antony—or, as they put it, "the idiot with the cowboy hat." The reason for this was that when Antony "died" and the Indian children had approached his "corpse" for candy, they had also asked for any shells or military souvenirs. In his best attempts to shield Rod's property from them, Antony had found himself lying on his side, gesticulating, conversing with the kids as if he were lying on a towel and chatting to friends at the beach.

In the evening, the lure of June and Rod's antelope steak seemed to be the obvious cause of the camp's increase in popularity. We were joined by most of the fort crew, including Bob, his wife, and Randy, one of the cavalry members. We all tried our best to keep Rod from dominating the conversation but his love of talking and being the center of attention was too much considering his that-reminds-me-of-another-story finger was in constant use.

For nearly half an hour, Rod attempted to explain how his pay and pension structure worked to the point where I don't think even he understood, and Antony and I started telling our favorite jokes. After an hour or so, it became apparent that Montanans use North Dakotans and Texans like the English use the Irish as their subject of ridicule, and that Randy would find a joke funny only if there was a rude or childish word in the punch line. Several hours must have passed before we decided to leave, and because Rod was such a good story-teller, no one had noticed the sun set below the rural horizon and his distinctive face become just a silhouette in front of a gas camplight.

*A*s the weather report had predicted temperatures as high as 102°, it was with great relief to realize when we arrived at Rod's camp less than an hour before the first of the day's two shows that the overcast conditions had lowered the temperature to the high 80s.

"Glad you could make it," said Rod sarcastically.

"Plenty of time, Rodney," replied Antony, as we made our way into the camper van to get changed.

Back in the fort, usual service was resumed. Lee Greenwood made everyone proud, the Indian descendant continued his nonsensical ramblings, and Bob shocked everyone with his cannon fire—quite literally scaring the shit out of Antony, who was in the portaloo at the time. Instead of helicopters ruining the historic authenticity, this time the show had to deal with a train, which took almost ten minutes for its four forbidding diesel engines to pull the eighty carriages past us. Trains are requested to stop for performances, and many in the fort were complaining. But I was busy picking bits of spiky thorns out of my leg. Because I was wearing sneakers, and not boots, they had managed to attach themselves to my sock. As I removed my shoes, Bob noticed me plucking them from my sock.

"Fuck tale?" he shouted.

"I beg your pardon, Bob?" I asked, thinking he hated them more than I did.

"Foxtails. They're called foxtails."

At some point that day, it became apparent to Antony and me that Rod wasn't the biggest fan of Pat and would ignore the stage manager when an order was shouted. I may not be a brilliant lip reader but I've watched enough football matches to know when someone is mouthing the words "Fuck off,

Pat." I later learned that Rod was asked to be the stage manager in only his second year, a job he accepted before deciding to step down because it took the fun out of the reenactment.

Minutes before the final battle, everyone was preparing themselves—except Jill, who decided she would remain in the fort. Antony, thinking about the previous day's warning from the committee and the tackle he'd received from his "killer," played things safe by quickly taking a shot and falling to the floor just yards into his battle sprint. I, on the other hand, had a much more interesting death, managing to attract the attention of a warrior who leapt from his horse and tackled me to the ground before taking a knife from his pocket and pretending to thrust it into my stomach.

The show ended, and all soldiers remained on the floor for "Taps" and rose to observe the national anthem. Before Antony and I could escape the postshow interaction with the audience, a member of the crowd and his son approached me and pointed at my rifle.

"What kind of gun is that?" he asked.

"It's a 1970 . . . no . . . 18 . . . hang on." I replied, trying to remember its name. "Rod! What's this called again?"

He was standing only a matter of feet from me, and Rod came to my rescue and informed the father and son that it was an 1866 Sharps Carbine Conversion. I must remember that, I thought.

Back at the camp, postshow conversations always began with how you died, and Rick, playing the most wanted part of Custer, always had the best stories.

"I was attacked by a young guy at first," he told us. "So as I pinned him down and pretended to punch him, his big brother spotted me and hit me with such force that I was thrown to the floor. I think I'm getting too old for this."

With a two-hour break between the end of the matinee

and the beginning of the evening shows, Rod had time to tell stories and, this time, complain about the state of journalism in the country. (I thought I'd best keep quiet about my own degree in journalism.) Rick had a copy of the local newspaper, which featured an article about the reenactment, and Rod's point was instantly proven right. Not only had the *Billings Gazette* used the word *losingest* in one of its front-page headlines, but they highlighted the reenactment's international appeal by including a quote from sixty-three-year-old John Jeffries, an Englishman who sat in the audience! All he did was sit in the stand. There wasn't even a mention for the two threshold protectorates who hailed from that fair nation, and who had already died for someone else's country twice.

In the second of the day's shows, I was invited to join the treaty party. Rod led the march, and took this role very seriously—you could tell he had once had military experience. He would shout things like "About turn!" and "About face," and because I didn't know what either of them meant, I simply did whatever everyone else did.

After the battle—in which I had to commit suicide since I couldn't find a single person to kill me—I saw some members of the audience making their way toward me. I grasped my rifle, repeating its name to myself: "1866 Sharps Carbine Conversion. 1866 Sharps Carbine Conversion."

"Hey," remarked one of two burly-looking men in baseball caps, pointing at the gun. "What do you call that?"

With an air of smugness, I pulled the gun down from my shoulder and laid it across my two open hands. Time to act! I may not have had a single line in the show, but this was my time to deliver. "This, . . ." I said with a smile on my face, ". . . is an 1866 Sharps Carbine Conversion."

"Oh yeah?" the other replied. "What caliber?"

Shit.

* * *

I was surprised that after three shows and two days, it had taken until the Saturday night for Rick, Bob, and Rod to make Antony and I try our hand at actually shooting some guns. After all, we were in Montana—a state that according to Rod and Bob had no rules (even the speed limit is just "a suggestion"). To begin with, Bob showed Antony that a blank could easily dent a can from close range. Good to know now that we were through most of the shows where we could have maimed each other. Bob then produced an 1860 Henry Rifle and an 1873 Colt Peacemaker (which I've always thought to be a stupid name for a gun), which he had used in the reenactment, and asked Antony and I to try them out.

"Where should I aim?" asked Antony.

"Just anywhere toward that hill," Bob replied.

Antony and I blasted holes in the hillside before we noticed that due to the kick of the gun most of our shots were missing the bank completely and continuing over the brow of the hill.

"What's over there?" inquired Antony as he turned to Bob with gun in hand, making him duck with fear.

"Nothing much," he replied. "Only the freeway."

Rod, not wanting to be outdone, and who by this time must have been incensed by no one listening to him, handed me the 1866 Sharps Carbine Conversion I had used in the shows and a bullet.

"Try this out," he said.

"Sure," I replied, knowing full well what little impact a blank had when shot from the rifle.

Unbeknown to me, Rod had handed me a full bore shell instead of the regular shells I had been using in the gun. Apparently, this was a trick played on new recruits when entertainment was hard to come by on western posts. The change made a lot of difference.

Holding the gun up to my shoulder and aiming at something green and unpopulated, I squeezed the trigger gently. An almighty blast produced smoke from the barrel, another shot was fired toward the freeway, and an instant pain ripped through my right shoulder. As I turned around clutching my collar, which was already beginning to bruise, and making what I'm sure was an hilariously surprised face, the rest of the camp began to laugh.

On the night-time drive back to Billings, Antony and I witnessed our first piece of road kill: a dead deer in the middle of the road. As quickly as it appeared in our headlights, it was under the wheels of our four-wheel-drive Suzuki, sending us a foot or so out of our seats. As I regained control of the car, we wondered aloud who would leave such a large animal carcass in the middle of the road with little or no warning. It wasn't until we returned to the motel that it suddenly dawned on us that with our erratic and inaccurate gunfire earlier in the evening, it may have been us who killed it.

On our arrival for the final day's reenactment, Rod and Rick stood side by side and Rod read from a piece of paper in his hand.

"Private Richard Smith. Having distinguished himself by his perseverance and dedication to his duty, while serving as a trooper in Company L, Seventh U.S. Cavalry during the 2007 reenactment of the Battle of Little Bighorn, is hereby awarded the rank of honorary corporal, and is entitled to all the privileges therein, and to expound at great length on his exploits. Given this twenty-sixth day of June 2007."

Both he and Rick shook my hand before handing me the certificate. Antony then received the same treatment.

"Wow . . . thanks, Rod," we chorused. What else *do* you say to that?

The final show was the best yet, with the exception of a car alarm resonating through some of the early parts. To be honest, as Antony and I ran into battle, you could tell that neither of us wanted it to end. By the look of things, neither did the Indians—I had to shout to a passing warrior to ask him to kill me.

Back at the camp, Antony and I handed out presents to Bob, June, and Rick. Because of his love of British sitcoms, we gave Bob and Jill something equally as British: a croquet set. To June, a glass paraffin lamp. As for Rod, a man who not only bought military clothing but made his own, we presented him with a British Bulldog belt buckle (complete with British flag reverse) we had purchased from the Fort Custer General Store. He promised to wear it—or at least make a belt that would accommodate such an item—when he returned home.

Bob and Jill decided that beating the Native Americans and the horse trailers out onto the road was the best bet and, after a parting handshake, left Antony and me with Rod and June.

"Thanks for everything, June, you've been great," I said as I extended my right hand. June ignored it and gave both Antony and me a hug.

"It's been great having you. A real pleasure," she replied.

Rod gave each of us a firm handshake, which I couldn't help change into a quick hug and pat on the back.

And why not? To Antony and I, Rod was more than our superior—he and June were perfect hosts, and had extended arms of friendship with unquestioning generosity. For the past four days, Antony and I were dressed and fed by them, and now, in the middle of a field, with the unfitting background drone of departing vehicles and horses refusing to enter their trailers, it was time to say good-bye. It was a wonderful start to our American trip, and we hoped that meeting pleasant and welcoming people would continue. It may have been a fake battle, but Bob and Rod were true compatriots, and there were no other people who we would rather have had by our side.

2. BASQUING

IN THE SUN

Herd not seen? Antony and I await the arrival of the bulls in Elko, Nevada.

We were in no particular rush to get to Salt Lake City when we left Billings, and so we decided that instead of driving to Utah using interstates, we would travel south through the northwest region of Wyoming. A major factor in this decision was that this particular route would take us through Yellowstone National Park.

The last time I was in Wyoming was with Bateman in 2005 when he was given a $220 speeding fine for traveling at 97 mph in a 75 mph zone. He later admitted that it was good the state trooper hadn't stopped him ten minutes before, when he was doing 120. Because Bateman and I simply flew home instead of paying the outrageously high fine or even appearing in court like his ticket instructed, I suspected that there was still a warrant out for his arrest. But I was confident that "accomplice to speeding" wasn't a crime and that I wasn't one of Wyoming's Most Wanted.

We entered Wyoming on a standard road that twisted and dissected its way through a surrounding mountain range in the Shoshone National Forest. The only way we could drive was upward. It wasn't until we had reached a vista point at 8,000 feet that I noticed the rental car was substantially low on fuel—we had enough to take us maybe ten more miles, and even that was being generous. Red Lodge, the last town we had driven through, was at least twenty miles behind us. I turned to Antony, who had the map in his hand, and asked how far it was until the next town.

"Um . . . ," he said, running his fingers between the map's

mileage scale and the road we were on, ". . . about eight miles, mate."

"Thank God for that," I exhaled. "Thought we were gonna have to walk for miles."

"Oh, no. Hang on," he added, "make that about thirty-eight miles. I didn't know where we were."

"Great."

For the next ten minutes, my eyes spent less time focusing on the road and more on the car's digital miles-per-gallon readout and the fuel tank display. The summit was nowhere in sight. We passed 9,000 feet and then 10,000 feet with snow by the sides of the road, the outdoor temperature plummeting from 92° to 41°.

Thankfully, at 11,700 feet, the ground transformed into a flat snow-covered plateau and the road began to descend. Instantly I put the car into neutral and coasted downhill, changing my miles per gallon readout from 26 to 99. But after several miles, the road began to level out and gears were required once again, thrusting Antony and I back into despair. Suddenly, though, as we entered a forested area, a small building came into view. The entrance sign informed us that it was a last-chance convenience store that sold food, drinks, souvenirs . . . and gas. I instantly pulled up by its 1950s-style pump and entered the shop to inquire as to how much it was.

At almost $7 a gallon, they really were cashing in on idiots like me who were in desperate need of fuel. And while most people would gasp at the prospect of paying such an absurd amount of money for a gallon of petrol, I was only too happy to part with my money. Although Americans are relentlessly complaining about the price of fuel in their country, $7 a gallon was still less than I paid back in the U.K., and so as far as I was concerned, I was still getting a bargain. We got enough fuel to get us to Silver Gate, where we could fill up before entering Yellowstone National Park.

On March 1, 1872, Yellowstone National Park became the world's first national park; it is best known for its geothermal activity, including the well-known geyser Old Faithful. Unfortunately, it's also home to a constant mass of tourists who hold up queues of traffic in order to take a photograph of a squirrel sitting by the side of the road. Covering 3,472 square miles, Yellowstone is impossible to see in just one day, and so Antony and I decided we would simply do the "touristy thing" and see the "good stuff."

Our first challenge was locating a parking space along the roadside beside the Mammoth Hot Springs. The springs are a series of limestone rock fractured terraces through which hot water can reach the earth's surface. Past volcanic activity has left the terraces in Technicolor splendor, and created shapes that even a great artistic mind couldn't conjure.

The region in which you find Old Faithful is dotted with hundreds of other geysers, giving you the unequivocal feeling that the earth is wild and most definitely alive. From a distance, the suppurating land looks as if a steam locomotive is coming around every corner—steam fills the air at random intervals and from arbitrary positions across the barren expanse.

The Old Faithful geyser is the most popular of all of Yellowstone's geothermic treats and, with this being America, is located near several shops, car parks, and hotels. The geyser itself is surrounded by enough seating to accommodate several hundred people and erupts every ninety minutes. By the number of people who had already assembled around the hole in the ground, it appeared as if Antony and I would not have to wait too long for the action to begin. Little jets of water shot several meters into the air, teasing the audience, before everyone felt the ground rumble beneath their feet. Just twelve minutes after we had arrived, Old Faithful let rip. As a wall of water was discharged over a hundred feet into the afternoon sky, it was easy to understand why people wait so long for the spectacle . . . and it also explained why the seated area is situated a clear 200 yards from the geyser. At the end of the eruption, after 5,000 gallons of water had been ejected from the earth's crust, the crowd departed quickly, rushing to their cars to beat the traffic. As Antony and I scrambled through the mob, it was perversely pleasing to know that the people we passed walking in the direction of the geyser had an hour and a half to wait for Old Faithful's next performance.

We arrived back in Salt Lake City late the next day and because our next festival was a long drive instead of a flight away, and we had days to spare, we decided to check into a Best Western in the south of the city. I figured we had enough time for me to meet up with an old friend; and we were in luck—due to some severe sunburn, he was off work for the remainder of the week.

Lee James and I have been friends ever since he lived in Cornwall in 2002, and in 2005 he and his girlfriend, Jen, helped Bateman and me hunt for whales in a local Utah reservoir. We called him and, using the Internet for directions, we were knocking on his front door in less than twenty minutes. By now it was late afternoon and so I invited Lee for some dinner in order to catch up. And, in honor of meeting up with one old friend, I thought it was about time I reacquainted myself with another.

Sadly, Hooters of Salt Lake City is certainly not the best of the restaurant's chain. The waitresses aren't in the same league as some of the Hooters girls I've seen before, and we found out that they are paid less than $2 an hour—we figured these ones wouldn't make a great deal in tips. Also, they don't accept U.K. driving licenses as proof of age because "they aren't in the big book of IDs." Their attempt at fish and chips was pretty awful too. On a lighter note, Lee was in a great mood, had a new job, had broken up with Jen some months before, and was living with his father.

As Antony and I ate our meal, Lee was on his phone constantly, trying to organize some sort of party for the evening. As we left the restaurant, Lee was on his fifth or sixth phone call, and by the sounds of it, the party arrangements weren't going particularly well.

As the sun went down, Lee made one final attempt, taking us to his cousin's flat just outside the downtown area. Here we met his cousin and flatmate, both of whom were in no mood for a party. Lee, who refused to admit defeat, tried one last contact and rang another cousin. And so it was that Antony, Lee, his cousin, and I listened to quiet music playing from my laptop as we sat in our motel room drinking low-alcohol lager. Hardly a contender for party of the year.

The following morning—on the day that saw Tony Blair's ten-year reign as prime minister come to an end after stepping down to make way for his chancellor, my e-mail in-box showed a startling coincidence concerning Lee. The top toolbar suggested a "word of the day," and that particular day's word was *factious* (adj.)—inclined to forming parties.

Regardless, Antony and I weren't in much of a party mood anyway. We had to save our energy for the 200-mile drive to Elko, Nevada, for the forty-fourth National Basque Festival.

The trouble with Salt Lake City is that once you have left the city limits, in any direction, the radio fails to pick up any radio station, and there is pretty much nothing of any interest out of the windows. This makes for a terribly boring game of I Spy. Once you have exhausted "road," "sky," "desert," and "road" again (which you used to fool your opponent into thinking it surely can't be a previous answer), there isn't much to do apart from set the car's cruise control setting to 10 above the speed limit and sit back in perfect silence, looking for something totally out of the ordinary.

"Look at those dogs!" Antony yelled, bursting into hysterics. I took a closer look at the vehicle we were about to pass.

On the back of a pickup, which was pulling a trailer holding a bundle of underground piping, sat two dogs. Because the trailer's attachment had taken up so much room in the truck bed cargo area, the dogs had been placed on top of a metal box that wasn't especially spacious and was higher than the sides of the vehicle. One sharp turn or a paw out of place would have sent one or both of the dogs tumbling to the road below. This didn't seem to bother the driver, however, who continued his drive at a safe 70 miles per hour.

We had passed the truck by this point, and in order to get another glimpse at the "wonder dogs," and to calm down Antony (who by this time was like an hysterical child, studying our car's mirrors and back window for a better view), I decided to pull into a rest area so that we could pass the pickup again. As we veered off the road, though, unfortunately so did the pickup—we would have to wait for him to leave before we could follow. While we were stopped, instead of talking to the dogs' owner, I became interested in where we had arrived by complete serendipity.

The Bonneville Salt Flats is an enormous tabular expanse and is one of the most unique features in America. A remnant of Lake Bonneville of glacial times, the salt plains are now more famous for being the place where automotive speed records are set. Ever since Malcolm Campbell managed to reach

301 mph in 1935, the plains have been the setting for all but three of the following twenty world record–breaking runs. With the salt as deep as 6 feet in places, the entire 30,000-acre landscape looks like snow heavily sprinkled on frozen water. Due to the curvature of the earth, it is impossible to see from one end to the other.

After studying the plains and returning to our car, we found that the pickup guy had apparently set his own land speed record. After spending only five minutes at the rest area, he and his dogs were nowhere to be seen.

Elko, Nevada, is a rather odd place and is more in the middle of nowhere than Salt Lake City ever was. The town isn't a metropolis but is home to more than 17,000 people and (being a Nevadan town) many casinos and places in which to gamble. It is also of interest that due to Nevada law—which states that any town with a population of less than 400,000 may have licensed brothels—Elko has four bordellos: Mona Lisa's Ranch, Inez's, Sue's Fantasy Club, and the rather unimaginatively named Sharon's Brothel. What's more surprising is that the town, well over 5,000 miles away from the autonomous Spanish region of the Basque Country (a small area of Spain and France that sees itself as a nation separate from its bordering neighbors), nevertheless plays host to an annual Basque Festival. Also, oddly enough, the town has a shop that sells traditional Cornish savory pies called pasties.

When mining became a stalwart source of income in the region, thousands of people descended on the area, including many from the Basque region of Spain and my home county of Cornwall in England. Today, mining is still the main industry in Elko and employs over a third of the town's male workforce.

It was because of the emigrating Cornish contingent that Antony and I had found ourselves in a town-center bakery contemplating which type of pasty to buy.

On the menu, five pasties were listed: beef, onion, and potato; beef and cabbage; chicken and rice; cheese and vegetable; and a breakfast pasty with egg and sausage. Even though I had explained that only one of the five was a true Cornish pasty, the shop assistant allowed us to sample one of each. The last time I had tried an American attempt at a pasty was in another town steeped in mining history, Mineral Point in Wisconsin. That had devastating results. The pasty looked more like a deflated scone, it was presented in a polystyrene box, and, for some unknown reason, came with chili sauce. As we sampled the array of oggies on offer here in Elko, we chatted with the shop assistant and asked him what we should expect from the weekend's Basque Festival.

"Oh, is it Basque weekend?" he asked breezily.

"Didn't you know?" I replied in amazement. "It starts tonight just a few streets from here."

"Yeah, but I've never been. I don't know a great deal about it to be honest. How are the pasties?"

Being able to garner little information (other than that we had arrived several months too early for the town's Cowboy Poetry Gathering Festival in January, and two weeks late for Elko's Motorbike Jamboree), we bought a couple of pasties—proper beef, onion, and potato ones—and headed in the direction of the Chamber of Commerce to learn more about the Basque Festival.

The Elko Chamber of Commerce is inside a log cabin and has hundreds of pamphlets and brochures of local attractions. There was not a single piece of literature on the Basque Festival, even though the town's lampposts were promoting the event. As I started to think the festival may have been canceled and we had driven for over three hours for nothing, the chamber's clerk asked if we were in need of any help. We asked her for any information on the Basque Festival, and her assistant handed her something. On a badly photocopied piece of paper no bigger than a postcard was the schedule of events for the festival.

"That's all we've got," she said, and we left the chamber.

The festival is a celebration of everything Basque including traditional Basque dancing, a parade, an entire day of athletic "old country" games, and, the most traditional of all, a running of the bulls. According to the schedule, the Bull Run was to take place twice over the weekend's festivities. We decided we would watch the idiotic men attempting to evade a skewering from the herd in the evening's run, and then, even though I had promised my girlfriend we wouldn't, Ant and I agreed to be two of those idiots in tomorrow's run.

Outside Stockmen's, one of Elko's largest and oldest casinos, a lonely refreshment stand and sign-up desk stood among a series of bleachers and a menacing-looking set of metal fencing that outlined the 200-meter course into which the bulls and their "victims" would be released.

By 6 p.m., a display of traditional Basque dancing had begun and the bleachers surrounding the run had already started to fill. The course, whose path followed two sides of the casino, certainly didn't look safe and wasn't particularly well organized. It was near what we presumed to be the start line that we met John, a traveling American who had arrived in Elko only earlier that day, and had taken one of the last remaining motel rooms in the town.

"I've been to Spain before," he said, "and this place may not look much like it, but the festival does have a lot."

"Like what?" I inquired.

"The dancers are authentic, the clothes are very good,

and the restaurants make fantastic food. Everything you'd expect to find in the Basque region is here," he continued. I looked up with a concerned look on my face. "Let's just hope ETA aren't here too!"

Elko's version of Pamplona's Running of the Bulls is known by what I believe to be the more accurate name of Running *from* the Bulls. At 7 p.m., it was time for the event to begin, and the crowd sat tense and eager expecting at least a few injuries. As a dozen or so competitors adorned in white T-shirts and some in a traditional red scarf (or *paliacate*) sat around, it became apparent that the stars of the show weren't present. By seven-thirty, the bulls still had yet to make their appearance and as the sun began to set, word was circulating that they wouldn't make it in time for the evening's run. At eight o'clock, the run was called off and a wood-chopping and weight-lifting display took its place. Because the crowd was there to see panic-stricken competitors and hilarious injuries, it wasn't long before the stands were vacated, leaving Antony and me with nothing to do but lose some money at a nearby casino's blackjack table.

The next day began in the same way that my Saturdays do at home: with a pasty. My weekends, however, don't begin with a town Basque Parade. Antony and I managed to find an adequate location to watch the morning's cavalcade, beside a woman who thought we were Australian and a dozen children with plastic bags. The reason for the carrier bags soon became apparent when the occupants of the procession's first car—a not-very-Basque pair of men dressed as crash-test dummies—threw sweets in the direction of the waiting kids. What followed was a mix of characters ranging from members of the local church to Miss Elko County, from a carpet-cleaning company to cowboys on horseback and a loudmouth radio DJ from the town's Mix 96.7 in a golf buggy. There was also a giant cuddly polar bear used to promote the casino who had taken our money the previous night. After almost an hour, near the end of the procession, the children found locating the sweets among the plethora of horse excrement was a near impossible task.

The afternoon's Basque Games were to take place at Elko's County Fairground, and because we didn't know where that was (and the pasty shop assistant's directions were incredibly difficult to understand), we simply followed the parade route—surprisingly, we located the fairground with ease. From what I could make out, the showground was much more used to holding livestock sales and horse racing than Basque dancing and a series of contests including weight carrying and a high-school tug of war. And on a day where the temperature reached 95 degrees in the shade in the morning, things didn't begin very well. For starters, the sign by the front gates read ENTRENCE; perhaps that's the Basque translation. We took our positions in the stand and, this being America, were asked to rise straight away for their national anthem. At this stage, I wasn't really sure as to which song was more annoying: Lee Greenwood's atrocities or the national anthem, which going by its usage in the country, was probably played before any true American even sat down for a meal. There was, however, an instant third contender as the "Oinkari" dancers from Boise, Idaho, began a routine to the "Birdie Song." They were soon joined by the local "Arinkak" group, whose dancers would also perform to the crowd before the games began. Three quarters of an hour later, Antony and I had sat through eleven separate dances and weren't exactly enthralled. When one of the commentators informed the crowd that "there are over four hundred and forty traditional Basque dances," we both knew we were in for a long afternoon.

By two o'clock, the games were finally under way. The first contest was the Bucksaw competition. Basically, teams of two able-bodied men share the job of cutting through an 18-inch-diameter log with a giant saw. After the contestants were introduced, I spotted a missed opportunity on our part: $150 was awarded for first place, the runners up would pocket $100, with third taking home a respectable fifty bucks. With only two teams entered, and an entry fee of only $5, Antony and I could have used a spoon and finished while the interval dancers were leaving and we would have still made up for our casino loss the previous night.

The remainder of the games, with the exception of the high-school tug of war, seemed more like a display of 101 things you can do with a piece of wood. They would stand on it and chop away at the piece from above, carry it around for a bit, or lift a log above their heads. Incidentally, the latter of the events was won by a guy who looked exactly like a traditional weightlifter you would expect to see in a nineteenth-century traveling circus, complete with leotard and outlandish mustache. As the dancing recommenced, Antony and I visited a nearby stall that sold items of Basque clothing so we could kit ourselves out for the evening's run. We each bought a red scarf, and I purchased a white T-shirt featuring the Basque flag for myself and a shirt depicting sheep for Antony. I cleverly planned on giving the sheep T-shirt to my girlfriend once Antony had used it as a sorry-I-broke-my-promise-and-ran-with-the-bulls present.

As we returned to our seats to witness yet another traditional Basque dance (which made any given contestant on "So You Think You Can Dance" look like Mikhail Baryshnikov), we decided we should stay for just one more event. Forty minutes of bell ringing and stick striking later, the junior weight carrying contest began. Anyone under sixteen whose parents had signed a release form (or anyone they plucked from the audience, so was the desperation for entrants) had to carry two 75-pound weights across a 100-foot course. The person who covered the greatest distance was deemed the winner. A local fifteen-year-old named Casey won the event with a distance measuring over 500 feet, narrowly beating a girl named Kelly who embarrassed her gender by failing miserably before finishing a single length. Still, it was hot. Out of the corner of my eye I could see more dancers preparing to fill the gap between this and the next event, and so before Casey was crowned, Antony and I left hastily.

I mean, why allow dancers to bore us to death when the bulls in tonight's run could take care of that quite nicely?

We had been told at the fairgrounds that if we wished to run with the bulls that evening, we had to find a member of the Elko Basque Club outside of Stockmen's and sign up. Because no one knew how many of the previous day's entrants would take part today, it was a mystery as to how many spaces would be made available for the evening's run. So Antony and I got there early and sat outside the casino for nearly an hour as more and more of our fellow runners joined us, sharing stories of the run from previous years and what laid in store for us. The rumor circulating among the crowd of entrants was that yesterday's cancellation was due to an accident in which one of the bulls had lost a horn. In the beast's fit of rage, he had put one of his handlers in the hospital—not the kind of thing you want to hear when you plan to be within a few feet of the animal.

As more and more people arrived to sign up, with still no signs of a Basque Club representative, we began talking to two young guys, Jonathan and Sam, who had traveled from California to take part in the run. Unfortunately, this is also where we met Mike. I didn't mean to be instantly judgmental, but when a man in his forties arrives wearing long shorts and a T-shirt with LIFEGUARD emblazoned across it, you just know he's going to turn out to be a bit of a prick. Next to him stood Geoff, his neighbor, whose only form of communication was to grunt whenever Mike felt the need to pause for breath.

"Hey, I'm Mike," he shouted enthusiastically as he outstretched his arm to shake all of our hands.

"Hi, Mike. Are you taking part in the run?" I inquired.

"Damn, right. Fourteenth year in a row!" he bellowed. "Woo!" He held an open hand aloft and was high-fived by the two young Californians we were talking to. Antony and I simply looked at each other wishing we were somewhere else: having a drink at the bar . . . losing money in the casino . . . watching more traditional Basque dancing . . . being gored by a vicious bull . . . anywhere but talking to Mike. I felt trapped. We couldn't leave the queue and lose our place, and yet the line was the last place on earth I wanted to be. I wasn't sure how we were going to handle the situation.

"So what brings two Brits out to Elko?" he asked, as if standing in a queue to sign up for a bull run wasn't obvious enough.

"We came to see you, Mike," replied Antony sarcastically.

Sarcasm, good old British sarcasm. That was how we were going to handle the situation.

Mike used the next ten minutes to bombard us with trivial information about his life. For instance, I know his house is 3,000 square feet, that his Samoan wife (yes, he's married) works for an airline and was in the crowd, and that he'd always wanted to do the famous Bull Run in Barcelona.

"Barcelona?" I questioned. "Don't you mean Pamplona?"

"No, man. The most famous Spanish bull run is in Barcelona."

"I think you'll find it's Pamplona, Mike."

"Oh, Pamplona," he teased in an aristocratic English accent, "Pamplona."

I wasn't sure if it was the heat, or the thought of being killed by an uncontrollable and tempestuous animal that was making me dislike a total stranger. Perhaps it was the constant dancing from earlier in the afternoon. No . . . it was Mike, I thought. He really was a bit of a prick.

After informing us that U2's Bono and Edge were of different religions and that his favorite film was *Braveheart*, he spotted my digital watch, which had a compass and thermometer built in.

"Well, *that's* a watch," he said. "What can that do?"

I paused for a moment. "It tells me what the time is."

By this time Mike had either realized that we didn't want to speak to him or decided that he had finished irritating us with his idle chitchat, and he left to annoy the hell out of somebody else. As he sauntered around the corner of Stockmen's with Geoff in tow, I think he may have said something along the lines of "Keep my place." I chose to ignore it.

Just as he disappeared from sight, the Basque Club representatives appeared, one of whom was checking the entry forms of yesterday's runners and working out how many newcomers they could sign up. Luckily for us (or unluckily depending on your way of looking at it) there were twelve spaces available and we were fourth and fifth in the queue. As Mike and Geoff came back, the final spot had just been allocated, and so a disgruntled Mike and just plain grunting Geoff had no choice but to watch the action from the stands.

Thank god.

As it was already an hour behind schedule, the run, we were informed, was to start almost immediately and so Antony and I made our way to the car to retrieve our red scarves. Upon returning to the enclosed run, it was clear that out of the twenty or so competitors—who by now were stretching, running on the spot, and preparing for the run of their lives—only four of us were adorned in scarves. We may as well have just painted red targets on the backs of our T-shirts. Antony had a look of determination on his face.

"I'm really ready for this. I can't wait," he shouted with a sense of eagerness. "Aren't you really looking forward to this?"

"Yeah," I lied rather convincingly.

Fortunately for me, I had a slight advantage over the other runners. A couple of years earlier, I had visited Pamplona, where the annual Running of the Bulls takes place every day for a week during the festival of San Fermin. I had experienced actually taking to the cobbled and curving streets of the Plaza Ayuntamiento, Calle Estafeta, and had made it unharmed to the finish at the gateway of the Spanish town's bull ring. Unfortunately, that was in November—a full four months after the Bull Run had taken place. The only thing that chased me down the narrow streets was the breeze. Still, I figured it should count for something.

To be honest, I wasn't looking forward to the Elko run at all. There was something ominous about the evening. An orangey red sun hung in the sky, the temperature had dropped suddenly, and there wasn't a breath of wind. Everything was still. The earlier torturous endeavors of Mike and the Basque Club dancers had passed, and we seemed to be entering the eye of the storm where the town remained at peace before rage and fury would besiege the streets once again.

"I heard these beasts are worse than the ones in Spain," shrieked one guy excitedly.

"They are," shouted his friend. "I've seen so many injuries here!" he added, before the two embraced each other with an impromptu high five.

As the sun began to drop, rumors reached us that the bulls weren't anywhere near the town and had been held up while on their way down to Elko. I turned my back to everyone and shrugged my shoulders disappointedly, but this was music to my ears. I definitely wouldn't have pulled out of the run, but I was certainly not going to complain or leave a dejected man if the bulls repeated their previous day's no-show. In fact, that was the best result—I wouldn't have to run but could still claim that I had really wanted to. Perfect.

Unfortunately, the shrieks from the crowd and the incessant beep of two huge trucks backing up confirmed my worst fears. The rumors, it turned out, were just that, and as the vehicles moved into position, the reverse warning beep was beginning to sound more like a death toll. The tremendous thudding coming from inside the trucks, as loud as a tribal drum preceding a sacrifice, filled the crowd with elation, my fellow bull runners with obvious excitement, and my heart with dread. I still had more than nine weeks in America remaining and didn't want to see the country through a hospital window.

As we jostled for position at the starting line, you could hear many tactics from my compatriots. Some were planning on jogging close to the horns of the bulls and a few had even mentioned running backward to taunt the beasts. My plan, however, was clear and concise: Run really, really fast.

There was no more time for thinking or contemplating what injuries might befall us. The runners were ready, the six terrifying bulls were certainly ready, and the crowd had been waiting for this moment since the last massacre in 2006. It was time.

No starter's pistol or horn sounded the start of the run, just a man who rather nonchalantly shouted "Go!" completely out of the blue (no "On your marks" or "Get set"). A throng of people passed me as my timing off the line wasn't the best, and I could tell by the reaction of the crowd that the bulls had joined the party. Because the course had been watered just an hour before the run had begun, building up a great speed was ill advised and treading carefully and precisely was definitely the order of the day.

From the sounds of crashing from the barriers and the yells from the crowd, it was obvious that the bulls hadn't enjoyed the long drive down to Elko and were very much appreciative of their sudden freedom. Antony was now by my side and we were sprinting around the corner of Stockmen's, neither of us knowing that by taking the inside route we would be crossing the path of a charging bull. I looked back. Just yards behind me were one of the Californian lads who had a definite look of concern on his face, and a rather angry-looking animal just a matter of feet from his heels.

"Watch out, Rich," Jonathan shouted, as he turned to dart straight up the rungs and to the top of a nearby fence, seconds before the bull would have sent him through it. I didn't need to be warned, I was nearing the end of the run anyway, and Antony was yards in front fast approaching the pen (into which only an idiot would run). I leapt onto the fence and clung for my life. It was only then that I realized how close the bull had been as I lifted my feet and it charged just below my shoes.

Antony wasn't so lucky.

He jumped on the first rung of the fence with the bull closing the gap, but slipped off again. As I began to climb to the top of the fence, the crowd's reaction alerted me to a problem, and I could only look on in utter shock and horror—it seemed that Antony stood no chance of evading the charging animal.

At first it appeared as if the bull had slipped, but as the beast lifted its head, Antony rose with it, rocketing into the air as flaccid as a rag doll. The T-shirt was ripped from his body by the bull's right horn and his body struck the ground with considerable force, landing shoulder first onto the hard and unforgiving concrete. The crowd wailed and applauded at first, but a sudden and somber silence overwhelmed the stands when it was obvious that something had gone horribly wrong. As blood began to pour from Antony's back, the bull changed direction. Whether an organizer behind the pen had affected the animal's choice in some way, or the lure of Antony's red scarf was too much for the bull to resist, the animal trampled on Antony's lower back and neck.

Antony lay motionless.

The bull continued on into the pen, and medics and organizers swarmed around Antony as the crowds, our fellow runners, and I looked on in disbelief. I raced toward the melee quicker than I had run away when the bulls were behind me. As I stepped aside to allow a paramedic through with a stretcher, it was obvious that things weren't going well.

"His name's Antony!" I yelled as the medic passed.

We were all told to stand well back to give Antony plenty of room, and as we did so, the crowd stood in deathly silence to hear of any initial news.

"He's breathing, but he's in a bad way!" yelled the medic who was first on the scene. "Is anyone with him?"

"He is!" shouted Jonathan, coming out of the crowd and pushing me toward the crew.

As the door of the ambulance shut behind us, it created an ambience of complete solemnity, and I realized that I was to blame for Antony's condition. As I looked down at his battered and bruised frame showing meager signs of life, I slumped into the corner of the vehicle and wept for my friend.

* * *

*W*ell, all of that *could* have happened.

The bulls didn't turn up again.

In reality, we paraded through the course and were applauded by an appreciative crowd for simply wearing a white T-shirt and saying we *were* going to run. I may not have run with the bulls, but at least I had (unwillingly) kept a promise to my girlfriend.

Shortly after the "event," Jonathan bought us each a beer, and Mike and Geoff came from nowhere to complain about the queue and his exclusion from the "run." (Well, Mike complained while Geoff simply stood in the background staring at the floor grunting occasionally.)

"Where are you guys staying tonight?" Mike asked.

"Um, in our motel, I guess," I replied, trying not to give the name of it away.

"You should come back to mine. The wife won't mind."

"Yeah, we just might do that," I said convincingly enough for him to believe me.

"We'll meet you in a bit," Antony added.

We both knew this was our one and only chance to make an escape. We darted around the corner of the casino away from Mike and Geoff, who had started to pursue. It was a day we thought might have ended in injuries from wild animals, and instead it ended with us attempting to outpace a man and a different kind of grunting beast. Instead of running from the bulls, we were running from the fools.

3. BIRTHDAY
GREETINGS

*There's always one, isn't there? A typical
American on the Fourth of July in Boston.*

$\mathcal{U}$pon returning to Salt Lake City, Antony and I were faced with a tough decision. Our next festival was still six days away and between then and now was July 4—America's Independence Day. The problem was deciding where to spend the country's birthday. I'd never spent the fourth of July in the U.S., and as I've heard it's the biggest annual party in the country, I wanted to see it correctly; and that meant finding the most appropriate city. Neither Antony nor I thought we should spend the day in Salt Lake City (due to the state's ridiculous alcohol laws), and there isn't another big city near it. To do it properly, we knew we needed to be on the East Coast of the country—an area that was steeped in history, heavily populated, and definitely much cooler.

In the end, it boiled down to two contenders: Washington, D.C., and Boston. One was selected because it was the capital, and therefore the political heart of the country, and the other because of its cosmopolitan feel, sense of American history, and pleasant surroundings. Luckily, I'd been to both cities on a previous trip to the States, and had definite opinions of each of the two.

Boston is the cultural capital of New England, is situated on the coast, has a mild climate, and was the type of city where pedestrians are more likely to be hit by another jogger than a car. Washington, on the other hand, is the nation's capital city, and its only drawback is that it's a horrible, dirty, filthy, stinking, odious, abhorrent, beastly, detestable, ghastly, repellent, disgusting, humid, litter-strewn dump, where shops and bars are replaced with monuments and museums.

Can you guess which one we chose?

Our early-morning flight to Boston would take us via Chicago, and once we boarded our connecting flight, we realized that for once the plane's audio entertainment channels weren't just the usual mix of jazz, spoken word, and cheesy pop. This time, they included a station on which you could listen to our captain's conversations with Air Traffic Control. I thought it was rather good; Antony most certainly disagreed. He thought it was nerdy and boring. I slipped my headphones on and listened in.

"This is United 536," came the voice from the cockpit. To be honest, most of the rest of it was foxtrots, tangos, and other exotic dance words used in the NATO phonetic alphabet. Then it suddenly got a bit interesting.

The flight in front of ours was apparently losing some sort of fluid out of the right side of its fuselage as we taxied our way to Juliet Foxtrot Left (good, right?). This delayed our take-off by quite some time, and the captain's voice came on the plane's internal public address system to explain the situation.

After the rather vague explanation, most people slumped in their seats to show their disappointment. I looked quite smug, removed my earphones, and turned to face Antony.

"I knew that."

At 30,000 feet, it got a bit boring listening to air traffic control twittering on about golfs, sierras, whiskeys, and something about irreparable damage to one of the wings of our plane (well, I may have made that last one up). Antony and I discovered that we had forgotten a fundamental travel accessory for when you find yourself on an airplane without a television screen mounted to the back of the seat in front of you: a book. With any luck, we could solve that problem in Boston. With a metropolitan population of over 4.4 million, I was sure they would have a book shop.

*B*oston is a lovely city. Sitting at the mouth of the Charles River, as it washes into a crystal-clear Atlantic, Boston has many nicknames: City on the Hill and The Hub of the Universe are two good ones. For me, though, there is only one moniker that truly reflects Boston's relationship to America as a whole: The Cradle of Modern America.

Since colonists first settled there in 1630, naming it after a small town in Lincolnshire, the city was the home of America's first public school and university and, most famously, was the scene of the Boston Tea Party, where America's Revolutionary War against the British was first ignited. Its many landmarks, including Boston Common, the statue of Benjamin Franklin, the Old State House, and the U.S.S *Constitution*, can all be located on a two-mile brick path known as the Freedom Trail, which has earned Boston the title of a "walking city." If there was ever a truly patriotic and cultured fourth of July, then surely Boston was to host it.

Our arrival in the city could not have been timed worse. Not only had we arrived during Boston's rush hour, but the subway train to our hotel was crammed with an exceptional number (even for America) of people in baseball caps. As Antony and I wondered aloud why so many people had chosen to wear similar hats, a young girl who was sitting quietly reading a book looked up at us.

"There's a game on tonight," she muttered helpfully.

"Oh, I see," I replied. As she noticed our accents, she laid the book over onto her thigh.

"Oh my, you're from England," she said. Top marks so far for not thinking we were Australian like most Americans.

"We are indeed," I replied.

"That's so cool." Nice bit of Colonial appreciation. "I've always wanted to go to England," she added.

"You should do, it's really nice," Antony said. We were both pleased with finding our first Bostonian to be so polite and informed. Then she really went for gold.

"Have you met the princes?"

Never mind. There are plenty of other people in Boston.

We checked into our hotel on Beacon Street, west of the historic Kenmore Square, where every other building is either a coffee house, restaurant, or a Dunkin' Donuts (they seem to have half of their worldwide stores in Boston). Instead of allocating hotel rooms with numbers, the Beacon Inn used famous names from Boston's history to name their rooms. Both the John Quincy Adams and the Mayflower room were available but we opted for the lesser known character of Paul Revere—a perfect choice for Independence Day.

The next day, a package arrived for me. I opened it immediately, like a child on Christmas Day. It was from Rod. I had e-mailed him the details of where we were staying in Boston and he had been so kind as to return my sunglasses, which I had left behind in his camper van. And that wasn't all he sent either. Accompanying my glasses were my kepi (which I had also left behind), a CD for each of us with pictures Rod had taken, posters advertising the Custer's Last Stand Reenactment, some sew-on stripes, certificates, and the prerequisite bag of sweets. It was more like a goody bag than a stash of military memorabilia. A rather touching letter from Rod and June was also included in the package. They thanked us for our presence in their camp and Rod explained why he had included more than just a "cheap pair of sunglasses" in the box. To not allow us to forget our military outing with him, Rod had included further certificates and "stripes," which we could add to the shoulder of an item of clothing. They both wished us good luck for the remainder of the trip and apologized for the brevity of the letter as Rod had to hurry in order to put the parcel in the "post" and then paint his flag pole for Independence Day.

As we stepped out of our hotel for our first full day in Boston, we made our way to the nearby subway station to await a train—we were headed for the site of tomorrow's celebration, the biggest party of the year. We wanted to see it on this, the eve of America's 231st birthday, before really digging in for the party tomorrow.

Boston's subway is the oldest in America and the fifth oldest in the world. Unfortunately, it shows. The rails don't seem as if they've been replaced since the railway's inception at the turn of the century, and the style of the stations and train cars look like what I expect the London Underground did in the 1960s. It is, however, clean and reliable, and so Antony and I made our way to the banks of the Charles River happily.

There we found a monolithic hatch shell stage surrounded by hundreds of seats. Because there is a concert (without fireworks) on the third too, and entry is free on a first-come, first-served basis, people were already beginning to queue for a show that was still more than seven hours away. As we weren't really in the mood to wait in a long queue for a party on an inappropriate day, Antony and I made our way to Cambridge, the area of Boston that is home to the prestigious Harvard University, not for a coffee shop or to breathe in the academic air, but to find a place where Antony could go to the toilet.

As Antony returned from a nearby café after abusing one of their facilities, we came across a man who seemed to own some sort of outdoor bookstore. Remembering that we were in need of something to read on future plane journeys, Antony began to peruse the three shelves and adjacent tables for something suitable as I began talking to the . . . um . . . "shop assistant."

"So how did all of this come about?" I asked, making small talk.

The assistant informed me that he had had to fight the government and various city courts for more than two years in order to be allowed to pitch up on the pavement. Meanwhile, Antony approached us and made his proud book purchase. It was called *Sexual Reproduction*, and to Antony's delight it included pictures (not a pop-up book, though). As I continued to listen to the "salesman" babble on about local bureaucracy and red tape, a book caught my eye. If the content was as ridiculous as the title, I was in for a treat.

The Humor of Jesus by Father Henri Cormier, C.J.M. (an acronym which identifies him as a member of the Congregation of Jesus and Mary if you wanted to know) is a study of the Bible and, as the title suggests, the sense of humor enjoyed by our Lord. If the hilarious title wasn't enough of an incentive to quickly swipe it off the shelf before anyone else got their hands on it, the $2 price tag and alluringly psychedelic yellow-and-blue front cover certainly sealed the deal. It was first published in 1977 in Montreal as *L'Humour de Jesus*, and this English translation had many chapters, with titles such as "Jesus, the number-one journalist" and "Jesus, the number-one caricaturist." It certainly had me laughing, and I don't believe that they were the jokes that Jesus had cracked either. For a thirty-year-old paperback, it was in quite good condition, and, as an added bonus, many of the pages had passages that had been highlighted by one of the book's previous owners.

Before making our way back to our hotel, we thought it would be a good idea to settle down with a quick pint just to make a nice start on our books. This, however, seemed to be an impossible task because in each of the three bars we stopped at, we were refused because neither of us had our American state driving license on us at the time.

It was funny—no matter how hard I looked in my wallet and trouser pockets, I just couldn't seem to find my Massachusetts driver's licence anywhere. I suppose it serves me right for being English and passing my test in the United Kingdom. Also, the DVLA were at obvious fault for issuing me with a British driving license. Silly people; what were they thinking?

What made it worse was as a result of us leaving the area earlier than we wanted, we had to squeeze onto another crowded subway car due to yet another Red Sox game.

July Fourth in America. To be honest, I wasn't quite sure what to expect, but I wanted some sort of ebullient party atmosphere. Of course, one of my reasons for selecting Boston was that I knew its population was more reserved than the rest of the country's inhabitants, and they wouldn't decorate themselves with face paint and gaudy stars-and-stripes clothing. I was hoping for that anyway.

As we ate our lunch on Boston Common, there were no obvious signs that it was a national holiday, let alone Independence Day. Only a handful of people were wearing clothes signifying the love for their nation, not a great deal more than you would see on any arbitrary day of the year. There were a few silly hats, the occasional flag-wielding family, and not a single person dressed as Uncle Sam, the national personification of the United States. So unimpressed were we with the lack of patriotic attire, Antony and I decided to visit a shop and stock up on American bow ties, boxer shorts, and top hats. Luckily, we came to our senses before any purchases were made.

Making our way back to the hotel—on yet another crowded subway train due to a 1 p.m. start time for the Red Sox game that day—we decided to visit a liquor store to buy some alcohol for our preliminary drinking before the evening's big party. There, I found it strange that in a bar, I must present an American state driving license in order to be served just a small beer, yet in a liquor store, with just my appearance as proof of age, I was sold enough alcohol to kill me.

On our return to the city, we joined a swarm of people who were heading in the direction of the Charles River. By this time, the sun was beginning to set and, for the first time in the seventeen days since we had left the U.K., rain began to fall. Hundreds of people were already lining a huge stretch of the dampening bank, hustling and competing for space on which to lay their picnic blankets and position their foldaway chairs in preparation for the day's firework culmination, which was still a good two hours away. However, even here there was little indication as to the significance of the day. Surrounding us were concession stands selling a range of different foods and, due to the weather, beginning to unpack their supply of ponchos.

After a quick visit to a bar and the nearly impossible task of using a portaloo in the dark back at the Charles River, we strolled down the embankment for a place in which to see the fireworks, I not knowing if my sneakers were wet because they were old and had holes in them, or because I had urinated on them earlier. After almost thirty minutes of walking, neither the rain nor the crowd showed any signs of alleviating and we decided to make our way to the Harvard

Bridge, which, according to a Boston newspaper's top fourth of July tips, was not normally congested and where a great view of the fireworks could be gained. By the amount of people fighting for position on the bridge, though, it appeared as if everyone in Boston read the same newspaper. It took us ten minutes to simply walk up the 200-foot zigzagged walkway to the closed-off road. When on the bridge itself, it was difficult to move and so Antony and I gave up trying to find a nice spot and remained in a tiny space just yards from the side, next to a couple who were in each other's arms (probably to save room).

As the first firework was shot into the air, the crowd silenced, solemnly leaving only the ubiquitous "Ooh" and "Aah" whispers to echo around the bay as the night sky was illuminated in astounding chromatic splendor. But five minutes in, the silence and awe were broken abruptly by screaming just several feet from Antony and me.

"Phone an ambulance!" yelled one man to the mass of people who had no choice but to huddle around a girl who had fallen to the ground. "Call 911!" Everyone reeled in shock at what might happen to her, and for a moment not a single person's interest was focused on the pyrotechnics.

Personally, I was more surprised that she had managed to find enough space in which to faint.

No sooner had someone dialed the emergency services, and reported our almost impossible position (which was hard enough for a human to reach, let alone an ambulance), than the girl came to and sat on the curb to recover.

With crisis averted we were morally justified in enjoying what remained of the fireworks display. For the following twenty minutes, Boston banged and flashed, detonated and discharged, and, with its breathtaking melee of explosions culminating in a dazzling array of rockets that continuously overwhelmed the crowd, the city rumbled and raged, causing its inhabitants to burst into a thunderous applause of unanimous appreciation.

The following day, our morning hangovers were improved significantly with the news that America's Independence Day was also the day that BBC Gaza correspondent Alan Johnston experienced his first day of independence after his 114-day hostage ordeal.

Because July Fourth fell on a Wednesday, we didn't have what had become our usual weekday break (since the festivals all happened on weekends). So it was the following day that we had an afternoon flight to Jacksonvile, Florida. Because check-out time was at 11 a.m. and traveling to the city center was a good thirty to forty-five minutes in the direction of the airport, we saw little point in leaving our luggage at the hotel. Instead, we thought we would study the subway map and select a suitable place near the airport to kill some time. With his name on the door of our hotel room as an omen (and the fact it was just five stops from the airport), Revere Beach seemed to be a perfect choice.

In 1896 Boston was home to the first public beach in the country and at the turn of the century more than a quarter of a million people would relax along Revere's five-mile shore on summer afternoons. During Revere's golden era, the Great Ocean Pier jutted a quarter of a mile into the Atlantic and housed a ballroom and large skating rink with half-hourly steamer services to Boston. What the resort was most famed for, however, was its amusements. Along with a Ferris wheel and businesses such as Bluebeard's Palace and the Fun House was the town's biggest attraction, the Cyclone: one of the largest roller coasters of the time, whose cars reached speeds of up to 60 mph and climbed to heights of over 100 feet.

Today, Revere Beach is a shadow of its former self. Just a handful of people take to its sands; nearly all of the town's attractions, including the pier, were demolished in a blizzard in 1978 and have been replaced with modernized housing units; and the only fast-food vendor that can be found on the seafront is located, rather woefully, on the ground floor of a government building.

The fast-food retailer, this being Massachusetts, is of course a Dunkin' Donuts, and having put off visiting one for so long, an equal measure of both curiosity and hunger sent us into the "world's largest coffee and baked goods chain." (Mind you, I can't really think of another.) Basically, the franchise is a cross between a glorified bakery and a poor man's Starbucks. As well as serving an array of breakfast meals and flavored coffee, the chain, as the name suggests and to presumably keep policemen happy, sells more than fifty different varieties of doughnuts and other dough-based products. As we purchased a bagel and coffee each, after waiting behind a small girl who stared at us because of our accents, we made our way in the direction of the beach, stopping en route at an area of covered benches in the center of a small patch of grass separating two roads. Two men sat at the bench opposite us and another was situated to our right. The place seemed dodgy, as did the men.

"Hey, is that thing online?" the man to our right asked me.

"I beg your pardon?" I replied, having no clue as to what he was referring. He pointed at my laptop bag. "Is that thing online?"

"Oh, no," I said. "It's just a standard laptop." I hoped he would believe the lie and not mug me for it. He stood up and joined us on our bench as Antony and I looked at each other for reassurance.

"You know how to work one of these things?" asked the man.

"What is it?" I asked while glancing quickly.

"It's one of those GPS systems. I bought it this morning and can't seem to get the damn thing off camera setting."

"Have you tried hitting it or looking at the manual?" Antony suggested helpfully. The man shrugged off Antony's advice and slipped the gadgetry into a black bag on the ground, suggesting to us that he probably didn't have the manual. We also suspected that he didn't buy it that morning.

As he rose from the bench to talk to the two men opposite us, it was just enough time for me to lean across to Antony and suggest we eat somewhere else. It was too late.

"Is that a Revere cop?" he asked the two men as he looked down the town's seafront road. As he rejoined us on the bench, a police car left the road and drove along the sidewalk to our covered seating area, answering his question perfectly. Yes, it most definitely was a Revere cop.

"Hiya, Brian," said the three men in unison as the policeman slammed his car door shut and approached them. The policeman exchanged pleasantries with the men and made his way through the area before looking over his shoulder. As the man with the GPS system began to mount his bicycle, Antony and I realized that the cop's pleasantries and exit were just a ploy to see if any of the men decided to make a guilty-looking move in his absence. The mounting of the bicycle was enough to rouse a suspicion.

"Hold it there a minute," shouted the cop as he approached the man. In a little under two minutes, the policeman had asked the man for some identification, another officer had arrived with sirens blaring, and all of the action had left Antony and I wishing we had popcorn with which to enjoy the show.

From our front-row-seat vantage point, we watched the policeman question each of the transients and request to see what they had in their possession. When a third policeman arrived, the first cop's attentions shifted dramatically to us.

"What's in the bag?" he asked, in the usual rude and abrupt way of American policemen.

"Um . . . clothes," Antony replied.

"What!?"

"Clothes."

"Where you from?" he asked.

After only thirty seconds, it seemed as if our accents and nationality proved our innocence, and the policeman made his way back to the three men and noticed the bag containing the GPS system. The other two men were free to go as the first man was read his rights, bundled into the back of a squad car, and driven away, leaving us with the first policeman. "What do you do?" he asked Antony.

"I'm at university," he replied.

"And you?"

"I've just left university with a journalism degree," I remarked.

"Right, you then, come here." Feeling proud to be chosen, I was led to the opposite corner of the seating area and interrogated. After explaining why we were in Revere and the reason we were found in the presence of such unsavory characters, the main question was asked.

"Was that his bag?" he asked in a let's-cut-to-the-chase-type way.

"To be honest, I can't say that it was his," I replied. "It was just on the floor. But it is where he put the GPS . . ."

Never have I seen three letters bring such a smile to someone's face. And nor can I think of a situation where it would happen again (well, perhaps "HIV" with the words "You don't have" spoken beforehand).

"That's all I needed to hear," he told me.

He invited Antony over next to corroborate my story, and, after taking our details and reassuring us we wouldn't be required for the future court case, he offered us a free ride in his squad car as a gesture of appreciation. When we discovered that the trip covered only the Boston metropolitan area, and that Jacksonville, Florida, was definitely out of the question, we thanked him for the offer and quickly returned to the subway station before we were involved as key witnesses in any further criminal acts.

Glad to be away from Revere Beach's tramps and cops, we checked in our bags at Logan International Airport for our afternoon flight to Jacksonville. We were about to head into America's Deep South to experience some good ole hospitality.

Luckily, I had the perfect book with which to start that journey.

4. THE OLYMP-HICK GAMES

Instant Redneck in 30 seconds—just add mud.

$\mathscr{I}$ haven't read a great deal of the Bible, but if *The Humor of Jesus* is anything to go by, I don't think the Lord has much of a future in stand-up. Not once did he make any rude and witty comments about any of his disciples' mothers or even visit a Nazarene pub on Open Mic Night to try his hand. Here's an instance of Jesus humor. One sub-chapter, titled "Humor stays with the "little ones,' " tells of a time in March A.D. 30 when Jesus was being besieged by a large crowd of followers. Zachaeus, a chief tax collector who was vertically challenged, decided to climb a tree in order to get a glimpse of the great man. At spotting this, Jesus approached him and, straight off the cuff, shouted "Zacheaus, come down quickly!"

Now, I don't know about you, but I'm unsure as to how Zacheaus didn't break his neck in his fits of laughter.

Even I can think of some lines which would have made Jesus seem as if he had some sort of comedic bone in his body. "Zacheaus, money doesn't grow on trees, you know," would have done fine; or another adequate tree-related pun would have been "I was wondering at which branch you worked." Even a simple "Fall, you tax-collecting bastard!" would have probably raised a few smiles in the crowd.

But instead of listing Jesus' favorite English, Irishman, and Scotsman jokes (or Israelite, Palestinian, and Mesopotamian jokes, I guess), the book prattles on with lame excuses to cover up the fact that Mr. Christ never did crack a one-liner. See, because humor isn't making people laugh, but

doing serious things without becoming self-conceited. Right.
I doubt the Last Supper was much of a laugh-a-minute occasion. Perhaps you had to be there.

As the two of us left the airport, I placed the book at the
bottom of my bag. We picked up our rental car and made our
way out of Jacksonville, through northern Florida and into
Georgia, where it seemed as if Jesus has moved into every
other building.

Visiting America's southern states (or the "Bible Belt,"
as they're sometimes referred to), is like stepping
into another country. The humidity during the summer
months is at an almost constant 100 percent, the temperature
rarely drops below 85°, and religion is very prevalent. In a
town with a population of just a thousand or so, it is not un-
common to see seven or eight churches as you pass through.
For someone from England, where churches are much more
rare, it was strange seeing all these religious edifices. I didn't
know there were so many different denominations, either. I
had heard of Baptists and Evangelicals, but The Assembly of
God, New Vision Fellowship, Pentecostal, and the Church of
God in Christ were new ones. Some of them had me thinking
that in choosing names they simply picked religious words
out of a hat.

East Dublin—situated almost in the center of Georgia
and, not surprisingly, to the east of the slightly larger settlement of Dublin—is a typical example of a Bible Belt town.
With a combined population of just under 20,000, the two
Dublins are home to more than a hundred places of worship
and the only Kentucky Fried Chicken in which I've seen the
Ten Commandments hanging on the wall beside the menu
(presumably to show any murdering, adulterous thief who
works on Sundays, uses the Lord's name in vain, and had

popped in only for a Crispy Twister just how much forgive-
ness and birching was required of him).

Under the Things to Do category on Georgia's official
government website about East Dublin, the only thing listed
is the Altamaha River. Once a year, however, the town plays
host to something that typifies the region's jovial attitude
and the pride they have in a name that others assume is an
insult: The Summer Redneck Games.

In 1996, when the Olympic Games were being held 150
miles up the I-16 in Atlanta, local radio station DJ Mac
Davies heard that many people were seeing the Games as
"being run by a bunch of rednecks who didn't know what they
were doing." As the criticism mounted, Davies and the station
decided that if that's what the people expected, that is exactly
what they would give them. They put together a true redneck
schedule of events that took place in tandem with the Atlanta
Olympics. When a crowd of almost five thousand people arrived (the organizers expected a tenth of that), they knew
they were onto a winner. Twelve years later, the radio station
still sponsors the annual event every July, and people are
drawn to the games from as far as seven or eight miles away.

For further information on this curious celebration,
Antony and I entered the Dublin information center and
approached a lady who sat on her own watching an American chat show to ask her if there was any literature on the
Redneck Games. She replied, but I wasn't sure if she did or
not. Due to her thick southern accent, she could have had a
cold and spoken Swahili through a hockey mask, informing
me that she had a detailed schedule along with all the records
from the previous eleven events and I would have been none
the wiser. Antony and I backed out of the center.

As we checked into our motel, the girl at reception had a
familiar reaction to our reason for being in town: "And you

came all this way for this?" It was the same reaction we'd received in both Elko and Billings. But you could have offered me a million pounds to guess what she would have said next and your money would have been safe.

"Are you going to Redneck Idol tonight?" she added.

"Um . . . Redneck Idol?"

"Yeah, I think it's taking place at the racetrack tonight, and the winner will perform at the games tomorrow." As if that didn't sound strange enough, she added the killer line: "All of that takes place after the mower racing, of course."

Of course.

The 441 Speedway is located 6 miles south of Dublin, off U.S. Highway 441, and for just $5 we could witness an afternoon of top-notch lawn mower racing as an aperitif to tomorrow's games. And if the action lived up to its rather melodramatic name, we were in for a treat. The 1st Annual Dublin Chrysler Dodge Jeep Cadillac Pontiac Buick Deep South Lawn Mower Racing Association Race of Champions (to give it its official title), didn't even take place on the speedway, instead using a small patch of dirt in the center. The MC, a rather large fellow with beard, baseball cap, and an XXL fluorescent green T-shirt, was not only a member of the Lawn Mower Racing Association but possibly its national leader—his intrinsic knowledge and love of the machines bordered on an unhealthy obsession.

Surrounding the lawn mower course, making full use of the rather dilapidated speedway, were several military vehicles as well as a mini monster truck and a similar vehicle which, we were told, could climb a vertical wall. Even with all of the vehicular attractions, the heat, the humidity, and the irritation of flies didn't do much to raise the morale of the crowd, which at 3 p.m. on a Friday afternoon was fewer than a hundred-strong. After an extensive explanation about the "sport" and the association's long-standing credentials and yearly events, the announcer got to the rules and regulations segment of the spiel, which got me thinking. To make races equal, the rules required the power of the mower to be limited depending on the age of the competitor and on the class in which you had entered, but for some reason, presumably safety, the blades had to be removed in all classes. Surely by removing the blades, the machine is no longer a lawn mower and is just a slow and aerodynamically terribly shaped go-cart. How can it be called a lawn mower when it is in no way capable of mowing a lawn?

From what I could work out, the mowers didn't seem to be equal in power or speed, and in the majority of races, the winner was whichever driver took the lead on the first turn of the ovoid circuit—he/she would remain there until they took the checkered flag. The races that followed included a girl representing Team Jesus, a mower dangerously tipping over, and the first successful overtaking maneuver when one mower reached a speed of over 40 mph, which, on a circuit with straights of less than 100 feet, was pretty impressive . . . for a mower that can't cut a blade of grass. Fortunately for us, the roar of the machines and the country music that echoed through the speedway's public address system during each race was enough to drown out the commentary of the MC who, by this time, was enjoying the racing so much that his relationship with lawn mowers seemed sexually gratifying.

As the practice races continued into the adult classes, where lawn mowers could reach speeds that almost rivaled our rental car, it became obvious that the day's racing wouldn't be finished for quite some time. As we made our way to a refreshment stand through the long blades of grass that surrounded the track, we had started to play a brand-new game—

trying to detect when one country and western song ended and another began. For two guys born and raised in England, where there aren't any songs about driving pickup trucks or attending barn dances, it's not as easy as you think.

As we returned to our seats, there was some good news and bad news waiting for us. Sadly, for reasons I still don't know, Redneck Idol had been canceled and would not be featured in the evening's festivities. But luckily, the organizers (with a lot of persuasion from the MC, I'm sure) decided on a back-up plan. The lawn mower races were now to include a greater number of laps per race and, later on, we would be shown a demonstration of the Dixie Chopper—the world's fastest lawn mower!

Woo!

So at this point it was time for the real racing to begin. The first few races were nothing special, and, as in practice, were won by whoever reached the first turn quickest. After four races, though, the crowd finally had a reason to get excited, as the mower duels were interrupted by the arrival of the *General Lee* (of *Dukes of Hazzard* fame). Of course, as people flocked around the famous orange 1969 Dodge Charger for a quick photo opportunity, the MC was eager to get the attention back onto the matter at hand, seemingly shocked that one of the most celebrated vehicles in television history could even come close to matching the attraction of a debladed lawn mower.

When the crowd's interest was back on the center track, the racing continued and the first of the adult division produced a photo finish . . . or, well, a shout-at-your-wife finish.

"Sherri!" he bellowed. "Who won that one? . . . Sherri!"

After a brief few seconds, Sherri raised her two hands and showed six fingers, as the MC turned to the two drivers.

"Number six won that race," he informed them. The

driver of mower 6 began to celebrate, as did his rival, who was at the helm of 06.

"SHERRI!"

After the confusion had been sorted out, the racing took a brief respite, allowing a pickup truck pulling a sheet of metal time to flatten the course. Meanwhile, the two monster trucks were brought into action to entertain the crowd. As the wall-climbing vehicle began to struggle with any sort of climb, the All-Terrain Monster was in full swing spinning and twisting its way through a mechanical ballet. As the truck skidded and slid its way around the concrete circuit, the driver was invited nearer the crowd in order to perform a maneuver known as a reverse hurricane (a "spin" to you and I). As he powered the truck into the central reservation, he applied the brakes and pulled hard on the wheel, sending dirt into the air, raising cheers from the small crowd, and, because it had all taken place on the freshly flattened lawn mower course, eliciting outcries of anger from the lawn mowerers. (I assume *lawn mowerers* is the correct term.)

With shouts of "Hey, what are you doing?," "Get out of here, buddy!" and other less polite remonstrations, I could barely hear the apology from the owner of both monster trucks over the angry shouting of the drivers and the laughter that was coming from both Antony and myself. As the pickup returned for a second flattening job, Antony and I decided we should head back to the motel, freshen up, and return when the temperature and humidity were more bearable . . . and hopefully when the lawn mower racing had been concluded.

After a quick shower, a swim in our pool, and a light snack, we returned to the track and, unbelievably, above the ubiquitous sound of insect cries in the grasslands that surrounded us, we could hear the MC commentating on a teenager's lawn mower race.

"And the best thing about this sport," he said, "is that as youngsters, it keeps them away from alcohol and drugs and they are doing something productive with their lives." Given the choice, I'd rather my son grew up to emulate Keith Richards than a grass-cutting Mario Andretti.

"You'd think they'd have short grass around here with all of those lawn mowers," Antony pointed out in frustration as we thwacked our way back through the high grass around the arena.

"Yeah, well, there're about thirty of them down there, and not a single one can cut the grass!" I replied.

When the races finally reached their climax, when the sun set and the stadium floodlights came on (although they didn't reach the center of the circuit), three and a half hours of excruciatingly boring racing was finally laid to rest and the organizers made good on their promise by introducing the world's fastest lawn mower to the crowd. Looking like a cross between a go-cart and a mobility scooter, the Dixie Chopper has a 990cc engine that produces a whopping 33 bhp. With a mind-blowing top speed of 15 mph, it has the ability to cut the grass of a football field in less than ten minutes, and turn 8.7 acres of grass into lawn every hour. Mind you, with a price tag of $10,000 you would expect it to take the kids to school and thrill you in the bedroom (which, again, for the MC, it probably does).

Due to the cancellation of Redneck Idol, the evening's entertainment was to be presented by a band called Deepstep, a quintet from Dublin that was weirdly named after a minuscule town 40 miles to the north. The stage, which had stood empty for the entire afternoon, began to attract a crowd of revved-up revelers, some of whom had brought their own chairs. Although the chances of the band's not playing any country and western music was slim to none, Antony and I

gave them the benefit of the doubt and decided to stand near
the expectant crowd in the hope that someone would speak
to us, or at the very least ask us how their stolen GPS system
worked. After fifteen minutes of nonstop, knee-slapping
country music and no chatting, Antony and I decided to
leave, but then we noticed a young man wearing a ripped
vest and sporting a rebellious baseball cap with the words
Jesus is a nobody written on it. I found this fascinating, in a
town so obviously and proudly devoted to Him. When on
closer inspection we discovered that the cap actually read
Jesus is my homeboy, my urge to speak to him dwindled and
Antony and I thought that it was the appropriate time to return to our motel to prepare ourselves for an even stranger
southern experience than the non-lawn-mowing lawn mower
races.

On the day when more than 150 musical acts at twelve
separate locations around the world were raising
awareness for climate change at the request of Al Gore,
Dublin's sweltering morning temperature made me wonder
whether the recognition of that particular cause had come
too late. With the mercury pushing into the 90s at only 11
a.m., along with the extreme humidity, the promise of the
events was the only thing spurring us into the car for the
fifteen-minute drive to Bukeye Park in East Dublin. The online schedule for the day featured curiosities such as the Mud
Pit Belly-Flop and the Armpit Serenade—how could we
miss that?

If the queue of traffic waiting to turn off the highway and
onto Buckeye Road was anything to go by, the Redneck
Games were very popular indeed, and, as I looked behind at
the huge line of traffic in which we were waiting, we were the
only two people in a conventional car. Everyone else was

driving 4x4s, SUVs, and, the most popular vehicle by far, pickup trucks—with four crammed into the front and enough room in the cargo area for a family of six.

For $5 we entered the hub of the Redneck Games, where the events, refreshment stands, and entertainment all would be crammed in an area no larger than a football field. At the very end of the park stood a boat ramp, which met the Altamaha River, where there were already a hundred or so people cooling themselves off. At the far bank, amid a flotilla of casual vessels sporting flags of the Confederacy, a tree whose branches were perfectly positioned to allow someone to leap from its height and fall into the river below was attracting a great number of prospective jumpers who queued patiently for their turn. The number of people waiting in line made me realize that the river really was the only "thing to do" in East Dublin—not even the earlier arrival of an ambulance at the water's edge had discouraged anyone from attempting the plummet.

At midday, the crowd were officially welcomed by some members of the Y-96FM staff, who still sponsor the event, and introduced to a character named Freight Train, a gentleman with long gray hair, a thin beard, and a Confederate flag–decorated hat, whose age was almost impossible to determine due to his youthful attire and lack of teeth. With a propane torch, made up of six cans of Budweiser with a flame coming out the end, it was Freight Train's job to light the ceremonial Barbeque Grill, the Redneck equivalent of the Olympic flame. With the grill lit ("Let the gas begin," said Freight Train) the games were officially under way. Freight Train took some time out to mingle with the crowd and pose for photos, distorting his face by placing his bottom lip over his nose (an expression that could easily have won the man a "gurning" world championship).

As we were informed by the announcer that the first event, the Armpit Serenade, wouldn't begin for another half hour, Antony and I decided to wander through the various stalls on the opposite side of the boat ramp to see what choices we had for lunch.

There was quite a bit of food available for a reasonable price, although much of it was slightly similar. Burgers were on sale at nearly every stand along with chicken, fries, hot dogs, the usual. To wash it all down, soft drinks, ice cream cones, and water were sold in abundance. Out of principle I avoided any sign advertising *burger's, hot dog's,* and . . . wait for it . . . *fry's,* and was drawn to the only vendor who hadn't used a single apostrophe incorrectly.

"You wanna try summin'?" she asked.

"Um, maybe," I replied. I pointed at a large sausage attached to the end of a wooden stick. "What's that?"

"That's alligator on a stick," she replied. "It's real nice. You wan' some?"

"Er. Not right now. I'll work up an appetite first."

Across from the alligator woman was a stand which, instead of selling food or merchandise, was advertising the Republican Party, a stalwart of the South. A man clutching books titled *Why Lincoln Was Wrong* and *The South Will Rise Again* along with fliers for a local candidate approached me, and I had no choice but to talk to him—the guy had left his stand (adorned in flags of the Confederacy) in order to speak with me. Luckily, I had the perfect excuse to get away, being from the U.K. and not exactly eligible to vote in the U.S.

In previous years the Redneck Games have appeared on several American television programs, including MTV's *Real World* and the popular talk show *Maury Povich.* As we joined the crowd for the Armpit Serenade—an event where actual adults produce fart noises by using a hand and a sweaty underarm—it became obvious that this year's south-ern extravaganza would be making a return to the small screen. Before the contest took place, so-called celebrities would demonstrate how the proceedings were run and could try their hand before the real competitors took over. With microphone positioned directly under his armpit, the first celebrity, Kyle, a young and shy-looking man who was a member of a regional television company based in Atlanta, removed his shirt and attempted to make a flatulence noise. On a day of such humidity and heat, a sweaty underarm wasn't difficult to produce, but after witnessing Kyle's disas-trous and not-very-crowd-pleasing attempt, it became clear that there was an obvious art to mastering the Armpit Sere-nade—one that a fourteen-year-old turned out to be most proficient in, taking the crown in the real contest and win-ning a trophy in the shape of a crushed beer can.

The Seed Spitting Contest followed and because so many people had entered, competitors' names were drawn from a hat. Once again, "celebrities" began the proceedings and Kyle embarrassed himself for a second time when, following an almighty exhale, his projectile slipped from his mouth, bounced off his chin, and landed just inches from his right shoe. Poor Kyle.

With my appetite back, I returned for some refreshments and as I sat on the bank of the river to watch the Redneck lemmings fall from the tree, I tucked into what I hoped wasn't the alligator's penis. Even though the arrival of yet another paramedic rescuing another injured jumper sweet-ened the afternoon, it did little to alter the taste of the meat, which can best be described as overly salted jockstrap.

Bored, Antony and I made our way back toward the re-freshment stands to wash the alligator out of my mouth and to see if we could sign up for any future events. As we walked, I spotted the most official-looking person within a quarter of a mile (a lady not dressed in dungarees with a pen) and decided she must be the appropriate person to ask.

"Hi. Just wondering if we could sign up for an event," I asked.

"Well, sure. Y'all're too late for the Bobbin' for Pigs' Feet, but you can still sign up for the Butt Crack Challenge, the Redneck Horseshoe, or the famous Mud-Pit Belly Flop."

Two of the events being self-explanatory, we inquired as to what was involved in Redneck Horseshoes.

"I really don't know," she replied with a large grin covering her face.

"I thought it had something to do with toilet seats," I replied, hoping to jog her memory.

"It could be," she replied, "but I really haven't got a clue."

"OK then. Can you tell me what time the Mud-Pit Belly Flop is?"

"Sorry. I don't know that either."

"Excuse me, but what is your actual job in this information booth?" Luckily, she just laughed and posted our entry forms into the appropriate collection bins.

As the only source of information we gained from speaking to the lady was that we were too late to enter Bobbin' for Pigs' Feet, we decided we had better see what that particular event was all about. I thought that it couldn't possibly be what the name suggested, and believed it to be similar to games such as Pin the Tail on the Donkey or Murder in the Dark, in which no one is ever really murdered and tails aren't ripped off and pinned back on real donkeys. But as we reached the front of the stage, we found that two see-through plastic tanks filled with water had been placed on the ground, and each contained eight real pigs' feet, skinned and looking like they had been pickled. Kyle was already showing the crowd how not to succeed—it seemed that the rules were similar to apple bobbing. His opponent, one of the ladies from the radio station, emptied her tank in forty seconds, as Kyle, struggling to grab his second pig's foot, looked more likely to drown than to finish in the ninety-second time limit.

Soon they drew names again to determine the real competitors. During the drawing, whenever someone's name was called who wasn't present, there was a large, shirtless fellow who without fail would call out "I'll do it," before taking a sip from his beer can and cheering on whoever was selected after the organizers ignored him. After four rounds of one-on-one pig's-foot-grabbing duels, and at least seven or eight "I'll do it"s, the winner was finally decided by a man who plucked the eight feet out in a Redneck Games record time of only twenty-six seconds, beating the runner-up, a middle-aged woman from London, England. After the third beer trophy of the afternoon was awarded, I went to hunt for the lady from London for two reasons. One was that I wanted to hear an English accent and to ask her what brought her to the Games. More important, though, the "I'll do it" guy had just began to speak to Antony and it was an excuse to leave.

I never did garner much information from the lady from London other than that she was with her daughter, but at least I was having better luck than Antony, who took a full five minutes to get away from Mr. I'll Do It. His real name, according to Antony, was Drew. We escaped into the maze that was the area of refreshment stands, but our anonymity lasted for less than ten minutes, as Drew caught up with us and introduced himself.

"So where are you guys from?" he asked.

"England. Not London," we both replied in unison.

"You boys are a long way from home," said Drew.

"Where are you from?" I asked.

"You see that hill over there?" he replied, pointing through the trees at a hill that looked to be just over a mile away.

"Yes."

"Just the other side of that."

"Oh," I replied. "Have you ever been abroad, Drew?" I asked. Drew's answer was blunt.

"Where's that?"

"To another country."

"Oh . . . um . . . I went to Michigan once."

After talking about what we did back home and discovering what Drew did for a living (he works as a delivery driver for a dump), he looked behind us and a sudden look of anger crossed his face—he looked as mad as if he were remembering catching his best friend in bed with his mother.

"I hate that!" he snapped. I looked around to see what he could have been referring to. There didn't seem much apart from the boat ramp and some alligators on sticks.

"What?" Antony enquired.

"That," Drew replied, pointing at two women, one black and one white, who were idly strolling near us side by side. "It shouldn't be allowed. Makes me so angry."

"Why does it make you angry?" I asked. Drew grunted, stuttered, and gestured with his arms, struggling for the correct words to sum up his feelings. "It just shouldn't be allowed. We weren't meant to live together."

Normally, at a point in a conversation such as this, I would find any excuse to walk away and not be associated with the person to whom I was talking and his/her views. However, in Drew's case, I made an exception, mainly because he was so mind-numbingly stupid and had the IQ of a boiled sweet.

"You know there are two different kinds of niggers. You

can get white ones, you know. I just hate the lazy niggers," Drew said loudly.

"You know, in England, that word is pretty bad," replied Antony cautiously.

"It's a bad word here too, but I don't give a shit."

At this point, some of Drew's friends appeared and he introduced us as his buddies from London. He seemed to call all of his friends "cousin" in the same way that the English use "mate," but actually, from the look of them, they could all have been related to Drew. It didn't take long for their second-favorite topic of conversation to dominate the conversation.

"You see I'm a Baptist. That means I can't drink," he said. Then he noticed me looking down at the can of Budweiser in his hand.

"Oh, no," he added. "I can drink; I just can't get too drunk."

"I see."

"Do you go to church at home?" he asked.

"No. I'm not a very religious person," I replied. Drew looked disappointed.

"You've gotta believe Jesus died and rose on the third day—how can you not believe it?" he questioned.

"Sorry, Drew. I just don't. How religious is this town? Many people go to church?" I asked.

"Most of 'em—probably about ninety, ninety-five percent of 'em."

I felt safe in the knowledge that Drew liked us enough to not hurt us at that point, and so I decided to see how vicious his views actually were.

"What do you think about same-sex couples?" I asked. "States like Massachusetts are legalizing gay marriage. What are you thoughts on that issue?"

"Oh, that ain't right, man. Just ain't right!" he snapped, before stopping and staring straight through Antony. "You two aren't . . . ?"

"Oh, no," I interjected quickly.

"That's OK then," he said before pointing at Antony. "It's just that with a haircut like that, you never know."

"Is that sort of thing not looked upon favorably here?" asked Antony.

"Well, at my high school prom, some fag came dressed in a skirt."

"Yeah?"

"Yeah." Drew said defiantly. "He went home in an ambulance."

On that rather solemn note, Drew decided to go sign up for the Mud-Pit Belly Flop and agreed to meet us there when it all began. He and his friends departed, leaving Antony and me by the side of a stand which, ironically, promoted love of the Confederacy as HERITAGE, NOT HATRED.

As a backhoe arrived in order to prepare the mud pit for the belly flopping, a man dressed in a long Confederate flag–patterned coat took to the stage and sang some classic country tunes to a crowd who were more interested in how the pit preparations were coming on. Thirty minutes later, the microphone was handed back to the Y-96 DJ, as a crowd about six thick surrounded the pit waiting to hear who would compete. First, though, as always, the "celebrities" would take to the pit before anyone else. An elderly lady known as Grandma Redneck—who wouldn't look out of place on a front porch in a rocking chair with shotgun in hand—was selected to lead these proceedings; she was to dunk herself into the 4-foot-deep pit, which contained muddy water an unhealthy shade of bright orange.

As Grandma Redneck stood at the bog's edge, adopting a

dive position for photos, a small child ran out of the crowd and ran right into her behind, attempting to force her into the mire. Due to her overall girth, Grandma Redneck didn't lose her footing (I don't know if she even noticed). But when she finally took to her downward plunge, her size and weight helped cover a large majority of the crowd in orange mud.

The rules are pretty simple from what I could work out: Each competitor was to fall into the pit adopting a belly-flop position. Judges would then decide on which "flop" was the best. If the contest was judged on how much water left the bog, Grandma Redneck had set the benchmark pretty high. According to the Y-96 DJ, the contest would take place in the form of heats, with the winners of each progressing to a flop final. When a name was announced, a shirtless newcomer would approach the pit, push members of the crowd back in order for a perfect run-up, dive into the mud, and return to the surface completely covered in a skin of orange, looking like a monster from *Doctor Who*. With each belly flop, the audience (especially Drew) shrieked and applauded as more and more mud splashed into the crowd.

Midway through the second heat, when a member of the audience was pushed into the pit, all hell broke loose. Everyone else saw it as an indication that they too could enter the bog, and in under a minute, dozens of people were crammed into the pit and many more looked for a space in which they could squeeze. This ended the official contest, which by now had no validity at all anyway.

"Shall we?" I asked Antony.

After removing our shirts and flip-flops, we entered the pit in a slow and methodical way so as to not trample on anyone. (Some other "swimmers" were running and jumping in, with no thought as to who would be in the pit when they came crashing down upon them.) The first thing I noticed was the incredible warmth of the water, and that the bottom of the pit was incredibly difficult to wade through—the muddy bed produced a drag effect on your legs similar to walking through a children's ball pit. As if rubbing shoulders with muddy rednecks wasn't enough of an enjoyable experience, in the center I met Drew, who decided to slap me on the back and show me a personal alligator-wrestling technique of his which he had earlier attempted to describe. Being sufficiently covered in Georgia's finest, I suggested to Antony that we wash ourselves off in the river and return to the motel for a proper clean and a spot of dinner at KFC (Kentucky Framed Commandments).

Only an hour had passed when we returned to the Redneck Games, but the scene had changed dramatically. People were still playing in the mud pit, which now had lost so much water, it looked more like a muddy paddling pool; the setting sun had drawn people out of the river and to the foot of the stage, and an entire day of drinking had taken its toll on a now energized and raucous congregation. Drew, who earlier had told us that his religion compelled him to drink responsibly, staggered around with a girl in tow, completely unaware of what was going on. But he finally showed some life when a Y-96FM staff member announced that a wet-T-shirt contest was about to start.

The four contestants were exhibited on the front of the stage to whet the crowd's appetite and to begin a charity auction for the right to hose the ladies down. This was eventually won by a German who paid $100 for the honor, and who also won the right to sit as a judge for "Mr. and Mrs. Redneck," which would precede the hosing.

From what I could make out, Mr. and Mrs. Redneck was a talent show, and the entrants didn't seem to have a single skill among them. One competitor showed that he could shout rather loudly. Another, a man named Cletus (yes, that was his actual name), could crush a beer can by placing it into his dungarees. The winner, however, was a woman whose "talent" was that she had given birth to five children.

As the wet-T-shirt contest became ever nearer, a careful listener could detect in the subtle nuances from the crowd that they were ready—they were shouting "WE WANT TITTIES" over and over again. On hearing this, a rather drunk girl ran to the front of the stage and lifted both her top and the spirit of the crowd. As event organizers forcibly removed the girl and the crowd got even rowdier, the host took to the microphone and tried to calm the situation.

"Hey, everyone, this is a family event," she said calmly. "Let's be classy."

Classy? At the Redneck Games? The crowd weren't going to buy that, surely. They had just witnessed a talent contest in which the ultimate in stereotypical rednecks was placed runner-up to someone whose only skill was in the art of procreating.

"WE WANT TITS! WE WANT TITS!" the crowd cheered. The host tried to laugh the chants off but finally they continued for so long that she stormed to the front of the stage.

"Hey!" she bellowed back. "There are children in the audience, so there'll be no more bullshit!" Whatever respect she had commanded flew straight out the window, and as the crowd responded by chanting "Bullshit" in unison, the wet-T-shirt contest was canceled, and it was up to the winner of Redneck Idol, which apparently had happened at some point after all, to play to the hostile audience.

Only five minutes in, the artist (singing—you guessed it—country music) was interrupted by the games' closing firework display. The attitude of the crowd, coupled with the sporadic fighting that had broken out in sections of the park, had probably persuaded the organizers that they should end the games as quickly as possible. Antony and I scrambled to a nearby bank to avoid accidentally getting into any skirmish, and found ourselves torn between which explosions to watch—the colorful ones in the air or the brutal ones in the crowd. As police and security guards were called into the darkness for the almost impossible task of finding a young man who had produced a knife, we decided to leave.

As the car door slammed, ensuring our safety, I took a last look at my fellow deserters. Suddenly, I felt out of touch with the human race. I knew that not everyone who had attended the games shared Drew's views and opinions, but it had been a shock to us to encounter such naked bigotry. In democratic societies, freedom of speech is embedded into constitutions and all expressions are allowed to be heard even if you don't like what they have to say. At first I assumed it to be a slang term, a funny insult, but to be a redneck is something held in high regard in the South and I found that it's a label that most of the working class wears with pride. For the best part of the day, the Redneck Games are a source of family fun and downright tomfoolery, but the outdated ideologies I'd heard that day made me wonder whether love of the Confederacy and its way of life is a case of heritage and not hatred.

The only thing that I was certain of, as I watched people stagger to their cars, stopping for the occasional vomit, was that there would be many congregation members nursing a severe hangover in church the next morning.

5. CRACKS AT THE TRACKS

Apparently, a member of INXS owns that
mansion on the hill. (I spent an entire day
mooning trains, so you'd think I'd have heard
something a bit more interesting than that.)

I hate Los Angeles. Absolutely loathe the place. I have ever since I first visited in 1997. Back then, I found the City of Angels to be an unrelenting urban sprawl of more than 18 million people residing in an area stretching more than 120 miles from the Pacific Ocean to the southwestern tip of the Mojave Desert. Due to the city's rather limited public transportation network, L.A. was home to no less than twenty-seven intertwining freeways, which still couldn't cope with the demands of the population's 65 million daily commutes. Even Hollywood, known for its prestige and allure, was no more than a street of souvenir shops where litter covered many of the stars on the district's famous Walk of Fame. Ten years later, fate had cruelly returned me to the city. But this time I decided to wipe the slate clean and start fresh, hoping things had changed and that the glitz and glamour had once again replaced the blitz and clamour.

However, this visit began even worse than the first.

In my eternal wisdom, to save a few dollars, I had booked our rental car with a company named Deluxe Rent a Car. Now, I know as well as you do that the name was most probably a name chosen out of irony and was not representational of their fleet, but at the time I was happy that I was making a huge saving of $3 per day. As Antony and I trudged away from the crowded baggage carousel in the airport, we made our way to the rental car pickup point located just meters from the airport's exit and awaited Deluxe Rent a Car's shuttle bus.

Twenty minutes of waiting later, Antony and I slumped

onto our bags to recover from the early-morning flight from Jacksonville to Los Angeles, which had taken eight hours owing to a 500-mile detour via Washington, D.C. The flow of rental car shuttle buses was becoming almost hypnotic and every one had passed at least once. Avis arrived and was quickly followed by Hertz and Advantage and Dollar; Thrifty preceded Budget, which made way for Avis and Hertz to arrive for their second laps. There was no sign of Deluxe, nor did any of the vans show the company's logo symbolizing some sort of partnership. A further ten minutes passed and with Avis and Hertz passing us for the third time, I made my way back into the airport terminal and approached the information desk.

"Excuse me, but I'm waiting for a rental car's shuttle bus. Do you know if they have one?" I asked.

"What's it called?" she replied.

"Deluxe Rent a Car," I said, rather embarrassed.

"I've never heard of it," she said bluntly. "Oh, hang on a minute"—she consulted some notes on her desk, running her finger down a list of names—"nope."

"Um, thanks anyway."

As I made my way back to Antony, I passed a pay phone with a telephone directory hanging underneath and decided to ring the company for instructions on how to reach them. There was a Deluxe Clothing, Deluxe Hair Salon, and Deluxe Jewelry listed, but then, where Deluxe Rent a Car should have been, it was Deluxe Rooter Sewer & Drain Service. Maybe it was the same company. As a last resort, I rang my girlfriend, who logged onto my e-mail account back in the U.K. and gave me the number for the rental firm.

I dialed the number from the pay phone with the useless phone book attached, and my call was sent directly to a recorded message that stated clear and concise instructions for reaching the rental center: "Hello, and thank you for call-ing Deluxe Rent a Car. To reach our rental center, please exit the terminal building and wait by the sign marked *Hotels and Courtesy Shuttles* for the white shuttle van that's marked *Jon-nypark*. It arrives every fifteen minutes and will deliver you safely to the facility. This pay phone will self-destruct in ten seconds." (I think I made that last bit up).

Of course! It was so simple. I'm surprised we didn't think of it earlier. To find Deluxe Rent a Car, we had to keep our eyes out for the van marked *Jonnypark*. It made perfect sense. Antony and I were kicking ourselves with stupidity for thirty minutes, until the van finally picked us up.

Upon arrival at the company's "headquarters," the sizable queue gave me some time to look around. The inside office was a tasteless 1970s mix of purple and gray. Outside, among the throng of cars parked in no particular fashion, stood a giant electricity box, similar to the ones found at the top of high-voltage transmission pylons. A small child standing just in front of me summed up the place rather nicely, tugging on his father's trousers and whispering, "This place is horrible, Daddy."

Finally, after an interesting conversation about why I had to pay $11 just because I had a foreign driving license ("We can control three pedals in the U.K., you know," I told her), I was handed the keys to our new rental car and we made our way outside to locate it. Much to my dismay, it was a Chrysler PT Cruiser. My three-hour wait had rewarded me with a car that was a cross between a 1930s limousine and a hearse. To make matters worse was the color of it—*they* called it gold. I thought "shitty brown" was a more accurate description.

Leaving the rental center to join the San Diego Freeway and the inevitable traffic jams that would be occurring at the time, I noticed two concerning facts about the car. It had very little fuel and, according to the digital display, an oil level of 0 percent. Fixing the problems was to be troublesome. After stopping in several petrol stations I finally found one that would accept my credit card. As for the rather disturbing oil level, I simply turned the digital display off—problem solved. I silently promised myself that I would return the car with an empty tank, even if I had to drive it around the block twenty times first.

Although our time in Los Angeles didn't get off to a flying start, we were sure that as long as the car didn't seize up (until the second we returned it to the rental centre), things were bound to improve. To that end, we headed for Santa Monica and its beach. At the entrance to its famed pier, one can see that Santa Monica has everything you would expect from a beachside city: golden sands, palm trees, a beautiful ocean, and an abundance of tramps basking in the summer sun. After a quick stroll along the pier, Antony and I made our way through Santa Monica's famous Third Street Promenade, past the expensive designer outlets and sports shops (which kept informing us that in just four days' time, David Beckham would begin playing football in a country where they don't even call the sport by its proper name . . . mind you, for £70,000 a day, I wouldn't complain).

Although David Beckham wasn't around to chat with, fortunately for us, ahead of me in a queue and having a bit of trouble with his credit card was ex-Arsenal and England left-back Lee Dixon. Antony and I collared him on the way out to see why the Premiership stalwart was in Los Angeles.

"Hello, Mr. Dixon," Antony muttered to get his attention.

"Hiya, lads," he replied quickly as if we were old friends.

"Must be great for you in L.A.," I interjected. "Must never get noticed," I added, instantly realizing that I myself was defeating my point entirely. I decided to move things swiftly along. "You out here for Football Focus or Beckham's unveiling?"

"No, but I've got a meeting with FOX. How long are you guys out here for?"

"Just a week."

"You've come to L.A. for just a week?"

Not wanting to go into the odds and sods of the entire trip, I decided to play it safe. "Yeah, kind of. Do you actually like it here? We aren't the biggest fans of this city."

"L.A. is great. My wife lived out here for fourteen years and you really need to know where to go."

With that, Lee left the shop and made his way into another clothes shop. As we headed in the opposite direction so as not to look like minor celebrity stalkers, it suddenly dawned on us that not only had we not asked him for his views on Thierry Henry leaving Arsenal just a week before, but, most important, we hadn't asked him where we needed to go to make the most out of such a horrible city. As we looked back down the street, he was being asked for a signature by a couple of guys who had recognized him.

*N*ext day, I wasn't sure if it was the drone of Los Angeles life or the fact that Antony and I had now spent almost a month together, but something was definitely wrong with the atmosphere between us. Neither of us was talking that much and things were strained. But we both sensed that it definitely wasn't so much of a problem between ourselves. . . . I think the hatred of Los Angeles was contagious and the thought that we still had three days to waste in L.A. sent a shared shiver of dread down our spines.

Stuff it, I thought to myself. Neither Antony nor I wanted to spend another day in this dump, so I was willing to throw caution to the wind and run the risk of the car breaking down in the middle of a desert. What Antony and I needed was a 500-mile round trip to Las Vegas. That should cheer us up.

Although Las Vegas is a city in the middle of the desert, established through gambling and expanding on greed, it is a truly fascinating, staggering spectacle. Where else in the world could I gaze at both the Eiffel Tower and the Empire State Building as a 40-foot Rita Rudner stared back at me through my hotel window? Due to the almost intolerable heat (during the summer, overnight temperatures are still in the mid-90s), we decided the best idea was to remain in our room with some cooling beers and take to the city streets when the sun had disappeared.

A walk down the city's famous strip is a strange experience and, if you can resist actually going in any of the city's 1,700 licensed premises, the stroll past 15,000 miles of neon lighting and free entertainment is enough to pass an entire evening. Each and every hotel dedicates itself to a theme, and with the pyramid at Luxor, the lights of New York New York, and the almost perfect replica of the St. Mark's Square Campanile amid the waterways of The Venetian, Vegas seems like a city into which the whole world has been squeezed. Treasure Island Hotel and Casino puts on a free seventeenth-century pirate show known as the *Sirens of TI* for passersby four times a night, and the luxurious Bellagio is famed for its 8-acre (32,000 m²) artificial lake and truly spectacular musical fountain display. As Antony and I perched ourselves on the casino's wall, "My Heart Will Go On" bellowed out of the speakers and the lake's hundred or so fountains, accompanied by 4,500 lights, danced to the melody. We decided to wait a further fifteen minutes for the next show, and the Sarah

Brightman and Andrea Bocelli song "Con Te Partiro" enrap-
tured the crowd. As the song reached a higher key, the carefully choreographed display made full use of its 1,200 nozzles,
dazzling the gathered crowd and passersby alike with a show
that befitted the beauty and elegance of the piece.

After returning to our hotel and consulting the Bellagio's
playlist, though, we found that it was a good thing that we
had stayed and watched the fountains perform only two
songs. Our moods could have been quickly quashed if the
casino's random selection of their thirty available tunes had
chosen to play Lee Greenwood's "God Bless the U.S.A." Fortunately it hadn't, and we found that Las Vegas and the fountains had done the trick—Antony and I were back to our
usual selves. And we needed to be. In a little over two days'
time, we weren't just going to spend the day together—we
were going to drop our trousers more than thirty times with
a bunch of complete strangers.

In 1979, K.T. Smith was drinking in the Mugs Away
Saloon in Laguna Niguel, southwest of downtown
Los Angeles in the wealthy area of Orange County. Smith re-
putedly told his friends that he would buy anyone a drink if
they approached the railway track opposite the bar, lowered
their pants, and "mooned" the next passing train. Many did
and, more than twenty-five years later, they continue to do
so one Saturday a year in July; however, K.T. is no longer
there to reward them. Still, today, the "Mooning of Amtrak"
at the Mugs Away Saloon is an event that attracts hundreds
of people.

When the Southern California's Metrolink regional rail
system began weekend service in 2006, the number of daily
trains that passed the bar on the selected Saturday between
dawn and midnight totaled thirty-six. Attending such an

event meant we would have to spend an entire day in or around a bar, but Antony and I were willing to make such a sacrifice. We made our way to the Mugs Away Saloon as soon as we checked into our nearby motel—we wanted to check the place out a day before the Mooning was scheduled to begin.

Located on a long dead-end road just off the San Diego Freeway, the Mugs Away Saloon looks more like a small business on an industrial estate than a bar. With a single pool table and a tiny outside area for drinking and smoking, the pub isn't the largest I've ever seen. However, as we approached the bar lady, preempting her request for ID by already reaching for our passports, a picture of a dozen pairs of bare buttocks from the opposite side of the rails let us know that we were definitely in the right place. Specialty cocktails were on offer for the weekend's extravaganza—with names such as a Wet Pussy, Dripping Dick, or a Royal Fuck, killing the subtle art of drink-naming innuendo—but Antony and I opted for a pint of beer each. We made our way outside just in time for a band to take to the stage and begin the saloon's Pre-Mooning Party.

In anticipation of the big day, there were already more than a dozen or so camper vans and RVs parked alongside the road next to the Mugs Away Saloon, and nearly every parking space belonging to the bar and nearby businesses had been filled. Above the door were two huge posters emblazoned with the northbound and southbound train times. If Antony and I were to take this thing seriously (as seriously as you can take showing your bare ass to commuters), we were going to have to arrive back at the saloon before the first scheduled train at 7:35 a.m. the next morning. So we arrived back at our motel early, for a good night's sleep before a day of mooning in the L.A. heat. It turned out that Antony had a pressing matter on his mind, and finally he shared his concern with me.

"Rich?" he asked with a serious look in his eye. "Do you think I should shave my ass?"

Even for me, 7 a.m. is a ridiculously early time to begin drinking. But outside the Mugs Away Saloon the next morning, people were already sipping from cans of Budweiser, and there were a lot of bikers congregated outside of the bar.

"You reckon we should go inside and get a drink?" asked Antony.

"I reckon we should go somewhere and get a leather jacket," I replied.

It was outside the bar that we met Mark Braconi, a young-looking thirty-eight-year-old who works with server operating systems, IP addresses, and other computer geek–related things I know nothing about. Mark was in the same boat as us—although he lived just five miles from the bar, this was his first Mooning of Amtrak.

"Most of the people here are W.T., you know," he commented, sipping his vodka and orange juice.

"Yeah," I replied slowly, not knowing what on earth *W.T.* stood for. Wearing T-shirts? Without teeth? Mark saw the perplexed look on my face. "White trash."

At this point, the barmaid who IDed us yesterday approached us.

"You were here last night," she commented accurately. "Have you been to bed yet?"

"Yeah. Had five and a half hours last night," I replied.

"Want a Bloody Mary?" she asked.

"It's just gone seven in the morning!"

She looked at me with utter disdain. "I have one word for you." I waited. "Pussy," she said.

"Ah, thought it may be something like that," I said, before turning my attention to the bikers. "Are they friendly bikers?"

"Them? They're the Capistrano Eagles, our local biker group. They're fine." She pointed out a burly fellow with a can of Budweiser. "Just don't piss him off."

At 7:30, Antony and I dragged an unwilling Mark to the chain-link fence to wait for the first of the day's thirty-six trains. Joining us across the road from the bar were maybe six or seven people—more than double that number were still in and outside of the saloon. At 7:40, the 7:35 came into view and the few who were present at the fence dropped their trousers and shorts and pressed their buttocks up against the chain-link fence. I noticed that, weirdly, the cold metal fence was somewhat comfortable on my bare skin and I felt at total ease. As the train slowed down for the benefit of the people onboard (the trains are booked up months in advance), everyone waved as it sauntered by, whistling in appreciation for the nakedness on show.

As the next train wasn't due for almost an hour, Antony and I made our way back to the bar and continued to talk to Mark. At eight, the Highway Patrol pulled up outside of the bar and two policemen exited the vehicle. A sudden undercurrent of comments such as "They have no jurisdiction" and "Rent-a-cop" echoed quietly through the ranks.

"What do you reckon they're here for?" Antony asked Mark.

"I reckon someone must have complained about your arse, mate," I replied.

At 8:20, we made our way back over to the fence for the first of three trains which were scheduled to pass in the following twenty minutes. It was here we would moon not only our first Metrolink train, but our first southbound train, too. The 8:23 whizzed by at 8:30 without slowing down or whistling. At this point, twenty-one people had joined us at the fence. One was a woman in her forties who was dressed for the heat in sunglasses and a small white dress.

"Are you from England?" she asked.

"Yeah, good guess," I replied, knowing how difficult it is for an American to distinguish between an English accent and the ghastly Australian twang (where every sentence ends on a high note as if something amazing has just happened).

"You live here?"

I scoffed at the suggestion. "No. I couldn't live here," I replied.

"England is home, then?" she asked rather compassionately.

"Yes. I suppose it is."

I leant against the fence to appreciate the kind words and the thoughts of home they had provoked. Suddenly, a few moments later, the crowd that had amassed to watch the mooning of the 9:09 southbound broke into uncontrollable cheers. Just a couple of feet from where I was standing, the woman who had just spoken to me about home had pulled her short skirt up and lowered the straps from her shoulders, revealing a vagina complete with stud and two medically enhanced breasts with what looked like Playboy bunny piercings attached to her nipples. Cameras were quickly whipped out by members of the excited crowd as the woman placed her hands on either side of her groin and showed off the piercing, of which she seemed immensely proud. In a little under a minute, she had gone from touching to touching herself. Ironically, the only item of clothing that was left in place was her crucifix necklace.

While most people were still awaiting the arrival of the train, she continued to prance around, much to the delight of

Kris, who she didn't describe as her partner or husband but as her "soul mate." He seemed quite content to stand back and admire her as other men ogled her and posed for pictures alongside her breasts. As the 9:09 Metrolink train zoomed by ten minutes behind schedule—but, as far as I was concerned, not a minute too soon—she turned, showed her bottom, and returned fully dressed to the fence next to me, continuing our conversation as if nothing had happened. "England's pretty out there, huh?" she asked. I didn't quite know what to say.

"Um, yeah. A bit. Think you'd fit in nicely though." She seemed pleased.

As the mooners dispersed, an elderly gentleman sporting a big white beard and wearing a Mickey Mouse T-shirt approached the woman. Any thoughts that he reminded me of Santa Claus were quickly dashed when instead of making her sit on his knee, he pointed at her breasts and said: "Can I look at your tits?" You didn't need to ask her twice, and as she swiftly acquiesced to his request, cameras focused on her again, transforming the mass of people into a horde of amateur paparazzi. Santa surveyed the woman's lower piercing like some sort of overzealous gynecologist.

During the commotion, Mark spotted a television crew and thought it would be a great idea if he informed them of the distance Antony and I had covered to attend the day's event.

"You'll get on for sure," he insisted.

"But I don't really want to, Mark."

"Yes you do. Hey, buddy! These guys came all the way from England."

Before we knew it, a father-and-son camera team had us sign disclaimers and were asking us our reason for attending.

"Um, just for a laugh" was the best reason both Antony and I could muster.

As the 9:27 Metrolink northbound passed, Mark introduced me to a woman called Laurie, a lady who (thankfully)
kept her replica Jeff Gordon NASCAR top firmly on, became
affectionately attached to the English word "bum," and took
obvious exception to my opinion of her beloved NASCAR (a
sport in which cars drive for hours on end turning left). As
we chatted by the fence, a newspaper reporter approached
and asked me for some quotes he could use for the local
paper. I struggled to find some words to say to him, but I
was luckily saved by the bell—the bell of the 9:47 passing
twelve minutes late.

By eleven, cars had blocked others in and the entire area
surrounding the bar looked more like a refugee camp—
although a really nice one with paddling pools, barbecues,
and giant caravans. Inside the bar, a band had already begun
performing, and the pool table had been covered with a sheet
of plywood so a girl dressed in only a bra, panties, and a bottle opener could dance on it. Reaching the bar now seemed a
near impossibility.

Outside, five men had arrived in ideal attire for mooning—
kilts. Presuming that the men or their ancestors all hailed
from Scotland, I was surprised to hear that they were Sicilian,
and that apparently kilts had been standard dress (no pun in-
tended) for the inhabitants of the Italian island since the
Seaforth Highlanders fought there in the late eighteenth and
early nineteenth centuries.

After the 10:34 (passing at 10:38) slowed down so much
that it almost came to a complete standstill (people managed
to take pictures from the back of the train's last car), boobs
were still on show, and the earlier woman's bra strap had
snapped—not that she needed it. Antony and I remained at
the fence in preparation to moon both the 10:54 northbound
and the southbound 11:01, but when a train shot by at 10:57

journeying south, we weren't sure as to which train had just passed. To add to the confusion, another hurtled by twenty minutes later traveling in the opposite direction.

Because there wasn't another train scheduled for fifty-nine minutes, Antony and I figured we had at least an hour and a half before it would actually pass. Antony went to buy a burger and hang out near the crowd, but I'd seen far too many breasts, and retired to the car to indulge in some air-conditioned relaxation. Antony decided to join me in the car with his burger, and just then we realized we were parked in between Mark and his wife, who had just arrived. Mark was leaving before "things got out of hand," so we exchanged mobile numbers and agreed to all meet up in far-less-bizarre circumstances before we left.

Such was the demand for a parking space that as soon as Mark's wife vacated her space, a man in a pickup truck quickly pulled in. "Fucking hell! There are more people here than last year," the driver bellowed as he slammed the door shut. "Why aren't you guys out there?"

"We've been here since seven and fancied a breather," I replied.

"Oh, man; so many people. We're giving out free liquor at a stand this afternoon for anyone getting their tits out. This is their Mecca."

He continued to talk to us. I struggled to keep up with his rapid pace of speech, but finally simply nodded my head at times when he stopped for air. It was clear he was excited about the prospect of what may happen later in the day, and as he bid us a good afternoon, he looked into the air with arms outstretched, in the same way as if a friend of his had just died and he was asking God why.

"Woo! Titties!" he shouted, and with that, made his way to the front of the building to join his people.

After our air-conditioned break in the car from hell, we both returned to the bar where the number of bikes parked outside totaled well over a hundred. The atmosphere had completely changed—what had begun as a frivolous day of fancy-free mooning had turned into a convention of bandanas and mustaches. The last time I had seen so many bikes in one place was when Bateman and I were in a town called Hagerstown, Pennsylvania—a town whose outlet store acted as a checkpoint for the 5th Annual 9/11 Commemorative Ride fours years after the attacks on New York—the day before I was to sleep on a refrigerator (it's a long story . . . about three hundred pages . . . ISBN 978-0-307-33942-4 . . .).

The scene that greeted us opposite the fence and just yards from the bar's entrance was nothing like what the atmosphere in which the early-morning mooning took place. The number of people in leather jackets had exploded, bandanas were prevalent, and the number of biker girls outnumbered the other female population by eighteen tattooed breasts to two. There was certainly no violence, but the crowd were boisterous and loud, and middle-aged women were being photographed topless and encouraged to either mount their bikes or their partners.

As Antony and I strolled through the bar's parking lot, we found that many of the bikers were trying, in their own imitable way, to see more naked women. Such men included Glen, a man who sat relaxing by a half-filled paddling pool where dozens of one-dollar bills and a single five-dollar bill floated on the surface. As he supped at his can of beer, he noticed our interest in his "creation."

"It's for women," he said. "But there aren't enough drunk girls. They have to be naked, you know."

"Could I have a go?" asked Antony. Glen simply turned in disgust. He encouraged us to find drunken girls who would flash their breasts at the George Washingtons, the one Lincoln, and, most important, Glen himself. Opposite the paddling pool, the man who had parked next to us had just opened his stall. With the name Shooters for Hooters, his earlier explanation of "drinks for tits" proved accurate. Behind the table, he and three other men stood with beers in hand, desperately waiting for thirsty women to approach them.

By 1:58—the time both the 1:27 and 1:39 passed the bar—the pipedream of mooning all thirty-six trains that day was fast becoming something I didn't really want to do. It was hot, the atmosphere had changed, and although a mooning festival wasn't the most dignified of activities, I never expected the Mugs Away Saloon to host a naked Hell's Angels reunion. Outside entertainment was provided by local band Ex-Paladin, a two-piece heavy metal band which, according to their myspace page, sounds like "the type of music you would hear if you were in the dark ages, and you heard a desolate wounded warrior rage about futile battles and failed courtships, alongside a rebellious maiden who is beating the hell out of her drums, ranting about her hamster that died."

Noisy. That's how I'd put it.

Back at the fence, awaiting the 2:18, we found the only innocent fun left—a dad had his young child on his shoulders, both of them lowering their pants in order to join in the action. Next to me, an elderly gentleman, who was engaged in a conversation about college education (he had paid over a quarter of a million dollars to help his daughter through a three-year course), noticed my height and eagerness for the train, and tapped me on the shoulder.

"Do you mind warning me when the train's coming?" he asked.

"Yeah, sure," I replied.

"Just say something like . . . " he struggled to find a perfect codeword or phrase.

"The train is coming?" I suggested helpfully.

"Um . . . yeah. Perfect."

There was something that was quickly becoming odd about the Mooning. It wasn't the fact that everyone was drinking—we expected that—but what they were drinking out of was very strange. Everyone appeared to be storing their beverages in a similar vessel, a container that I had seen on many American films and television programs but had never seen in real life, at least, not outside the United States. That day in Orange County, there were hundreds and hundreds of plastic red cups. If you are American and reading this, you'll wonder "What's the big deal with some red cups? We see them all the time," and you'd be right to think that. But I'm not used to seeing these things, and everyone had a red cup. Everyone. To me that was just plain odd. I have never seen a single red cup outside the United States: They're in Hollywood movies (traditionally when some sort of high school party is in full swing) and stacked high in U.S. shops and supermarkets; a cup even provides the centerpiece for a poster I saw advertising a new ABC Family television show about college life called *Greek*.

A red plastic cup *is* America. It's a symbol that typifies the nation, like the bald eagle, the Liberty Bell, the Statue of Liberty, and obesity. If the stereotypical Frenchman is a bike-riding, baguette-carrying, onion necklace–wearing artist in a black-and-white–striped sweater and tilted black beret; and a German is dressed in lederhosen, dancing strangely and drinking from a huge half-liter beer glass, then an American would be enjoying a burger and drinking from some sort of red plastic vessel.

By late afternoon, interest in mooning had all but dwindled and people would bare their buttocks only while concentration was on other things. Antony and I decided that the sordid and raucous atmosphere that had enveloped the event wasn't a scene we wanted to be part of. As we made our escape, negotiating the car carefully through the parked bikes so as to not clip the first and begin a domino effect that would anger a hundred bikers, my last glimpse of the Mooning of Amtrak was of several hydraulically aided cars bouncing and a navy T-shirt informing me that the acronym for the The War Against Terrorism is TWAT.

*W*ith only two days of our time remaining in Los Angeles, Antony and I were determined to find something positive about the city. The following day, we finally did.

Twenty miles south of downtown Los Angeles lies the city of Long Beach, a shining jewel in the decaying crown of L.A. Its quiet, palm tree–lined streets and quaint shopping districts draw your attention away from the myriad of corporative skyscrapers and dockyards that dominate the majority of the city's coastline, and its cosmopolitan feel exudes an air of prosperity on a level with that of Monte Carlo. There's even a Grand Prix held there each year.

Across the bay from Long Beach stands the RMS *Queen Mary*—once the pride of the Cunard White Star Line—an incandescent reminder of the British Empire and her historic stature as a nation of elegant fleet builders. Today, as the world around her looks to the future, the ship, now a hotel and museum, remains embedded in tons of concrete more than seventy years after her regal launch, looking out rather forlornly at the Long Beach skyline.

In the evenings, the city's peaceful streets are a joy to stroll, and following a history of gang-related crime, Long

Beach has imposed an evening curfew on unaccompanied youths. This, coupled with the fact that the local police force question anybody who blinks awkwardly, creates a splendid ambience of safety in which an evening drink can be enjoyed.

On our last full day in Los Angeles, we spent our time paying a lengthy visit to an outlet mall, taking advantage of the favorable exchange rate. In the afternoon, we rang Mark from our motel room and agreed to meet him and his wife, Aleks, just a few miles from the Mugs Away Saloon, at the Yard House, which was somewhere in the Irvine Spectrum Center, a huge outdoor mall based on the architectural magnificence of the Alhambra in Granada, Spain (complete with a twenty-one-screen cinema complex, extravagant fountains, and a Ferris wheel).

The Yard House boasts of having the largest selection of draft beers in the world—and with 147 from which to choose, it may in fact be right. Opening the menu, we found that it was more like reading a J.R.R. Tolkien novel than simply deciding what to drink. The waiter approached our table and asked Mark for some ID. Mark, don't forget, is a thirty-eight-year-old man, and although he doesn't look quite his age, believing him to be under the age of twenty-one is really pushing the imagination to its absolute limit.

"I just don't get it," both Antony and I said, interrupting each other. "Why on earth are they IDing you? It's obvious you're older than twenty-one," I added, concentrating my speech at Mark so as to not make Aleks feel old.

"I kind of like it," Aleks replied. "Makes me feel young."

I took an instant liking to Aleks. Not only was she attractive, funny, and intelligent, but also well traveled and definitely switched on about American cultures and her opinions on them. She was a defiant patriot and proud American but flew the flag only on Independence Day, a stalwart supporter of the Democrats but hated Hillary Clinton. With the ID request leaving a bitter taste in our mouths, we decided to enlighten our new friends to some of the foibles we found with America and certain things that had irritated us over the course of our month's stay. With quite a list already forming in our minds, we decided we had better begin on a rather cheery note.

"We like the car pool lane," I said. "But you don't use adverbs."

"Pardon?" replied Aleks, probably expecting to hear the same old complaint about obesity or the fact that Americans drive on the incorrect side of the road.

"*You* might," I replied. "But most of the American public never use adverbs. They use adjectives instead. They will often forget all about the *l* and *y* on the end of a word. 'You drive too quick' instead of 'quickly,' for example. And the worst one, 'You did bad' instead of, 'You did badly.' That one really annoys me."

Aleks simply nodded in agreement.

"And your coins are rubbish," I added anxiously. That should win them back.

"In what way?" questioned Mark.

"Well, the five-cent coin is bigger than the ten for starters. How stupid is that?"

"Oh, yeah. I've never thought of it like that before," he replied.

For the following half hour, Antony and I listed our annoyances, and Mark and Aleks listened intently as if they were getting some sort of twisted kick out of it. These included such major flaws as America's international dialing code, which is somehow 001 even though we invented the phone, and minor discrepancies like the fact that vinegar isn't readily accessible in restaurants and that toilets are often called bathrooms even though I've yet to see even a bidet in one.

I expected some sort of backlash from Aleks after discovering her patriotic streak, but much to my surprise she agreed with every single one. You could tell Mark had some points to make but after admitting he once bought a pickup truck (after Aleks and I agreed that Americans drive unnecessarily large vehicles), he thought better of it.

The evening continued much in the same vein. We liked the turn-right-on-red rule and beer glasses kept in fridges, but not the constant advertisement breaks on television, fully grown adults wearing baseball caps, dangerous two-prong electrical sockets, the adding of sales tax at the counter, American sports' failure to accept ties, and the teenage-girl phrase "I was like."

Aleks and Mark either enjoyed our company a great deal, or the drink had gone to her head and she was getting frisky with her credit card, because she decided to split the bill with me even after I had insisted on paying. Either way, after sharing the cost of the evening, she disappeared for fifteen minutes and returned to the table with a Yard House pint glass and hooded sweatshirt for both Antony and me.

Outside of the bar, we bid farewell to Aleks and Mark and exchanged addresses in the faint hope that we would one day spend another evening together, perhaps in a British pub listening to a list of their own.

It had been almost a week since Antony and I landed in Los Angeles, and we had wanted to leave after only a day. However, the evening spent in the company of Aleks and Mark and our time gently strolling around the streets of Long Beach had all but made up for L.A.'s shortcomings. We both left the Irvine Spectrum Center with a newfound respect for Los Angeles, with only the Chrysler to dampen our spirits.

Antony and I had to leave the home of movies, as we were scheduled to attend our very own premiere. The only problem was that with just a week before the opening night, we were a thousand miles away and the movie didn't exist.

6. AND THE
WINNER IS...

The film crew and me (in the Armani suit seven yards too big).

$\mathcal{E}$arly the next morning I was back at Deluxe Rent a Car, and I don't mind admitting that I had cleverly rationed the fuel to the extent that with just a few minutes of revving the engine around the corner, the car was down to running on fumes. As I handed the keys back to the woman behind the counter, Antony and I started moving our luggage from the trunk of the car into the airport shuttle bus we had managed to miss for two hours when we first arrived. It was only on slamming the hood shut that I noticed that the car's license plates had expired over a month before.

LAX is the fifth busiest airport in the world by passenger traffic, and handles more origin and final-destination passengers than any other in the world. Two hours after dropping off the horrible car, we had made it through all the many lines in the airport and were finally sitting in the departure lounge awaiting our flight to Portland, Oregon.

$\mathcal{C}$ompared to the polluted air and urban sprawl of L.A., Portland was a literal breath of fresh air. As our plane touched down, a quick peek out of the jet's windows showed a view pleasing to the eye. Desert plains and clogged interstates had been replaced with alpine horizons and the gentle flow of winding rivers. Portland is definitely a pleasant place to be—a city that is home to half a million people and that has a manageable downtown area, with the distant and domineering Mount Hood overlooking the metropolis.

After a night in a nearby Econo Lodge, we returned to

the airport to pick up a rental car so we could make the eighty-mile journey south to the city of Corvallis, where the premiere was now a day closer and the film hadn't taken a single step closer to completion. In fact, right now, it wasn't even an idea in someone's head.

After the hassle of Deluxe Rent a Car and the awful PT Cruiser, a reputable company (complete with obvious shuttle bus) was selected for our week-long Oregon car. Dollar even offered us a free upgrade, and we departed Portland International Airport in a 2006 Ford Mustang—a car complete with fuel, oil, and unexpired license plates. With a whole day and feeling no rush to check in to our motel, we decided on driving 40 miles to the coast to follow the Pacific coastline down until we had to head back inland. As we departed Portland, the interstate gave way to winding U.S. highways (allowing the Mustang to show us what he—yes, he was male—could do). The sky turned an overcast and daunting gray, temperatures plummeted into the mid-70s, and it started to rain. Life couldn't get any better.

The Oregon coast is rugged and certainly not the paradise one might imagine of the Pacific in summertime. Cliff edges were windswept and beaches were long, empty plains of dark yellow sand, and for the first time since arriving, I was reminded of home. At first the road snaked its way in a constant shadowing of the shore through towns with names like Tillamook and Neskowin, until finally we started hitting more ordinary names such as Lincoln City and Newport, and began traveling inland to our destination—Corvallis, two days before the beginning of the city's annual festival of art, science, technology, and kinetic energy.

Corvallis' rather eccentric da Vinci Days is the longest-running festival of its kind and, although the three-day event bears his name, celebrations are concentrated less on the artist himself and more on his legacy, the ideas and inventions that were centuries ahead of his time. During his sixty-seven-year life, da Vinci sketched early designs for a helicopter, an odometer, a catapult, a tank, and a machine gun and still had time to thrash out a couple of paintings here and there. It's the creative and conceptual part of the fifteenth-century polymath's life that the people of Corvallis choose to embrace in their festival. As the brochure puts it, "Where else would you find art that makes you think, mini race cars built by school kids, juggling physics lessons, a race of human-powered, artistically designed kinetic vehicles, award-winning music, a film festival, a keynote speaker, street performers, and interactive art and science activities and events . . . all in one weekend festival?"

See, I thought you couldn't. (I thought of Cannes, but that covered only the film festival bit, really).

The city of Corvallis has a population of just over 50,000 and was briefly the capital of the Oregon Territory in 1855, before the state was welcomed into the Union four years later and Salem was selected. The city is home to Oregon State University, a college which during term time adds a further 20,000 to the population. Nothing could speak more profoundly on Corvallis' character and geography than the top three programs studied at the university: forestry, engineering, and environmental studies. OSU's motto, also befitting of the region, is "Open minds, open doors."

Since leaving Boston, Antony and I had endured a tiresome couple of weeks of exhausting heat and intolerance in Georgia and the frustration of traffic-ridden L.A. Corvallis seemed the perfect antidote. Not only were we surrounded by rivers, mountains, and forests in a bucolic alpine environment but Corvallis was recently voted one of the top ten bicycle-friendly cities in America and the nation's twentieth safest city, and, ironically enough, Benton County (of which Corvallis makes up the majority of the population) has the lowest church-attendance rate per capita in the entire country.

The following day, the eve of da Vinci Days, Antony and I took a short walk through the leafy streets of downtown Corvallis to the tourist information center where our weekend tickets were being held. The "tickets" came in the form of colored wristbands, which would allow us access to all events, activities, exhibitions, and general revelry taking place during the weekend. I consulted the brochure stand to see what was in the local area that could pass the afternoon. It boiled down to two choices—a drive through the spectacular volcanic Cascade Mountain Range or a self-guided tour of Oregon's most popular covered bridges.

It was an easy decision to make.

The Hayden Covered Bridge—located just off Highway 34—was built in 1918 and is one of the oldest in the state. At 91 feet, the bridge spans the Alsea River and was of absolute no interest to us as we traveled east out of Corvallis in search of the Cascades.

Of the entire 700-mile Cascade Range—which stretches from Northern California through America's Pacific Northwest and into Canada—Oregon contains its fair share of volcanoes, and we were near enough to pass the northern trio: the Three Sisters, Mount Jefferson, and Mount Hood. This is where my map, which had served me well for three previous trips to the U.S., was proven useless. We navigated our way through the bizarrely named towns of Sweet Home and Upper Soda smoothly, but then the four-lane U.S. highways changed to more modest country roads. When we turned onto Route 22, roads became single lanes and directional signs were either painted on the ground or written on crockery.

Yes, crockery.

If road-sign pots and pans didn't tell us we were in the middle of nowhere, the Mustang's radio sure did. In an urban area in America, a scan through the FM band normally results in the discovery of nearly thirty or so stations between the 87.8 MHz and 108 MHz frequency. Here, though, where soup bowls and plates informed you of your position, only one station came through Russell's speakers (Russell is what we had named the Mustang). Unfortunately, the network's playlist was exclusively Christian rock. We actually found that it wasn't too bad, as long as you didn't listen to the majority of the lyrics. And after an hour of nonstop Bible ballads, we finally reached the thriving metropolis of Detroit. Not the huge city in Michigan, you understand. But with a population of 260, Detroit, Oregon, was easily the largest town within a 30-mile radius of our current location. Having not seen a single one of the town's people, we continued on to the NF-46 (at least I think that's what was etched into the colander).

After a further hour of such classics as "It's All in His Hands" and "You're So Inviting," Russell delivered us safely to Mount Hood, Oregon's tallest peak, and the Cascade Mountain Range's most-likely-to-erupt volcano. Unfortunately, in the town of Mount Hood we had somehow missed the turning to Trillium Lake—where the best views of the stratovolcano can be gleaned. How we drove straight past an 11,000-foot mountain without noticing I'll never know. We turned around.

On the shores of Trillium Lake, surrounded by a family of ducks feasting on the remains of our Doritos, Antony and I stood in awe of the magnificent spectacle and natural beauty of Mount Hood. There was a striking mirror image of the peak in the lake. Its 11,249-foot peak disappeared into the drifting clouds and snow seemed to trickle down its slopes as if poured on by God's own hand. Either that or I had probably left the radio on for too long and had listened to the lyrics subliminally.

As Antony and I returned to the car with a vision of un-rivaled environmental artistry forever etched in our minds, we made the discovery that the mountain is over 500,000 years old, is made up of twelve separate glaciers, and last erupted at the end of the eighteenth century. We also learned that as much as ducks enjoy Doritos crumbs, they aren't the biggest fans of malted milk balls.

As we made our way on U.S. Highway 26 toward the interstate for a quick and easy return to Corvallis (and metallic road signs and a range of radio stations), we realized that the Mount Hood Highway may as well have been called Silly Name Drive. In just ten minutes, we had passed the town of Government Camp at the foot of Tom, Dick, and Harry Mountain and the slightly larger settlement of Rhododendron and its neighbor Zigzag. In the thirty miles which followed, we were welcomed to the towns of Wildwood, Salmon, Sandy, and, at the end of the highway, the town of Boring—where we enjoyed such sights as the Boring Fire Department, the Boring Square Garden Center, Boring Middle School, and Wally Road where the Boring Farmer's Market was held every Sunday morning during the summer.

Although the campus of one of the largest universities in Oregon sits on the outskirts of the town, Corvallis doesn't really have the kind of nightlife one would expect, and little bars with a live band are as crazy and exciting as it gets. Still, a Thursday-night promotion at the Peacock Tavern had drinks at just $1.50 (the favorable exchange rate meant the pints were less than 75p), and we were fed and made significantly merry for less than twenty bucks . . . leaving us with hangovers for the opening day of the festival. But because da

Vinci Days didn't officially start until the evening, we didn't miss a single minute and even had plenty of time to make our way back to the bar to try and locate a pile of vomit Antony produced outside, and to try to remember why a girl had slapped him. We never did remember.

Running concurrently and in conjunction with da Vinci Days was the eighth annual da Vinci Film Festival, a celebration of independent film that included short films, feature films, and documentaries submitted by local and national filmmakers that had been whittled down to a small selection of a dozen or so, which would be shown at two of the college's auditoriums. Although a mini film festival was of only minor interest to Antony and I, the companion film competition certainly was of more interest, and we were gearing up for victory.

The rules were simple. The da Vinci Fast Film Project, according to the program of events, involved teams writing, shooting, and editing a ten-minute film in just forty-eight hours. All a team needed to do was to arrive at the LaSells Stewart Center in the college campus, be given a theme for the piece and a prop which must appear at some point within the film, and then make and turn in the movie. We quickly decided that if we could scam the borrowing of a camera from the organizers, we couldn't help but win. We had no experience in filmmaking and no editing software, so we would have to do things like writing credits on pieces of paper and singing loudly whenever music was required, and the entire half-assed effort complete with horrendous acting and British accents would get us enough sympathy votes to ensure us victory.

That was the plan anyway.

At 4:45—a clear fifteen minutes before the competition began—we arrived in the LaSells Stewart Center and approached the sign-up desk under our new guises as Rich

Hitchcock and Antony Spielberg. Behind the desk sat a young woman and a small man in his midtwenties with short, curly hair.

"Are you directors?" asked the woman.

"Um. Not really," Antony replied.

"We'd like to be, though," I said. "Is it possible to enter the Fast Film Project?"

"Yeah, sure."

"Can we borrow a camera?"

She shook her head. "You can't borrow one. You have to use your own."

Plan B it was: We would stand around waiting for a team to arrive who would allow us to latch on, appear in the background of one of their scenes, and claim victory for ourselves.

As we waited, it transpired that the short man sitting beside the woman wasn't a member of the organizing committee and was in fact a competitor on the Fast Film Project. He talked almost exclusively about himself and his film course at OSU as he sat back in his chair, and it made Antony and I not take a liking to him at all. He was the kind of smarmy guy who would try to always one-up you in conversations, and instead of listening to anyone else would change the conversation around to something that reflected well on himself. What was worse was that he also looked like the sort of person who would wear a scarf. Terrible. Because of this, Antony and I didn't ask to join his one-man "team" and instead of asking his name, we simply dubbed him the Turd.

We had a new purpose in Corvallis. Our main priority was beating the Turd; winning the competition was just an added bonus. By the look at the number of teams who had arrived, though, things seemed bleak. It was looking more and more likely that we would have to abandon our plans and instead try to join forces with the Turd, create some sort of elaborate inside job, and destroy him from within. As we basked in the thought of treason and treachery, a young man with blond hair and glasses tapped me on the shoulder and muttered, "I hear you're looking for a team to join."

Without the need to wow him with my A in high school Drama or the fact that Antony can do a masterful impression of Borat. Our new crew consisted of Andy Foster, the guy who invited us to join the team in the first place; Mary Jeanne Reynales, a middle-aged woman with long, dark hair and a Bluetooth earpiece; and her husband, Dave Grucza. They had already drawn "fall from grace" as the film's theme, and had been given a booklet of da Vinci's inventions as our prop. As they welcomed us onto the team and we shook hands with our new partners, Mary Jeanne suggested we should head to the Lower Campus area where the da Vinci Days festival had just begun and where we would meet the rest of the team to hatch a plan.

Following Mary Jeanne and Dave was easy enough, but managing to actually find a parking space near the campus was a different matter whatsoever. It wasn't that the streets were busy or that parking was prohibited, but every time it seemed as if we were making good progress, there was either a ROAD CLOSED sign in our way or a battery-powered car shooting across our path. The ENTEK International Grand Prix Electrathon, the first race of the festival, had started, and, according to the organizers, it was the longest-running Electrathon America-sanctioned event in the country. (I'll take their word on that as for all I know it may be the only one.)

Eventually we all found a place to park a couple of blocks from the campus and we made our way to a park just outside of the main da Vinci Days exhibition venue to sit down beside a painted wagon they had used in a production of the *Wizard of Oz* (it was now serving as an information stand). We began to discuss the brief outline of the movie. Luckily Dave had a plan.

"The plan is that it's all based around a focus group," he said. "Da Vinci is planning on marketing his helicopter as some kind of commercial airline." He continued talking for quite some time. After a few minutes I switched off, though— I didn't know what on earth he was talking about. I tuned back in just as he said, "So all we need is a punchline."

"Right," I said, not knowing what he was talking about. "Well, I just want to beat the Turd," I added helpfully.

"You two go and get some food," said Mary Jeanne. "You must be hungry."

After purchasing some chicken-fried rice from one of the many food stands, we perused some of the exhibition stands. Nearly every one was similar and promoted things like more efficient energy use. "Paint with soil" was a particular favorite stand of mine. Opposite them was an energy-efficiency desk where members of the public were invited to list ways in which energy could be saved. Before returning to our team, I happily joined in, scrawling the words, "Leaving the television on standby is the Devil's work."

Settling back into lawn chairs the group had brought with them, we were introduced to team members Bill Powell (a friendly faced man with short gray hair and matching mustache) and his effervescent wife, Michele, and learned more about our team's backgrounds and the skills each was bringing to the table. (It was quite like the dossier scene at the beginning of *Mission: Impossible*. Not the terrible, gung ho films starring Tom Cruise, but the classic and cleverly written 1960s television series). It appeared that we were in good company. Mary Jeanne was part of the Corvallis Community

Theatre and although she was a spitting image of the actress Kathy Bates, she had decided against appearing in the film, instead bringing her experience as theater director to the film. Her husband, Dave, was a whiz with editing software and could also solve the problem of creating a life-size model of da Vinci's helicopter by superimposing a model of one a friend of theirs had already made. And Andy was an experienced cameraman and part-time video production person. It was he who then stood up and seemed to be in charge as he began to explain an idea I actually understood.

"Right, we have the plot now, guys," he voiced proudly. "Basically it's a news report about a scientist who has created a helicopter from da Vinci's designs. The report will be of the first launch—"

"At Grace University," Mary Jeanne interjected proudly.

Andy continued. "The report will be of the first launch and as you are British, we thought you, Rich, could play the reporter—"

"Nigel Huffington," Mary Jeanne interrupted. "Antony, you'll be the voiceover announcer."

Due to our short walk, I hadn't been there to interrupt their thinking process, and as a reward was handed the lead role. I quickly turned around to check if my name had been written on the back of my lawn chair (it wasn't . . . yet). But before I could accept the role, I needed to make one point absolutely clear.

"I'll be a BBC reporter, right?" I asked. "Because I'm not gonna pretend I work for ITV."

Bill was the first to act on my sudden mood change. "Why? Don't you like ITV?" he asked.

"Don't get him started on ITV, Bill," warned Antony.

It was too late. He had.

"Bill, it's a channel that doesn't broadcast a single program I enjoy, their sports coverage is appalling, and all they seem to show are soaps and terrible "documentaries" about fat people or celebrities. Basically, its target audience are the morons who read things like *Take a Break*, *Heat*, or *OK* magazine. Now you can even get ITV two, three, and four! Why have those when you can't even get ITV one right? The only reason it's popular in the U.K. is because it's left on in retirement homes twenty-four hours a day and the old biddies can't be bothered to change the channel for something more beneficial to their dwindling and stagnant lives. . . ."

"BBC it is then," bellowed Mary Jeanne, defusing the situation as I paused for breath. I calmed down, sat back in my chair, and learned more about our film.

During the report, the helicopter would eventually crash, and the punchline would be that the failure was due to a cleaner at the lab turning the design of the craft upside down. Antony and I didn't find their idea of a punchline particularly amusing, though, so we sat back in our chairs thinking of other jokes and gags.

"We have to have that annoying satellite delay and touching of the ear," I said.

"Good thinking," Mary Jeanne replied.

"When it crashes, can I shout the exact same lines as that Hindenburg commentator did? You know, the 'Oh, the humanity' line?"

"I like it."

I was on a roll. And they hadn't heard the best one yet.

"Can't I have a double-barreled surname? If I was called Nigel Huffington-Fall, I could end my report by saying, 'This is Nigel Huffington-Fall from Grace University.' You see, a very cheeky way of getting the words 'fall from grace' into the piece."

Clever, hey?

The group was impressed. They turned their attentions to Antony—it was his turn to produce a comedic gem. Antony raised his finger to his lips thoughtfully. "You know, Rich, we only needed to buy one wristband—we could have passed it through the fence."

As the meeting drew to an end, we realized that two hours had passed already and we had only forty-six hours until the deadline. Mary Jeanne headed home to write the script, advising us on her way out to enjoy the evening's performance by Pink Martini, a local band who had "made it big."

We remained in the audience for only an hour or so, though. Not because Pink Martini weren't that good (quite the opposite, in fact). We had an unearthly start time of eight the following morning, and we didn't want to make the mistake of arriving late for our big acting debuts.

Antony and I arrived back at the park at 8:20 the next morning. Luckily, we weren't even the last to arrive. As a couple of organizers marked an area of the park in preparation for the Canine Frisbee competition later on that morning, Mary Jeanne and Dave stood beside a table of filming equipment with the script. At over ten pages, the prose seemed quite substantial until I realized that the words were written in a large font so the pages could be held above the camera as some sort of rudimentary teleprompter.

After Bill and Michele appeared, Mary Jeanne handed me an Armani suit with shirt and tie, and asked me to put it on, before informing me of its $3,000 value.

"I hope you have a belt," she said. "It belonged to my brother-in-law and he was a larger man than you."

Bill and Michele adopted the role of wardrobe by brushing random hairs from the jacket and even straightening my tie before adding a clip. It soon became apparent what "larger than me" meant—the trousers would be put to better use as an expensive wind sock. The jacket, although perfectly comfortable, was very loose around the chest, having just about enough slack to hold our crew and most of the equipment. Luckily Mary Jeanne had a solution. She presented me with two giant plastic clamps, which were then attached to the back of the jacket, making me look as if I were the victim of a brutal stabbing by an army of Lego men.

As I went through my opening line in my head, Andy arrived clutching a tray of drinks from Starbucks, supplying everyone else with an early-morning cup of coffee, and Antony and I with our first cup of tea in over a month.

After a quick tie-straightening by Bill, who now donned an authentic brown leather bomber jacket with a white scarf around his neck for his role as test pilot Brent Collander, we were ready to begin. The camera was facing in my direction and Mary Jeanne had thrust a microphone into my hand.

As not to confuse me and Antony too early into the filming process, the first scene we were to shoot was the opening one of the film (I obviously began to pick up the terminology). However (and try to keep up with this), the scene would end with me introducing another scene which I proclaim the "BBC" had filmed earlier . . . but in reality, we were to record it later. It would be spliced into place in what is called "editing" (media studies students will be familiar with the concept).

With several attempts already filmed—some not delivered quite to Mary Jeanne's liking and others resulting in a complete balls-up-by-me flubbing of my lines—we continued to work on the opening bit for quite some time, until it seemed there were a hundred different versions from which the best (or "least worst," in my case) could be extracted and placed into the final edit. So we moved on, thankfully relieving me of ever having to say the words *gyroscopic* and *Professor Cornelius Whalborne* for the remainder of my life.

The following scene was very much straightforward. The line was simple—"And you rejoin me here at the launch site where the anticipation is palpable"—and then I had to turn away from the camera. We filmed the five-second line so many times searching for one for the final edit that it became apparent why big Hollywood blockbusters take many months to shoot. The reason for my turn at the end wasn't apparent yet, but then Mary Jeanne marched across the park with a small crowd of confused-looking people in tow. It seemed that I was meant to be turning to the audience, and the next scene to be edited in would show that the crowd who had arrived to witness this historic launch would total only a dozen or so (one of whom appears on his disability scooter, takes one look at what all the fuss is about, and simply continues on his way).

With the helicopter existing only through the wonders of computer technology, a double-rung ladder was positioned where the craft would be placed so the crowd and I had a common target on which to focus. The helicopter's "launch" and subsequent "crash" was demonstrated by Andy's right arm—when raised higher into the air, the crowd would look happy as if the experiment was turning out to be a huge success, and when he dropped it back to his thigh, the crowd would turn dejected and leave in disgust. That left me to look at the camera, apologetic and defeated, amid a plume of smoke created by a fire extinguisher set off by Mary Jeanne.

We shot almost ten minutes of videotape featuring a dozen attempts. Finally, Dave shot close-ups of the (by-now-impatient) crowd, and my work was effectively complete. Bill, the test pilot, was then filmed approaching the craft, then dying in another scene. I then shouted the Hindenburg lines into the microphone (several times of course) so it could be edited in when the helicopter fell to the ground, and I finished with a typical sign-off line and the clever "Fall from grace" line.

In all, almost an hour of film had been shot, of which only two minutes would make the final edit.

I removed the suit, changed into my usual clothes, and was shocked to discover that it was already the early afternoon. Mary Jeanne suggested that the entire crew should meet up later in the evening in order to grab something to eat and meet the final members of our cast, including a few extras and Peter Platt, a proper actor with on-stage experience who would be playing the crucial role of the professor.

The Fox and Firkin pub in downtown Corvallis (before you look it up, a *firkin* is an old English unit of liquid volume equal to 40.9 liters, and not an indiscreet way of getting a swear word into the name of a drinking establishment) is a pleasant way to spend one's evening, and not just because of the company. Fish and chips, curries, pies and ploughman's suppers all appeared on the "English pub's" menu, and so it was with a fond thought of home that I opted for the mashed potato and sausages, which the pub had correctly named Bangers and Mash. By a strange coincidence, we were also reacquainted with Jean Dick, an OSU student whom we had met in the bar when we first arrived in Corvallis. She was joined by three fellow students, Julia Clark, Alex Svela, and the fantastically named Kendall Zwang. Luckily none of these was the girl who had slapped Antony.

Over an hour late and still appearing to be in some state of urgency, Peter Platt arrived and shook both Antony's and my hands. Peter was nothing like what I expected. Our "professor" was in his late twenties, had olive skin, and although he had a full set of hair and a beard, both were jet black and neatly trimmed. For me, a professor should have glasses, he shouldn't care about his appearance, and he should look as if his hair was just as eccentric as him. Mind you, if Peter had seen me earlier on wearing a pair of trousers four hundred sizes too big for me and with two giant clamps hanging from my jacket, he probably would have thought that I didn't look much like a BBC reporter, so who was I to judge? And anyway, Peter had already appeared in countless amateur dramatic productions and was a graduate of Harvard University. The closest I have come to acting stardom is through my granddad who appeared as an extra in the 1977 war movie *A Bridge Too Far*. Also, I once starred as an Oompa-Loompa in a primary school production of *Charlie and the Chocolate Factory*.

By now our cast and crew totaled twelve people and we had only the last few scenes of the film to shoot. For this we required Peter and a set that looked like a professor's laboratory. So, whether we were allowed to be there (let alone film) or not, the dozen of us made our way to a federal laboratory where Bill worked on the outskirts of the town.

The Environmental Protection Agency building wasn't much to look at from the outside and appeared to have more in common with a middle school than a government building. The rear door could be opened only from the inside, and like thieves involved in an inside job, we parked around the back of the building and waited to be let in by Bill. Once we got in, Bill led us through narrow corridors, past locked doors, and finally into a room that looked like a lecture classroom. As I undressed to don the Armani suit once again, Jean, Alex, and Julia scattered miniature models of da Vinci's designs around the room and put on white lab coats in an attempt to make the classroom look more like the den of a da Vinci–obsessed science professor. Peter put on his own lab coat and a pair of plastic safety glasses, and perched himself on a stool beside an overhead projector to await Mary Jeanne's instructions.

It was only then that Antony and I experienced just how good Peter was, and what a sublime choice to play the role of the professor he had been. Clutching the da Vinci design booklet—the prop that had to appear somewhere within the film—Peter went through his repertoire of accents, characteristics, and general idiosyncrasies. Professor Whalborne was first a French aristocrat, then from the Deep South, then an eccentric doctor who was angered at people's lack of understanding of his work. Such was the brilliance of each take that the laughter from me and the rest of the crew were ruining the scene and beginning to irritate Mary Jeanne, who wasn't enjoying the range of characters on display and wanted something more sensible than a Dutchman or a Jamaican drug baron.

After a dozen hilarious takes, Peter finally presented the professor as a restless, slightly schizophrenic character who made me, the BBC reporter, feel uneasy about interviewing him. He was brilliant and unnerving, and I was convincing, too—every now and then I smiled encouragingly as to not show my unease.

"Success!" Peter blared. "Absolute, incontrovertible success!"

With that, my work was done, and as Andy and Dave filmed the final scene where Kendall plays the cleaner lady who turns the projection upside-down, I changed back into my casual clothes and set off down the corridor—I figured since we were here I could uncover some sort of illegal biological experiments or governmental cover-ups. Twenty minutes of some serious sleuthing later, all I had discovered was that we were in the Western Ecology Division of the EPA's office of Research and Development; the facility's primary mission was to study the response of terrestrial, coastal, and regional-scale ecological systems to pollutants and other human stresses; and that the face staring back at me on the wall of reception between George W. Bush and his vice president, Dick Cheney, was that of the EPA administrator Stephen L. Johnson—and I didn't even find that one out myself; Bill told me.

With filming completely finished (or is that called a wrap?), Antony and I were invited to Mary Jeanne and Dave's house along with Bill, Michele, and Andy for some quick last-minute voice-over work. We were only too happy to accept and caught a lift with Bill and Michele to the north of the city.

As soon as you enter Dave and Mary Jeanne's house, it is clear from the framed movie posters, motion picture soundtracks, and musical scripts littered in every room that they really love show business. So much do they enjoy the thrill of a live audience and a theater, that in May they were married in one, live and unrehearsed in front of an audience who had turned up to watch a matinee performance of *Ragtime*. Before the show, Dave had shouted the proposal from the balcony and Mary Jeanne, trying to look shocked, paused before accepting. After the closing of the curtain, the musical conductor began the "Wedding March"; Dave appeared in a tuxedo, Mary Jeanne's cousin performed the ceremony, and the audience were left considering whether what they witnessed was real. Only a handful of people were let in on the secret and Mary Jeanne got the no-gifts, no-nonsense, spontaneous wedding party she had always wanted.

Andy and Dave locked themselves in the computer room

editing the film, while the rest of us talked. Someone asked what Dave did for a living, giving Mary Jeanne an idea to pass the time.

"We'll play twenty questions," she said, excited by the prospect, "twenty questions to try and identify Dave's job."

I was never any good at this game, and Antony and I played this time at my usual standard. After all our questions were used up, all we knew was that although he was very competent in digital editing, Dave didn't work with computers, but that he was a tradesman, worked indoors, used tools, modified and repaired things, and made a mess in his line of work, but he wasn't a plumber, carpenter, builder, plasterer, decorator, or electrician.

Give up?

So did we.*

As if Dave's job wasn't difficult enough to figure out with twenty questions, Michele ran a yarn shop in Corvallis. We could have played *five hundred* questions and I would never have guessed that one. We never played to guess Mary Jeanne's job (a nurse), which was too bad as I was hoping she had forgotten she gave me her business card earlier in the day. Meanwhile, in the editing suite (or the study), Andy and Dave were ferreting away in full nerd mode. Eventually they called all of us in and showed us some of the scenes they had already pieced together. I didn't want to see a great deal, and purposely looked away, saving myself for the premiere.

Antony and I recorded quick voice-overs for segments of the film, and Bill and Michele decided it was time they had better be leaving, an indicator that we should make a move,

---

*He was a cobbler. Incidentally, his business was called Dave's Family Shoe Service (a name that he must have spent many sleepless nights thinking up).

too—partly because it was late, but mostly because they were giving us a lift back to the motel.

As we were led through another hallway of their more-than-modest abode, a certain picture caught my eye. It was of Tony Blair, Gordon Brown . . . and Andy.

"What's that all about, Andy?" I asked.

"Oh, yeah. I used to work for the Labor Party," he said rather breezily.

As it transpired, Andy worked as an intern for Blair and co. in 2003 and as a contractor during the 2005 general election. If only I had known this information before, I wouldn't have agreed to join his team.

We left Mary Jeanne's house, where Dave would be working through the night on the editing. We realized as we passed the night lights of Corvallis that our final day in the town would end with us either leaving as bona-fide winners or feeling like the Hollywood actors and directors who are constantly being nominated for Academy Awards but never pick up a trophy.

*T*he previous day's full schedule of filming had meant that with the exception of the "Paint with Soil" stand and the hour we had spent listening to Pink Martini, we hadn't really seen a great deal of the da Vinci Days. So early on the Sunday morning we headed down to the Crystal Lake Sports Park for one of the many "kinetic races" that take place over the three-day weekend (a kinetic race being an event in which the vehicle was powered without an engine or other means of propulsion other than human movement—like a bicycle).

The Kinetic Challenge Mud Bog is the third leg of the weekend's race, and is like a bizarre dream. The previous day, the entrants had pedaled their way up a steep sand dune and then showed how quickly their vehicles can travel on the road. Today, they were pitting their creations against 100 feet of knee-high mud, before entering the nearby river for the fourth and final section of the race. Due to the four wildly differing terrains, there is no ideal design and so the vehicles come in all different shapes and sizes. A black school bus with the words *Deliverance Truck* on the side waited patiently for its turn behind an old black Ford named *Henry Ford Goes Surfing*, a high-wheeled structure called *Chariots of Tire, and a giant caterpillar.*

Things turned even more surreal when a giant tomato with huge wheels took to the mud. The crew onboard yelled "Hiya Del Tomate" over and over again, and an elderly lady dressed as a tomato garnered support from the crowd. When the vehicle became stuck, the crowd cheered and yelled encouragement until, bizarrely enough, several Vikings appeared from nowhere to help move it through the substantially bulky and gummous course. A big, yellow school bus followed and after a vehicle named *Patriot Act* entered the fray, I thought of what a perfect festival the da Vinci Days was for its location and the people of Corvallis, and wondered if such an event would work anywhere else. I would imagine Rod and Bob would have lost interest due to the lack of guns, and the people of Elko would have gotten bored due to the absence of Basque dancing. Even Drew might have been a casualty—had he heard there was a festival dedicated to the genius of an artist called Leonardo, he'd be on the lookout for the other three ninja turtles. Being a liberal and science-embracing university town, Corvallis is the ideal home for the festival.

Corvallis was also the town that could turn Antony and me into winners, and so we headed to the LaSells Stewart Center to breathe in the atmosphere of the film festival before the evening's decisive premiere.

Before stepping foot on the red carpet that led the way to the double entrance doors of the LaSells Building, Antony and I got interested in the Reser Stadium opposite. We couldn't believe that such an impressive construction was home to just a university team (of American football, where the players hardly use their feet but still insist on calling it football). As "phase two" of the renovation work was being completed on the southern end of the structure, we crept inside for a closer look . . . and discovered that the inside was just as impressive as the outside. With a seating capacity of more than 46,000, the stadium could almost house the entire population of Corvallis. It rivals any stadium found in the English Premier League. It was so awe-inspiring that we didn't arrive at the LaSells Stewart Center for another thirty minutes.

The previous day, between leaving the park and meeting up at the pub, we had managed to watch a selection of different films ranging from a terrible mafia-style movie called *On Top of Spaghetti* to a feature film called *The Mini*, a feature-length movie about a futon salesman who takes part in a mini-marathon. We approached the information desk to ask what films would be showing soon.

"There's an excellent comedy called *Last Stop for Paul*, which starts in the Construction and Engineering auditorium in a few minutes," she said.

"What's in the other auditorium?" I asked. She consulted her list.

"It's called *Fairy Tracks*. It's a documentary about whether there truly is a nature fairy and how we can define nature."

I paused for a moment. "What time does *Last Stop for Paul* start?"

After the movie (which if I had to describe in one word

would be *watchable*), it was already three in the afternoon, and the forty-eight-hour deadline was less than two hours away. I rang Mary Jeanne's mobile and she told us that Dave was still in the process of finishing the DVD but would be at the auditorium within an hour. So Antony and I killed time by watching a short documentary about Kamikaze, a bicycle messenger in New York City, whose nickname certainly fits his character.

With an hour until the premiere and none of our crew to be seen, I phoned Mary Jeanne for a second time and asked if she was anywhere near the auditorium. It turned out that she and the rest of the crew were sitting at the Hilton hotel across the road from the LaSells Stewart Center—they must have arrived when we were busy watching a middle-aged man weave in and out of traffic by "surfing" the back of vans and buses.

As the bar at the hotel was yet to open, Mary Jeanne, Dave, Andy, and the rest of the crew were all sitting around a large table drinking glasses of water. Unfortunately Peter couldn't make it that day due to a rehearsal for *Much Ado About Nothing*. We were, however, introduced to John Herrmann, the creator of the miniature model of the helicopter we used, who demonstrated his genius further by offering us some whiskey out of a hip flask he had managed to smuggle into the hotel.

"Apparently there are ten teams entered," Mary Jeanne informed us.

"Yeah, and I think the organizers are having some problems with some of the DVDs," I replied, relaying some gossip I'd overheard after I'd left the auditorium.

"Really?" Dave said, looking in Andy's direction.

"We'd better check that ours isn't messing up," remarked Andy, and the two left the hotel.

At ten to five, we made our way into the auditorium and discovered that only seven entries had made it to this final showing and that our DVD was one of the ones that the organizers had been having trouble with. Filled with concern, we watched the same woman who had been behind the desk all weekend appear at the foot of the stage and introduce us to the showing of the da Vinci Days Fast Film Festival.

The rules were simple. Each of the films would be shown, and the winner would be decided at the very end by a good old-fashioned voting system—applause. There were more than two hundred people in attendance, so Mary Jeanne's plan of bringing as many people as she knew along in order to raise the volume of our combined clapping seemed a fruitless endeavor. Without knowing in which order the movies would be shown or if the technical problems had hampered our entry, we all hushed into silence as the auditorium's lights dimmed to darkness and the first movie appeared on the screen.

The film was about two men who met at a bus stop. Each day one of the men would unintentionally impede the other's progress onto the bus. For a week (which is also how long the movie seemed), the same thing would happen every day until, at the very end of the film, the driver was revealed to be the man who had never managed to board the bus, and who purposely made his passenger's life hell. I think.

The second film was completely bizarre and was something about a vortex or something. The cast of the film didn't aid my understanding with their constant screeching and shouting, and the script was impossible to follow. Antony summed it up perfectly when he leaned over to me during the lackluster and quite brief applause following the movie and whispered, "What the fuck was that all about?"

Film three was something to do with a fitness-obsessed

man and his lazy friend. One would constantly sit on the sofa eating junk food while his friend was in the garage making use of the multigym or jogging down the street. It ended with the health freak being knocked down by a car or some other tragedy. To be honest, if the entrant wasn't ours or the Turd's, it wasn't really of that great interest to me. Finally, though, the group of people sitting around the Turd grew restless and began to tap each other on the shoulders. I knew his film was next.

We'd overheard a brief chat he and Andy had had in the foyer, so we knew the Turd's theme was gossip. He didn't like this at all, and had admitted to Andy that he had simply added a minute's worth of footage over a documentary he was making for college . . . the cheating bastard.

His movie wasn't the greatest. It was basically a selection of clips of people regaling the audience with inane anecdotes, broken up by blank screens with a sentence like "That was nice, please tell us another" written on it. As the film ended, I stared in disapproval at any of our entourage who dared to applaud his unscrupulous efforts. The rest of the audience sadly began to applaud the movie, although the most noise by far came from those sitting around the Turd. It soon became obvious that due to the voting system, any old piece of shit could win the award (remember, *Titanic* won eleven Oscars!).

The fifth film was so short that if you'd taken your eyes off the screen to adjust your shoelace (or have an angry word with anyone who applauded the Turd), you would have missed it. It must have been on for less than a minute with the credits doubling the duration of the film. I think it was set in a shop and had no speech—relying on subtitles to carry the story. Unfortunately, I had leaned across to Antony to insult the Turd's entry and by the time I glanced back at the screen, the film had finished.

A Rubik's Cube was the main feature of the following film, which was the first movie, other than the Turd's, to have my attention from start to finish. It was basically a mild horror film in which no matter what the owner of the Rubik's Cube did, the handheld puzzle would return to him until it had been completed. To be perfectly honest, I thoroughly enjoyed the film. Dave was not so impressed and argued that there was too much in the movie for the team to have been able to shoot and edit in just forty-eight hours.

The room fell silent for a few moments, and we feared that our DVD's technical problems had kept it from entering the film festival competition. Just then, the BBC logo appeared on the silver screen and Antony's voice filled the auditorium. "And now we go live to Nigel Huffington-Fall on location."

Antony and I eased back into our chairs, I appeared on the screen with not a single clamp in sight, and we began wishing we had some popcorn with which to enjoy the show. My opening line linked in with the lab scene brilliantly, and the superimposed model of the helicopter looked . . . well . . . superimposed. My close-up reaction to the professor, the one which I had been so proud of for a perfect look of uncertainty and unease, was a bit of a disappointment. . . . In reality it seemed more like I was midway through a giggle. My turn on the "palpable" line made perfect sense and worked well with the size of the crowd, and the sound effects and launch worked brilliantly with the fire extinguisher blast. If there was a performance worthy of some sort of recognition, though, it was Peter's. The scenes which were shot in our absence—of the professor giving his final test instructions to the pilot, and his hilarious reaction to the entire launch ending in disaster—were sheer comical gems and certainly made the film. If I had to focus on some negatives, it would have been that the Hindenburg line had been removed (it will probably be in the deleted scenes on the DVD extras) and that the final punchline did anything but punch. At least we managed to get a groan of puny dissatisfaction from the audience after my "Fall from Grace" sign-off line. At less than four minutes, however, at least we hadn't wasted a lot of everyone's time like some of the entrants.

All seven movies had been shown and now it was time for the all-important judging and the completely unfair clap vote. It was a method that could let the Turd take the crown due to his cortege of classmates. In fairness, I thought the Rubik's Cube film was at least equal to our movie. Fortunately, I've watched enough Eurovision Song Contests to know that going last is a huge advantage, and although the stars of the Rubik's Cube were in attendance, we had the Eastern Bloc on our side.

After applause was offered for all seven films, the organizer paused for a moment and announced that the winners of the da Vinci Fast Film Festival would be . . . decided by a clap-off. She couldn't seem to separate two of the teams: us and the Turd's! Now it was time to be serious. Everyone in our team and who had come in support of us were ordered to keep their hands at arms' length when the Turd's film received its applause, and break the rules of "clapping only" by bellowing in a boisterous and obnoxious fashion on our own turn. It did the trick.

"And the winners are the 'Fall from Grace' team," she said. "Can I invite the team up to the front?" Mary Jeanne darted from her seat and we all followed her to the front of the stage.

With the auditorium now quickly emptying, there was no need for an acceptance speech (or berating the cheating Turd). There was also no award for us to receive, but we were told we would be sent certificates in the post . . . no cash prize but our film would be on the official da Vinci Days Film Festival website.

It was all rather anticlimactic.

However, although it had taken two attempts, the Turd had been flushed, and that's all Antony and I cared about. Victory was ours, and I had the pleasure of being mobbed by a fan as I departed the auditorium. A girl in her late teens approached us, noticing my accent.

"Oh, my god! I love your accent," she screamed as if I were a member of a hunky boy band who had just handed her a pair of my boxer shorts. "It's real, isn't it? Oh my god!"

After following Andy to the nearby university campus to inform Peter of our victory, disrupting his rehearsal and frustrating his colleagues, we made our way to McMenamins, a bar just a few blocks away, for our postvictory party. With all tables already booked, and with our sizable group, we decided to perch ourselves at every available seat at the bar and ordered our food and drink.

By now, the sun had started to set, and with an early-morning flight to catch from Portland, Antony and I quickly cleared our plates and said our farewells, shaking hands and hugging each and every member of the group. Following our active role in the Custer's Last Stand Reenactment, we hadn't had a chance to actually take a competitive role in a festival (barring bare buttocks in California), since the bulls hadn't arrived in Elko and our names hadn't been drawn at the Redneck Games. But this time, finally, we had competed . . . and better yet, *won*. We were both going to miss our crew, Oregon, its people, its mild climate, and the Mustang.

Our next flight was to return us to the Deep South after only a two-week hiatus. Once there, our task was to build a boat in just four days. For Antony and I, the thought of something involving construction filled us with dread (camping in France once, we struggled to pitch a simple tent). Luckily, I had a secret weapon and a trick up my sleeve . . . well, maybe not up my sleeve. But aboard a flight from London.

7. BACK ON DRY LAND

The Pirates attack us in the bay—presumably to plunder our hundreds of yards of duct tape!

$\mathcal{A}$rriving in Little Rock was a shock to the system. After days of being in the cool mountain air, we were once again in a huge, hot city with flat surroundings.

In five days' time, the 21st Annual Cardboard Boat Races were to take place in the little town of Heber Springs, 60 miles to the north of Little Rock, and Antony and I were going to enter. The only problems were that we had no boat and no materials with which to build one. Plus, our plans were completely up in the air. Literally, 30,000 feet up. Perhaps I should explain.

In order to protect both my visions of a second victory and my relationship with my girlfriend, I had flown her out to meet us in Little Rock. On Bec's insistence, she would travel with us for two weeks before returning home and, as an added bonus, she was bringing six packets of pickled onion–flavored Monster Munch potato chips. Also, her dad, Dave, is an engineer, and although he is more familiar with designing parts for mechanical machinery, the idea of drawing up a cardboard-boat blueprint was well within his capabilities and a task that saw him sit at a table with a blank sheet of paper in front of him and a pencil behind his ear. I put him to work before I ventured out to the States and now, without entrusting the documents to the mercy of the United States' postal network and instead requiring the services of the most expensive hand-delivered method, the fruits of his labors were en route.

Antony and I touched down at Little Rock National Airport in the early evening and found that Bec's flight was delayed and not due for several hours, so we picked up our rental car and drove in search of a motel. Citing reasons such as privacy, noise, "It's been a month," and other cryptic messages to which I was none the wiser, Bec insisted I check into a room separate from Antony, across the hall. We kept in touch using some walkie-talkies I had bought in Billings. Tracking Bec's plane on my laptop, I glanced occasionally up at the television, changing the channel until something caught my eye. CNN had coverage of all of the Democratic candidates for the 2008 presidential election taking part in a debate the likes of which I'd never seen—members of the public had been asked to use the video sharing website YouTube to record questions, a selection of which were put to the likes of Barack Obama, Hillary Clinton, and some people of whom I'd never heard. Elsewhere, a shopping channel was offering me an indestructible razor, built from carbon and stainless steel, which eliminates the need to ever buy another razor again—weirdly, if I rang straight away, I could get a second one absolutely free. And on *CNN Headline News*, there was live coverage of horrendous flooding which, according to the host, was devastating parts of "Glow-ster-shire" and "Wer-sester-shire." I lay back on my bed and breathed a sigh of relief. From the familiar-looking images of the live pictures and aerial shots of the flooded plains, I was beginning to think that something had happened in England.

Bec's plane finally touched down at ten-thirty and I set off in search of my blueprints. I was eager to bring Bec back to the motel, too, so we could all find something to eat. Of course, by eleven o'clock, most of the restaurants and bars surrounding the motel had closed, and we were left with a nearby Taco Bell, which had just closed its doors to the public but were still serving people through the drive-through. It was a great chance to show Bec the type of service one expects from

American eateries—although it's difficult ordering food via a speaker installed into a menu board (and the person on the end usually comes through sounding like they've been kidnapped and gagged), the genuine kindness and common courtesy demonstrated by people in the service industry stateside is second to none.

The only problem I have with Taco Bell is that the pictures on the menu don't really represent the product well and a degree in Spanish or modern languages is helpful when ordering. The situation wasn't made any easier that night by the speaking menu board, which didn't even understand me saying, "Hang on a minute," much less any attempts at a language I don't speak. Take a quesadilla, for example. Living the sheltered life that I have, I had never seen that word before and when I came to ordering one, pronouncing it exactly as it was written, as "Cwos-a-dilla," I managed to make it sound less like a Mexican dish of melted cheese and more like an Australian prehistoric reptile.

The menu board reacted, sounding as if he had placed a welder's mask over the top of his ball gag. We went back and forth a bit, I trying to add a soft drink to the order and at some point finally using the simple numbering system they had in place, but even that was garbled. With that, transmission ended and I was left to drive to the window to see what our incoherent conversation had produced in the kitchen. I drove several yards forward and the attendant aggressively pulled his window open. "Here's ya food," he shouted, thrusting three tin foil–wrapped packages into my hand.

"Um, thank you," I replied.

"You really English or were you fucking with me, dawg?" he asked.

"I beg your pardon?" I replied, as politely and English as

I could. "Yes, I am English, yes." I've never sounded more English.

"Oh!" he exclaimed. "I thought you were . . . um . . ." He struggled to find the words as I prepared a perfect English accent.

"Fucking with your dog?"

"Yeah. Summin like that."

Without drinks to go with our "meal," Bec's introduction to the delights of American cuisine was in the motel room with something or other from Taco Bell and a can of lager we bought from a twenty-four-hour gas station.

The next day, we had two things on our minds: to get a decent meal without having to speak through a garbling machine and to find some cardboard so we could start work on our boat. Making an early start and checking out of our motel at nine in the morning, we headed toward a Yamaha and Honda bike dealership, which Bec assured me her dad had previously contacted about giving us cardboard, and which was conveniently located just 2 miles from our motel. What she failed to inform me until we pulled into the dealership's forecourt was that the shop never replied to his e-mail. Considering Bec has a good knowledge of bikes owing to her father's amateur career in motocross, coupled with the fact that I once crashed into a hedge on a moped, I let her do the talking so that if need be she could talk about bikes in a confident charm offensive. After a conversation with her about a Yamaha YZ125, Jeremy, the assistant, seemed impressed and invited Bec into the back. She'll do anything for cardboard.

We left the business with several flattened boxes, enough sturdy, corrugated cardboard for the sides of the boat, though it was nowhere near robust enough for use on the base of the vessel. As we began our 60-mile drive north to Heber Springs, we left the interstate on the outskirts of Little Rock and pulled into a café for some breakfast. The host was affable and kind . . . but rather ill informed of the world.

"Oh, I love your accents," she said after we had asked for a table for three. "Where are you from?"

"Have a guess," I replied. A puzzled look covered her face before she replied. "Where's that?"

Showing us to our table after learning where in the world the United Kingdom was, the waitress presented us with the menu. Each breakfast meal was cleverly named after a southern state of America, inserting a pun if the circumstances were propitious. Well, I suggest clever; there was "Yolklahoma" for the meal with two eggs instead of one, but then the menu seemed to have lost its linguistic flair as the other breakfast choices were simply named Missouri, Kentucky, and Arkansas.

As we left the interstate and joined the northern Highway 5 toward Heber Springs, main roads and large settlements gave way to quiet, scenic byways and the obligatory churches. So ubiquitous were places of worship that to pass the time, we would look at the map, find the name and population of the next town, and guess how many churches we would pass. The game continued until we reached our destination of Heber Springs—population: 6,500; churches: 16.

Usually when we check into a motel, we do so based on one thing: price. The amenities, comfort, and location came as a mere afterthought. Heber Springs, however, was to give us more of a challenge, as not only were there only five motels from which to choose, but we needed to find one with an owner who was sympathetic to our cause and didn't mind us using his motel as a temporary dry dock and cardboard shipyard.

The Budget Inn, conveniently located just a few blocks from the center of town, half a mile from where the races were to be held, and owned by an Indian family, was perfect. It was quiet, close to a supermarket and hardware store, and, because the owner had someone with whom he could talk about cricket for the first time in ages, he was more than happy to allow the construction of a cardboard vessel in his parking lot. He even suggested that his family would attend the event for the very first time, and offered to load our boat onto the back of his pickup truck to transport on the day of the races. Brilliant.

With both accommodation and a construction yard secure, all we needed before undertaking such a monumental development project was alcohol. Famous British engineer Isambard Kingdom Brunel wasn't quite the same without a cigar in his mouth, and so, to create the HMS *Bateman* (lovingly named in his absence)—a ship that would rival both Brunel's SS *Great Britain* and *Great Eastern*—we needed our own iconic trademark to guide us through the long, hot days of construction: beer. A quick trip to the supermarket was required.

Just across the road from the motel lay the welcoming parking lot of Harps Food Store, a large place which seemed as if it was last remodeled in the 1980s. As Antony marched up the aisles in search of beer and wine, Bec and I perused some of the shelves for items we could use as cheap tools for the boat. Soon, Antony reemerged empty-handed.

"I can't find it," he said.

We all walked to the far aisle where the beer was usually sold and found nothing alcoholic. A young girl in her Harps Food Mart uniform was near, and we asked where the beer section was.

Nothing at all could have prepared me for her response. "Oh, we don't sell it," she replied. "This is a dry county."

Bec and Antony looked on, puzzled by the girl's words, but I knew exactly what she meant. If you are in the same boat (see what I did there?) as Antony and Bec were, I shall explain.

In 1933, the Eighteenth Amendment, more commonly known as prohibition, became the only one in America's history to be repealed, leaving states to decide whether they wanted to relegalize the sale of alcohol. Today, most counties in America do sell alcohol (and are called wet), but there are some, most in the South, which are "dry," meaning that the sale of alcohol is forbidden. Because certain cities and municipalities in the country have the right to make their own laws, there are cities within dry counties that have declared the sale of alcohol to be legal. These are called partially dry or moist counties. This system is a complete contrast to what we are used to in the U.K., where *wet* or *dry* wouldn't be appropriate. To describe the scenes one would witness in many places on a Friday night, the terms *drenched* or *piss-stained* would be much more fitting.

Seventy-four years after the repeal of prohibition, 10 percent of the country remains completely dry. This is true for almost half of Mississippi's counties, where it's even illegal to transport alcohol across any of the dry counties in the state. Although recent research has shown that dry counties have a higher proportion of alcohol-related traffic accidents from people driving back from a wet county, forty-two of Arkansas' seveny-three counties still prohibit the sale of alcohol.

I realized at that point that whoever came up with the crazy concept of a cardboard boat regatta did so when he was sober!

Now, I'm not an alcoholic or a heavy drinker, and in the thirty-six days Antony and I had spent in the States together, we must have been inebriated only two or three times. However, with a large task of hard work and camaraderie required for the construction of the boat, some refreshment was definitely needed. I headed back to the motel to check on the Internet which of our neighboring counties sold the stuff.

Heber Springs sits almost central in Arkansas' Cleburne County and the district is surrounded by five adjacent municipal areas. Traveling to Stone County would mean a drive around Greers Ferry Lake to the north, but would be a futile endeavor as that county is also dry. There was the Searcy Country Club, one of the few venues in White County to the southeast of Cleburne that was allowed to sell alcohol, but I wasn't prepared to join a golf club to enjoy a pint. Cleburne's southwestern neighbor, Faulkner County, is just as dry as it is, and Van Buren, whose border stood less than ten miles to the west, was dry too and had been for almost two hundred years. Our only hope was Independence County, whose name made it sound as if it embodied the spirit of the right to free choice. We were sure that a county named Independence had duly repealed the only amendment in the American constitution that *removed* freedom rather than ensuring it.

Nope. It was dry.

So our only choice was to embark on a 100-mile round trip to Pulaski County, home to Jacksonville, which is one of the few "dry" towns within a "wet" county. With little time to spare, we all leaped into the car and made our way south on a courageous expedition of chivalry and unwavering valor, worthy in merit to that of Marco Polo and Sir Francis Drake. Kind of.

Driving in Arkansas was a real frustration—the roads were wide and empty and yet the speed limit was a pitifully slow 55 mph. There were few schools to pass, as the road meandered through only a small number of towns, and the only houses on the side of the highway were large farms, which were set back a considerable distance. I didn't put my foot down, but I think the ease of driving and the wide road subconsciously made me speed up.

In the rearview mirror I could see the bright glare of flashing blue lights and a police car's headlights. Goodness knows how long he'd been following me; I looked into the mirror only to wipe away a smear. I can vividly remember exactly where I pulled the car over to the side of the road—it was less than 50 yards short of the White County line. As the cop took his time departing his vehicle, I wondered if edging the car across the county line would have made as much difference as it does in the movies, resulting in no jurisdiction for the officer and a clever escape of a fine for me.

It was too late. All of my contemplation of *Smokey and the Bandit*– and *Dukes of Hazzard*–style escapes had given the officer enough time to leave his car and approach my window.

It's not the first time I've been stopped by the police in America. In fact, I can't remember any trip I've taken to the States where I haven't been pulled over for something. My dad and I were stopped in Seattle for not pulling over to the side of the road when an emergency vehicle was making his way through the traffic, even though the paramedics already had a clear 50 yards of space through which to charge. And the last time Bateman and I were in America, he was stopped by the police in Wyoming for speeding . . . and a week later we were held nearly at gunpoint by three undercover police officers just because of a Cornish flag on the parcel shelf of our car (it's a long story, about three hundred pages, ISBN 978-0-307-33942-4 . . . I'll keep trying). Anyway, I digress. Where was I? Oh, yes, the police officer.

As he tapped on the window, I remembered the two main points in escaping fines in foreign countries: act very British and very ignorant. I pressed the button that operates the electric windows and realized the keys weren't in the ignition, and so I fumbled around until the keys were in and the window began to lower, perfectly demonstrating general ignorance without even trying.

After asking for my driving license, car details (and Bec's passport for some reason), he began the questioning while trying to make sense of a United Kingdom driver's license.

"Do you know what the speed limit is on these roads, sir?" he asked.

"Um, well in England . . . ," I said, making sure to get the word *England* into my opening sentence to verify that that is where I was from. ". . . these sorts of road are sixty mph, and I must admit, I don't know what it is out here. I've only been here a few days," I lied.

"Well," he said, breathing out a sigh of disappointment. "Most roads in Arkansas are fifty-five mph. When we approached you, you were doing sixty-five and then you sped up to seventy-one."

"Oh," I replied, realizing that the policeman must have thought I was trying to evade his capture. "Sorry about that."

"You in a hurry to get somewhere this evening?" he asked.

"Yes, officer. I'm setting off in search of a week's supply of alcohol which I intend to bring back and store in your dry county while we build a cardboard boat."

Obviously I didn't say that. That would be madness. "Nowhere special," I said.

After more questioning to which I lied—no, *withheld the truth*—he returned to his squad car for a moment or so and returned with mine and Bec's IDs, my rental car details, and a blue piece of paper.

"I'm giving you a warning, Mr. Smith, because I wouldn't

want you to have to return on vacation here again to appear in court," he said sternly.

"Oh, that's OK, officer, give me the fine," I didn't say. "I would just fly home and not pay it anyway."

In actual fact I simply said, "Thanks," and we were back on our way to the Promised Land. It was only after a few miles that I realized I had given the policeman the rental car details for the Mustang in Oregon.

After forty police-free minutes, we finally reached the interstate and were just several miles from the Pulaski County line. Such is the number of dry counties in the state that I saw the colossal *Ace Liquor Store* sign before the county's welcoming sign. Liquor stores and alcohol-stocked gas stations cluttered the first hundred yards of Pulaski County, and simply crossing the county line was similar to disembarking a ferry into the port of Calais on a booze cruise.

Because Ace Liquor Store was on the other side of the highway, we pulled off and visited Harvey's Liquor, where we made the employees' day by simply speaking in an English accent. In return they made our day by selling us three cases of Coors, some wine, and several other bottles of beer. With our expedition at an end, we safely returned to Heber Springs with no interference from the law, smuggling the alcohol into Antony's room and filling every available space in his fridge with the contraband.

*D*ay one of construction began with the realization that I was wearing the same T-shirt for the sixth straight day and I required a launderette before the search for tools and more cardboard could begin. The Sugarloaf Laundry Mat was run by a genuinely amiable and polite gentleman who didn't at all mind washing Antony's vomit-stained clothes, which he had kept with him since his episode at the Peacock Tavern in Corvallis. The owner also took a keen interest in our boatbuilding endeavors and revealed that he had once entered the competition.

"Have you got any tips?" Bec asked.

"Elephant glue," he said. "Elephant glue will stick anything down and it doesn't take a lot of time to dry."

With a full day before we could return to collect the clothes, we decided we should return to the motorbike shop and see if Jeremy had any more cardboard for us. Jeremy remembered Bec and had taken the trouble of logging on to the official website of the races—he'd read the regulations and had put the correct type of boxes to one side for us. He was a jolly nice man. Sadly, although we were very appreciative for his interest in our cause, the boxes were still not enough to complete an entire boat and were definitely not sturdy enough for the base of the vessel.

We continued on the interstate toward Little Rock, wondering where a mass of cardboard of adequate thickness could be found. Then we came across the most fortuitous of billboards, one that proved that someone or something was definitely on our side and had summoned the cardboard genie. Hovering 70 feet above the interstate was a sign advertising a cardboard box factory! Due to the utter shock of seeing such a conveniently placed billboard, I managed to see only that the business in question was proud to stock "Over 500 different sizes." I was forced to leave the interstate and turn around to see and record the name and address.

I don't know about you, but I've never seen a billboard (or any advert in any publication or medium for that matter) promoting cardboard boxes. Yet the only time in my life I have been desperate for such a thing, one appears. Perhaps, I thought, there is a god after all.

Whether it was the work of a deity or just a stroke of

luck, on the second time around the billboard gave us the name of the company, Riverside Box Supply, and instead of staring blankly at the sign in awe, each of us memorized a segment of the telephone number. With no phone to contact the company, and no map on which to mark their position, we decided that the best course of action would be to find a suitable tourist information center and use them instead.

Located in downtown Little Rock was the most beautiful tourist information center, set in a magnificent historic ante-bellum home. Below a glistening chandelier sat a small table with a computer. In less than ten minutes, I had the directions to the cardboard-box–supply store and the nearest hardware store, and was finally ready to hunt for our very own cardboard version of El Dorado.

Riverside Box Supply is located in a barren landscape on a minor service road leading to the airport. By the look of the business' foyer and reception area—where a tacky aerial photograph of the business was surrounded by effigies of Jesus and framed psalms and passages from the Bible—it seemed that if it was, indeed, God who was behind the placing of the billboard, now he was attempting to complete the job and convert us. The husband-and-wife managerial team welcomed us, called Tony to come out from the back, and encouraged us to talk—"Just say anything"—so they could listen to our accents as if our pattern of speech was angelically melodic in some way.

Tony finally came out, relinquishing us from our clown duties, and led us into the back of the store. Piled to the very top of the room, just short of the 30-foot ceiling, stood hundreds of pallets of flat-packed cardboard and boxes of varying size and thickness. We were just after some materials for a sturdy base and support joists for our tiny vessel, but there was enough cardboard in the Riverside Box Supply to assemble an armada.

For our base, I opted for one of the thickest sizes they had, a triple-corrugated piece of cardboard, which took two of us to carry. Several pieces of the double-corrugated variety could be used as the sides and support joists of our boat. As I drove the car around to the side delivery doors, it soon became apparent that due to the size of the saloon-style boot, loading the vehicle with the four large sheets of cardboard was going to be a bit of a struggle. Tony helpfully suggested that it would be easier if we put the car in the box instead of the other way 'round, but really we were left with no choice but to bend the base sheet in half and force it sideways into the back of the car. With the vehicle crammed with cardboard, Antony contorted his way into the backseat, where he remained uncomfortable but without complaint for the two hours it took us to visit the hardware store and return to the motel. The cardboard god who led us to the box-supply store watched over our safe passage back to Heber Springs, keeping us at a far distance from the policeman who had stopped us the previous day and the remainder of the Cleburne County sheriff's office.

Finally, on Wednesday evening, with less than three days until the big race, construction on the HMS *Bateman* was underway. We quickly made the startling discovery that despite their dry county location, the handles on the Budget Inn's cupboard made brilliant bottle openers.

As with most construction jobs, there was a budget we needed to keep within for the HMS *Bateman*. The cheapest spray paint was bought; a clothesline was purchased in place of the more expensive rope; Elephant glue was substituted with the low-cost Gorilla Glue; and instead of proper oars with a price tag of well over $30 a piece, I opted for the more economical solution of using three $4 dustpans (the brushes were an added bonus).

Bec's dad knew only too well of mine and Antony's constructional foibles and had made the design sheets huge and easy to follow. If we followed the plans correctly, the HMS *Bateman* would be 7 feet long, 3 feet 10 inches wide, and would cut in at the front of the boat to produce a 2-foot bow. We would sit in a central hull measuring five foot six by three feet, which would be held in position by twenty-six rolled cardboard joists, adding strength to the main sides of the boat. That was the plan, anyway.

Construction began in the early evening, the Arkansas heat at 90 degrees as I cut my way through the thick base cardboard with one of my four steak knives (which I had bought to escape the price of a hacksaw). Antony and Bec measured and cut precise amounts of cardboard for the body of the boat. As darkness fell on Heber Springs, using the car's headlamps as our only source of light, the first day of construction came to a close when the varnishing had been completed and there was nothing we could do but retire to allow the cardboard to dry. We finished our beers, collected the tools, and swept away the debris with the "oars."

Early the next morning we checked on the varnish and decided we should continue construction. After only an hour in, we were already forced to take several breaks due to the intolerable heat and the lack of shade offered by the motel's courtyard. It was a unanimous decision that efficient work on the boat could be achieved only in the evenings, when temperatures had dropped and the sun wasn't as intense.

To be on the safe side and to make sure we weren't unintentionally breaking any of the stringent rules laid down by the race organizers, I decided to visit the town's chamber of commerce to see if there was any literature on the regulations. I left with not only an eighteen-page booklet on cardboard boat basics called "What Floats Your Boat" but also an entry form and the knowledge that, to our surprise, there was a twenty-four-hour Wal-Mart Super Center on the opposite side of town.

The rules of the race stated, not surprisingly, that the structure—with the exception of the propulsion system, oars, and the steering device—must be made entirely of cardboard. Check. There was one rule, however, that we had overlooked—every member of the team must wear a life jacket, which was something we definitely did not pack. With Wal-Mart charging an extortionate amount for something we would use only once, and our finding that arm floaties are apparently not a sufficient life-saving device, we headed to a nearby marina to see if we could rent some life jackets.

The nearest ocean beach to Heber Springs is a nine-hour drive away in Louisiana, but the town is situated on the banks of Greers Ferry Lake, an artificial reservoir named after the town situated on the opposite shore. It was formed by the creation of the Greers Ferry Dam in 1962 and was dedicated in 1963 by John F. Kennedy the following year, his final major public appearance before his ill-fated trip to Dallas a month later. Due to the newly formed lake, both towns profited well from a tourism boom, which helped the area become one of the country's most popular destinations. Today, the popularity of the region may have regressed but the Heber Springs Marina is one of many dotted along the shores of the lake where many out-of-towners still moor their boats for weekend breaks on the water.

As we wandered up the jetty to the building at the end, the overhead sun shone on the surface of the water, and large fish could be seen between the hull of the boats and the bed of the lake. After waiting patiently for a woman and her family to rent one of the many boats available, I approached the counter and asked if they hired out their life vests. We were in luck. For $15 and my "fascinating" driving license as collateral, we could borrow three life jackets and were even offered two oars for free, meaning that only one of us would have to endure the embarrassment of using a dustpan during the race. With two days before the big race, we agreed to pick them up the following day.

In the early evening, work recommenced on the HMS *Bateman*, but the heat was still a major problem. The base was taped together and the varnish had dried nicely but the glue we had used refused to dry in the overwhelming humidity. Our best bet was to use duct tape and, finding that its use would be of integral importance to the structure and support of the vessel, I visited the local hardware store and bought 125 yards of the stuff. At the checkout, my confidence in our project took a bit of a knock when the assistant revealed that he too was entering a boat into the race.

"Yeah, I'll be there," he said before adding the real confidence booster. "I've been working on it for about six months now and she's still not finished!"

Upon my return, Antony and Bec had managed to duct tape the base together and were starting work on our central seating section. By nightfall the inner hull was complete and had been varnished, ready for gluing to the base, but insect bites to my comrades were adding to the already problematical heat and impending deadline. When tools were put down at the end of the working day, though, at least the inner hull stood firm and would hopefully be completely stuck to the base of the boat by sunrise.

Friday would be the last day we would have to work on the boat, and if it was too hot for us to work during the daylight hours, we would be left with only the evening hours and early morning to get the HMS *Bateman* ready for Saturday's 9 a.m. registration. The glue would need adequate time for adhering—if it was applied too late, the boat would leak almost instantaneously, condemning our hours of work to a watery grave. Construction was going to go down to the wire; we had only seven hours remaining and just twenty-four cans of beer left in the fridge.

*F*riday began with a trip to Wal-Mart for some bug repellent and itch cream, which we could all use on the injuries we had sustained the previous day, and a visit to the marina, where we collected our life jackets and oars. By the afternoon, we had dragged our boat to the rooms on the opposite side of the motel's courtyard so we could shelter from the sun's glare.

As we created a production-line system to make the twenty-six rolled joists—Becky on rolling duty, Antony sticking, and I as the duct-tape cutter—we began to notice that the motel was quickly filling up with weekend customers. For the entire week, we had effectively been the only people staying at the motel, but now, early Friday evening, half of the rooms had vehicles parked outside. One pulled into the space beside our working position with a cardboard kayak attached to the roof.

The Neumaster family from Missouri had entered their ten-year-old son, Hunter, into the youth division of the cardboard boat races. Hunter took an interest in our construction and couldn't disguise the sound of disdain in his voice.

"That gonna float?" he asked.

"Probably not," I replied. I pointed at the roof rack of his car. "That yours?"

"That's *Skeetle*, my boat."

"That's right," his dad interrupted. "What's a boat, honey?" he shouted to his daughter.

"A hole in the water," she responded as if rehearsed.

Hunter and his dad were only too happy to offer equally helpful hints on construction and suggest materials we should buy to ensure the buoyancy of the boat. As the children's grandparents were due to arrive and would need to park in the very space in which we were working, we had the perfect excuse to drag the HMS *Bateman* back across the courtyard to escape the constant interference from Hunter. Stupid name anyway.

We continued on the boat as more and more people checked into the motel. Before too long, the NO VACANCY sign came on, and our efforts came under further scrutiny from our new neighbors. We glued the sides to the base of the boat and nearly emptied our rooms, using heavy objects to weigh down the flaps to help them stick. Two wooden desk chairs along with two armchairs were both put to good use, and to compensate for the potential deficiencies in the bonding of cardboard to glue, I was sent to Wal-Mart for yet another roll of duct tape.

With duct tape beginning to peel and the strength of the boat coming into question, we began to work tirelessly into the night, attempting to ignore the man who had checked into the room next to ours. Smoking a cigar, he paused to watch us for several minutes before returning to his room and reappearing with a camera. There he stood, just feet from us, among several tools and cardboard scraps, not saying a word. For minutes he sidestepped his way through the work area taking pictures without an expression on his face. As Antony, Bec, and I hinted in his direction with our eyebrows, displaying our queries and wondering what he was doing or from which mental illness he suffered, he finally removed the cigar from his mouth and broke his silence.

"Is that a boat?"

Cheeky bastard.

By midnight, there was nothing more we could do. The glue required hours to take effect, we had no more durable cardboard at our disposal, and although we had wrapped it in almost 200 yards of tape, and HMS *Duct Tape* was a far more appropriate name, all we could do was wait. Owing to the Arkansas temperature, an early-morning paint job would dry in no time and with any hope, once the HMS *Bateman* was emblazoned in the Cornish colors of black and white, it would transform from a shit state to become shipshape.

"That looks great," Bec called across the motel parking lot the next morning to the grass bank at the back, where I was busy spraying the finishing touches. A thick, white cross covered all four visible sides on a black background, creating the flag of Saint Piran anywhere you looked, with the words *HMS Bateman* emblazoned across the stern. The boat seemed sturdy enough and the drying of the glue had turned the previous evening's structural frailties into a vessel that was, if not beautiful or amazing . . . well, whole, at least. One single entity.

As we decided against an official naming ceremony, just in case the boat wasn't able to withstand a collision with a bottle (empty or otherwise), the owner of the motel parked outside our room and pointed at his cargo space. "We go?"

Complete with board shorts for when (not if) the boat went under, and a captain's hat (which I had purchased from a Dollar Tree store earlier in the trip), I helped Antony tie the boat to the frame of the pickup using the clothesline, then hopped into the cab. Dollar Trees are incredible shops. With the favorable exchange rate, everything was less than 50p for us—including a pregnancy test, which Antony and I saw in the their Corvallis branch. (Of course, for that kind of money, the quality of the test was probably such that tossing a coin would be just as accurate.)

Sandy Beach has everything you'd expect from a standard seaside location. It has a car park, an area for volleyball, hordes of people in revealing swimwear, and golden sand. The only thing it lacks (and I must admit it's a bit of a clincher) is the sea. The Greers Ferry Lake, however, makes up for the lack of an ocean, and its clear waters and flat conditions create a pleasant artificial seaboard.

As we located the organizers and registered our boat into the adult team division—the only people not from the states of Missouri, Oklahoma, Arkansas, or Mississippi to enter—we found that our international entry would truly make this year's event a "World Championship." We grabbed a schedule of events and found a suitable location on the sand, away from the crowds and in the shade. The course was pretty simple. A semicircular swimming area had been cordoned off by continuous lines of plastic tubing, and approximately 30 feet farther into the lake a row of buoys provided a boundary where yachts and speedboats were moored; the bridges of the thousand-dollar flotillas were used as grandstand seats. The cardboard boats used the central division in between and would have to navigate the roughly 200-foot arching course.

According to the schedule, awards weren't just presented for the fastest boat—a team could pick up a trophy for a wide array of achievements (all of which I doubted we would be collecting at the day's end). The Pride of the Fleet award would be handed out to the team whose boat had an innovative and unique design, and who had taken into account the important matter of science and physics. A Cornish flag and a name that meant nothing to anyone (in addition to the fact that I had tried to incorporate Archimedes' principle without any luck) would definitely see us miss out on that particular medal. Our discordant dress sense and fears that our vessel was one of the worst in the competition wouldn't aid us much in picking up the prize for Team Spirit. Our best hope was to aim for the Titanic Award, won by the team who suffered the most dramatic sinking and who demonstrated the best efforts to prevent such a disaster. This, at first, seemed easily attainable; sinking was the one thing at which we were all sure the HMS *Bateman* would excel. Unfortunately, to "win" the award, the boat had to travel at least 50 feet, and that was at least 48 feet farther than we had anticipated reaching.

From our vantage point, by the side of a spacious and tall dry-docked power boat, we had a great view of the course and wondered why hardly anyone was sitting by us, with the watercraft's supports providing a pleasant backrest and adequate shade. By 10 a.m., it became apparent.

A sharp, eardrum-shattering squeal came from a speaker right near us and filled the beach with a booming voice welcoming everyone to the 21st Annual World Championship Cardboard Boat Races. Sitting alongside the commentator, former chamber of commerce member Gary Redd, was Laine Berry, better known as Mrs. Arkansas 2007. The beauty queen would be cocommentating with Gary and presumably was there to provide the crowd with detailed analysis of the races and the crafts involved from her expansive understanding and encyclopedic knowledge in her specialized field of pageantry and makeup.

Just when we thought the space and shade would compensate for the noise, Gary announced that he was going to throw to the viewers some merchandise from Sonic, a chain of drive-in diners, the sponsors of the event. In little under a minute, a multitude of beachgoers had gathered in front of us, unintentionally kicking sand in our faces and aggressively competing against one another for Frisbees, mobile phone pouches, and inflatable beach balls; continually begging for more freebies with arms outstretched as if they were refugees at a UN food-package drop.

With utter relief, the tossing of the tacky gifts ceased, and we were free to admire the view of the last few races of the youth division, and the marvellously encouraging sight of Hunter struggling against his competitors and traveling in the wrong direction.

As the races continued, we enjoyed the brilliant commentary skills of Mrs. Arkansas. At the start of each race, she would read the names of the boat and crew from a sheet of paper and then, when one of the boats led its adversary by several feet, she would bring the microphone close to her lips and say: "Wow! They have a commanding lead." That was about the extent of her analytical talent.

The youth races came to an end, and as they left the water, preparing themselves for their second run, the announcement for the beginning of the adults' heats was sounded. This was our call, and we left our perch beneath the commentators and dragged HMS *Bateman* to the far shoreline to meet our fellow competitors. Two rows of cardboard boats in front of us, collecting plaudits and looks of awe, was the boat likely to win the Team Spirit Award. With the crew dressed in matching bandanas, the *Pirates & Paddles* boat was a piece of papier-mâché perfection. John Bartlett was the chief designer and captain of the stunning miniature replica of an eighteenth-century frigate decorated in the style of a pirate ship. His team were proud of their creation and had already decided not to enter it in the afternoon's finale—the demolition derby, open to any of the boats that survive the trials of racing.

Next to the pirates stood the *Sprocket Rocket*, a floating cardboard platform powered by a bicycle mounted on top, an invention whose engineering genius made it an absolute shoo-in for Pride of the Fleet and put an end to our incredibly slim chances of picking up any award. Because there were twenty-five teams in all adult classes, most heats were between two or three entrants. Viewing wasn't easy due to the bustle down in "the pits," but at least I was within audible distance of Mrs. Arkansas and could hear which boat had a commanding lead.

The *Pirates & Paddles* may not have been the quickest team in the competition and wouldn't be winning the overall title, but the ship took to the course gracefully in a chorus of horns from the boats and cries of encouragement from swimmers who had sprawled themselves on the floating boundaries to gain a closer look.

Soon it was our turn . . . probably.

"HMS *Batman*?" asked a man with a clipboard.

"*Bateman*," I corrected.

In the waist-deep water we were positioned alongside *Flower Power Unsinkable* and a brown boat with a yellow bolt of lightning drawn on the side called *White Lightning* (even though they had misspelt their name and had *White Lighting* written on the hull). According to the captain, it wasn't a mistake and *Lighting* was a colloquialism in Mississippi. He was definitely lying. I've heard *Lightnin'* as a different pronunciation, but *Lighting*? What would they say when they really needed to use the word *lighting*?

As attention was turned to the mayor, who stood with the starter's gun on a speedboat behind the grid, we each clung to the rim of our vessel, all hesitant to step inside in case it would provoke a flooding before we had even begun. No one wanted to be the catalyst of the boat's sinking.

A loud bang filled the air and water splashed in our faces as our opponents raced off. We all jumped in and for the briefest of seconds things appeared to be going well. We may have already been a good five or six lengths behind *White Lighting*, but we were all aboard and paddling furiously, Bec at the front using her dustpan as a rudimentary rudder, attempting to steer the boat in the right direction. But after only ten or so seconds, it became obvious that the only direction we were headed was down.

"We're leaking!" Antony shouted, trying to keep his panicky giggling to a minimum. He wasn't joking, either. We were all kneeling in the boat and already the water was up to our thighs.

"Bail, Bec. Bail!" I yelled.

Any water that wasn't seeping through the badly glued gaps at the side, evading the seal of over 200 yards of duct tape, was managing to cascade over the stern, which protruded out of the surface of the water by only a matter of inches. As Bec converted her dustpan-cum-oar into a dustpan-cum-oar-cum-bucket, Antony and I paddled like madmen just to see how far we could get. Not very. Before we knew it, we were up to our necks in the Greers Ferry, still kneeling on the base of our boat which, in turn, was now resting on the bed of the lake. We had sunk and things weren't going swimmingly (well, actually, I guess they were). As we dragged the soggy mess out of the water, all I could hear was the jeering of the crowd and Mrs. Arkansas exclaiming that *White Lighting* had a commanding lead.

To the best of my imagination, that is how our entry into the races would have gone . . . had we registered. (I promise this is the last time I'll lead you on, readers).

In the early hours of Saturday morning, wilting under the tireless task of reapplying peeled duct tape and adding further coats of inadequate glue while battling the heat, humidity, and insect bites, the decision was made to abandon ship. If you had seen the exhaustion and sweat on our faces and the devastating state of our "nautical vessel," you too would have probably admitted defeat.*

With only the evenings in which to work, our cardboard having to be folded and therefore weakened to fit into the car's trunk, and the temperature preventing the glue from setting, we were facing an uphill struggle. And although Bec insisted it would float and we should continue working through the night until its completion, the fact that the sides wouldn't stand firm against the light breeze told me that it probably wouldn't have held up to thousands of gallons of water, either. Antony and I knew when we were beaten. After what I had paid to build the piece of crap, I wasn't prepared to spend a further $50 registering it and a $25 deposit I could lose if we failed to drag the stricken vessel from the depths of the lake.

Bec may have been correct, however. The following morning, before we headed to the races, we tested the boat for durability. We had already angered the owner of the motel by not appearing from our rooms in time to catch a lift with him, wasting his time, and so we didn't really want to try the boat out in the pool. Instead, we opted for a far more strenuous

---

*You can see an artist's impression of what it should have looked like, and what it ended up resembling, at rich-smith.net. Abysmal doesn't even begin to describe it.

trial, as Bec drove the rental car into it. At approximately 10 mph, the car simply moved the boat across the ground, trapping it beneath the grill. So I asked Bec to reverse the car and really have a go. This time, at about 25 mph and a longer run-up, the HMS *Bateman* stood no chance.

Bec was quite impressed. "See? It survived the first one," she said.

As we headed back to Little Rock the following day, the atmosphere in the car was hushed and strained. Bec was still upset that we hadn't entered and I was regretting the decision. The rental car test had shown that it was durable, and would have withstood whatever the nautical equivalent is of being hit at 10 mph by a Nissan Sentra.

We pulled into the same motel we had left five days before, feeling defeated and downhearted. Avoiding Taco Bell, we ordered a pizza and decided that as we were lodging in a wet county for the first time in almost a week, we should drown our sorrows with a drink at a nearby bar or grab something to drink back at the motel. We didn't even succeed in that either. Arkansas doesn't sell alcohol on Sundays.

8. THE LONGEST YARD

Guns galore, and secondhand swastikas—just your usual southern American yard sale.

ight, thanks for everything," said Antony. I shook his hand and Bec wrapped her arms around him and kissed him on the cheek.

"Right. We'll see you when we get back, mate," I replied. "Hope everything goes well."

This Monday morning was especially depressing.

While we were in Heber Springs, Antony had learned that his grandmother had been diagnosed with a brain tumour and had been given just two weeks to live. For the next hour, Antony agonized on his course of action, whether to stay for the remainder of the trip or fly home before it was too late. He decided that after the boat races, he would return to Cornwall.

The doors closing behind him, Antony made his way toward the check-in desk while Bec and I returned to the car. We both hoped that he would arrive home safely and that his nan would be well enough to see him. I thought of all the good times Antony and I had experienced together during our fifty-day adventure. For some reason my mind could only muster images of him being sick in Corvallis.

It dawned on me that if it wasn't for Bec's arrival, I would be on my own. We changed all of the remaining flights to be in her name instead of Antony's. Whether or not I thought she and I would have as much fun as Antony and I had been enjoying, it was clear that Bec's two-week stay with me was to get considerably longer.

Our final day in Little Rock was to be our first as a duo,

and we had a day to waste in the city until our flight later in the evening. I hoped to avoid malls (more precisely the Build-a-Bear Factory outlets that lie within them, as I didn't want to be forced to buy clothes for Bec's companion bear, Gary), so I suggested we visit the William J. Clinton Presidential Center, one of twelve buildings in America that preserve papers, records, and historical materials from presidential tenures. The library is the second largest of its kind and is housed within a futuristic glass structure, which arches over the Arkansas River, echoing Clinton's 1992 presidential campaign promise of "building a bridge to the twenty-first century."

Covering 20,000 square feet of exhibition space, including a 110-foot timeline of the eight-year Clinton administration and a life-size replica of the Oval Office, the library contains 2 million photographs, 80 million pages of documents, and nearly 80,000 artifacts from Clinton's time as president. The Presidential Center is a truly magnificent sight and does a fantastic job of demonstrating what a popular and productive presidency Clinton had. After seeing exhibits documenting his work for African Americans and his handling of the Kosovo Crisis (a conflict that didn't see a single death of NATO peacekeeping forces), you leave with a distinct sense that although Arkansas is the origin of some crazy alcohol limitations, the state had at least managed to produce someone of significance and of great benefit to the modern world.

By the way he loaded our bags into the back of the shuttle bus, you could tell that the driver was either in some pain or had experienced some sort of long-lasting injury at one point in his life. He appeared to be blind in one eye and walked as if one of his fists weighed a substantial amount more than the other. As we locked in our seat belts, he jumped into the driving seat and lowered the volume on the stereo.

"Guess what happened to me?" he asked. Without giving us any time to guess, he exclaimed, "I was shot!"

"When?" I asked.

"Oh, many years ago now," he replied, breaking into a childish giggle as if he had fond memories of the event. "Yeah, it was at a motel I was working at twenty-three years ago, when I was twenty-two," he added, resorting to a second juvenile chuckle. I was less shocked by the shooting and more by his age. He certainly didn't look forty-five.

"So you from London?" he asked.

"No. Not really," we replied.

"I used to live in London."

"Oh yeah? Did you like it?"

"No. It was cold and it rained a lot." He laughed.

I enjoyed the bus ride a great deal. He may have painted a pretty bleak picture of street life in Louisville (and London's climate for that matter), but the driver's heartening and humble character was as infectious as his childish laugh, and I wanted to keep talking to him all morning.

As he arrived outside the terminal, he looked up at the rearview mirror, looking at us, and laughed again. "The shooter got seven years."

Until now, the festivals I had attended had each been concentrated in one town, city, or (in the reenactment's case) field. The next festival on my agenda (if one can call it a festival) doesn't take place in just one city, but is concentrated on a single road—a route with bargains on every corner as it snakes its way through five states. I was headed to The World's Longest Yard Sale. Also known as the Highway 127 Corridor Sale (named after the road the hundreds of yard sales line), the annual event began in 1987 and was used as a way of luring travelers away from the nearby interstates to prove that the back roads still had something to offer. And it certainly does, all 450 miles of it.

The 2007 event was the first in the yard sale's history to include an additional 180-mile segment, which would take the shopper through Ohio and extend their itinerary to an unprecedented 630 miles. Because the event operates only from the first Thursday in August through the following Sunday, we decided we would stick to the traditional 450-mile trail to give us some sort of chance of completing the route while having enough time to experience the sales.

It was only Tuesday, and we had two days before we began our long bargain-hunting trek. So instead of making our way to the starting point in the most northerly part of Kentucky in Covington, we continued across the Ohio River and into neighboring Cincinnati to get to our lodgings for the next couple of days. It was here we were to experience the Budget Host Town Center Motel.

When I'd booked the motel online two days before, there was only the one picture: a motel situated in a shaded, leafy area of the city. It had a pool, the rooms looked clean, it had easy access to the downtown area, and it was just off the I-75, perfect for getting to Covington for the start of the yard sale. Also, at $56 per night, it was one of the cheapest in the area, but I had paid less than that before and had been happy with the resulting accommodation. I reserved two nights without a moment's hesitation.

Upon our arrival, Bec remained in the car as I made my way to the front office to check in. It was only four in the afternoon, but there was already raucous noise coming from the bar adjacent to the front desk. As the clerk turned in his chair, raising his eyebrows in acknowledgment of me, I told him my name and reservation details before noticing that along with the usual office signs informing you of the check-out time and policy on pets, there was a third notice stating NO DRUGS. I know that should have been a clue as to cancel my reservation right there and then, but frankly I was too British and too polite.

Our room on the ground floor was located just two doors down from the chained-up and abandoned swimming pool, and I entered the room a full five minutes before Bec (as she took a 50-foot detour to avoid the hornets' nest that lay just a couple of feet in front of where one might find a welcome mat). When she entered, Bec headed straight for the curtains, pulling them open and flooding the room with light. She was not impressed with what she could see.

Although it was a nonsmoking room, there was a definite smell of tobacco that clogged it and couldn't be expelled because the windows didn't open. Bec found chewing gum stuck to the walls, there was what looked like blood on the back of both the curtains and on the ceiling, the carpet looked like it hadn't been cleaned since Ronald Reagan was president, and all of the table surfaces were sticky. I won't even comment on the state of the sink and shower. Suffice it to say, Janet Leigh had a more pleasurable experience in her bathroom at the Bates Motel.

"It's not that bad, Bec," I said, trying to remain upbeat and positive. "It's got wireless Internet access at least."

Bec didn't care and sat still on the bed, not willing to walk around the room or unpack any of her belongings in case they became "contaminated." She hated the place. And she wasn't the only one.

I know you didn't buy this book as a travel guide or AAA accommodation handbook, but allow me to just share some reviews of the Budget Host Town Center Motel I have found on various travel review sites. I won't bore you with the entire

passage, and will simply list a selection of the titles the review-
ers used when they summarized their stay.

At the time of writing, Tripadvisor.com has seven reviews on the motel and they are titled thusly: "No Way Jose,"
"Keep Driving," "Absolutely Disgusting," "Too bad to even
stay," "Don't waste your money . . . ," "Stay Away," and "Why
can't I give it a rating of 0/5?" (that one's mine). Yahoo
travel isn't an improvement—it posts six reviews including:
"We thought it looked clean until . . . ," "Keep Driving! Do
Not Stop Here!" and "Gunshots outside the door."

The accommodation's only tick in the positive column,
the Internet access, proved a godsend as it helped us to get
immediately out of the Budget Host and into a Super 8 motel
in the north of the city that was not only far superior but
cheaper, too.

The first day of the yard sale was upon us, and after two
nights' sleep in a place that *wasn't* home to some of
the world's most infectious diseases, we were ready to begin
the monumental task. I had planned to turn the entire four
days into a competition of epic proportions between me,
Antony, and Bec—we would all have $30 with which to buy
goods before we arrived in Gadsden, Alabama, where we
would use the remainder of the Sunday attempting to sell
them to see who could make the most profit (or suffer the
smallest loss). Antony's departure had left the game in doubt
but since it was quite a good idea and we both still harbored
bitter feelings about our time in Arkansas, we agreed to compete. We each wanted to win at something to remove the
nasty aftertaste of failure.

U.S. Highway 127 was to be our home for the next four
days, but it wasn't clear as to where it was from the center
of Covington. Despite having the official yard sale brochure

in my possession—which also pointed out areas of historic and general interest along the route—locating the correct road was by no means an easy feat. Finally, though, having taken Pike Street to the Dixie Highway, a conveniently placed road sign confirmed we were traveling south on 127 and had officially begun on the trail of the World's Longest Yard Sale.

Fifteen minutes in, on the outskirts of Covington, we passed the first of the sales—several tables set up in a gap between two buildings. No one was standing behind any of the tables, and although children's toys, $1 sunglasses, and some secondhand batteries were mighty tempting, we decided to move along before the owner of the goods appeared and persuaded us to part with our money.

We had driven past only one sale thus far, so even though this one garage sale, which was trying to get in on the act, wasn't right on the highway, we decided to follow signs leading us off the road to a housing estate. Outside of a garage stood an assortment of lamps, lampshades, and badly damaged furniture. Inside, three members of a family sat in silence until one of them overheard Bec and I talking.

"Australian?" asked one of the two women.

"Um, no. We're English," Bec replied.

The lady pointed at me. "Well, he's definitely got something Steve Irwin about his voice."

"Yes. Although I doubt there's a similarity in our voices now that he can't speak," I remarked, quieting everyone.

We finally left Covington and came across our first large-scale yard sale, one that had dozens of vendors, numerous refreshment stands, and hundreds of shoppers. And how could we not stop at a sale in a town called Beaverlick?

We were determined to buy the first of our stock to resell later, and so we started trying to surmise what would or wouldn't be of interest to Alabamans (and then haggle for it). That meant things like pickup truck paraphernalia and anything linked with the Confederacy we were in, while you could forget about trying to flog such items as books.

I decided against buying an antique-style map of Great Britain, and Bec dabbled with the decision on whether to purchase a Jesus figurine. No one was operating the stall, though, so we moved to a nearby booth where merchandise included a North American road atlas from 1967 and a VHS tape of the John Candy film *Uncle Buck* that the owner had recorded off television.

The Beaverlick yard sale wasn't a complete waste of time, however—both Bec and I managed to make a purchase. After haggling the owner down from $5 to $3, I secured a product called Tic-Tac-Putt, a molded plastic putting practice game where balls are putted into spaces using the same rules as Tic-Tac-Toe.* Bec was pleased with her purchase, too—an unofficial U.S. Army cap for $5. The only problem with my purchase was that there was a golf ball missing—an orange one.

With our first items purchased, feeling good, we solemnly swore to stop at every yard sale on the route—that way, we could claim to be the only people who had truly experienced the event in its entirety (and I could search the golfing stands high and low for an orange ball replacement). There couldn't be that many, surely. We had already traveled outside of Covington and had seen only three. And it's not as if 127 passed through many large towns and cities. Plus, it was a Thursday; probably a lot of people were at work and others wouldn't want to spend three whole days roasting in the southern sun

---

*I've just scoured the Internet for Tic-Tac-Putt and found that Dick's Sporting Goods are selling it for $32.95. Bargain!

trying to flog their junk to unsuspecting travelers. I mean, there couldn't be many yard sales at all.

How wrong I was.

In the three and a half hours that followed, we managed to travel just 37 miles (that's an average speed of 10.5 mph), passing and stopping at forty-six separate sales. At that speed, assuming the yard sales would be available to view between ten in the morning and five in the afternoon, we would have needed until the following Tuesday to see it all (and the Friday after that if we had chosen to travel down the new 630-mile route).

The next sale we came across was in a field at the side of the road, and although I was tempted to invest in some John Deere coasters, I decided against it and moved in the direction of a stall that sold guns, guns, and more guns. It's remarkable that in the U.K., even a farmer would have to wait for weeks and wade through tons of paperwork and red tape to purchase such a weapon, but here in Kentucky, I could buy any firearm I wanted, no questions asked, from a guy in dungarees in a field. In the corner of this medium-sized "yard" sale stood a pair of hillbillies (only way to describe them) who had positioned themselves behind a table with random junk sprawled across it and were playing banjo music as an incentive to approach them. If only, at that precise moment in time, I had one of those cameras that not only captures the image but records just a few seconds of audio to set the scene (similar to those annoying birthday cards that also play a bit of music when opened), my American photo album would be a much happier place.

We knew it was impossible to stop at every single sale, so we decided to avoid smaller sales like this one and to venture into a yard sale only if it was one of the big ones (or if there was a chance I could find a replacement golf ball). We returned to the car and traveled all of 800 yards up the road.

This one was the daddy of all sales. It was situated in a huge field on the outskirts of the town of Owenton, Kentucky—named after Abraham Owen who died at the Battle of Tippecanoe in 1811 (quoting from the brochure here). I immediately found a stand selling golf bags and clubs, and quickly located a big, blue tub full of hundreds of golf balls. White and yellow dominated, and as I delved deeper, it became clear that not a single one of the balls in the container was orange. Bec, on the other hand, had secretly made her second purchase after locating a rather unique stand while I was up to my neck in golf balls. She came up to me holding a necklace. "Look at this, Rich."

"What is it?" I replied.

"It's an alligator tooth."

Bec had purchased the item for $7 from a table which had a wide array of similar collectibles. Horns of different animals sat alongside crocodile heads and bits of leather; even human teeth were up for sale. What made the stand just that little bit more unique was that sitting alongside the anatomical oddities sat a sports almanac of the Cincinnati Reds' World Series winning season of 1976.

By six o'clock all the sales were packing it in and we had checked into a Best Western in Frankfort, the state capital of Kentucky. With a population of less than 30,000, Frankfort is by no means a metropolis, but the small city is a charming blend of old and new. Modern financial institutions and Georgian antebellum buildings, evident of a bygone era of historical significance, stand as if united overlooking the Kentucky River, which roams calmly beneath bridges of varying age. Today, Frankfort only just sneaks into the top-ten list of Kentucky's largest cities, which was evident as Bec and I entered an Italian restaurant in an eerily desolate and somnolent town center.

Over a dish of spaghetti and meatballs, we realized that we would have to pick up the pace if we were going to make it to Alabama with enough time to sell our haul. My idea to stop at each and every big sale because there "couldn't be that many" was proved inarguably and thoroughly misguided, and as a result in just one afternoon we had stopped at 231 of the bastards and managed to cover only 77 miles of the 450 required.

With three more states after Kentucky to pass through, we were determined that Friday would be used to make up lost ground—the next motel we checked into would be in Tennessee, we decided. By ten, we had already passed by several minor yard sales to stay true to our commitment, and we had covered 10 miles before we were finally enticed by a sale at a church. There wasn't a great deal to buy, but for obvious reasons the sale would be held there only until Saturday. This instantly started alarm bells ringing; the farther south we traveled, the less likely it was that sales would be held on Sundays, and I began to wonder if Gadsden, deep in the Bible belt, would have anywhere for us to set up on the Sabbath. And worse, there wasn't a single orange golf ball at this sale.

The second yard sale of the day was the biggest we'd seen so far, and with more than three hundred vendors featuring in both an air-conditioned warehouse and a large outdoor area, it would be the largest we'd pass during the weekend's festivities. The bulk of the indoor merchants specialized in guns and firearms, and likely explained why so many people were strolling casually down the aisles clutching rifles and handguns, creating the atmosphere of a car trunk sale during a military occupation. Among the plethora of sports-orientated stalls, I was frustrated when after searching for over fifteen minutes, I came away from all of them orange ball–less. The

closest I came to my dream was when I came across an un-
opened pack of Wheaties, clearly years old with a picture of
Tiger Woods on the box advertising a special giveaway in
conjunction with the 2002 PGA Championship, which included two free golf balls. But the risk of spending $10 on a
breakfast cereal four years past its sell-by date, in the hope
that one of the two random colored balls would be orange
didn't seem smart to me. I was, however, coerced into listening to a spiel from a nearby vendor who tried to make me buy
a pair of $30 sandals (the kind old men wear over socks)
which, according to the seller, made the wearer feel as if "he
was walking on marshmallows."

At this point, we were only six miles away from the motel
in which we had woken up two hours before. We decided that
if we weren't going to make the same mistake as the previous
day, we wouldn't stop for another sale until the town of
Danville, 40 miles farther south. Just 2 miles later, I pulled
off the road and parked up on the side of the road alongside
another yard sale. Well, I had to. There was a sign claiming
it sold "Golf clubs, balls and shoes."

No luck.

Not stopping at any (other) yard sales helped us claw back
a lot of time, and as we passed no fewer than ninety yard sales
en route to Danville, we were certainly saving a great deal of
time, which would have been otherwise wasted looking for
golf balls and other random tat. The lengthy car journey also
gave us time to devise another game we would play in addition to our amateur adaptation of *Bargain Hunt*. While we
scoured and searched through endless items for our personal
plunder, we would now be on the lookout for a certain item
selected by our opponent. To keep things simple, things that
weren't likely to exist were barred from selection, such as an
Edwardian pneumatic drill or a 1984 A-Team annual signed

by Joan of Arc. For Bec, I had chosen any dish, plate, or type of crockery that depicted either George Washington or Abraham Lincoln. Bec, on the other hand, had managed to come up with a challenge extremely cunning.

"So, what do I have to find?" I asked.

Bec smirked and her face lit up. "An orange golf ball."

Clever bitch.

Our first chance to find our articles presented itself at the first yard sale in Danville, a city famous only for an international news story in which a female fraudster with a sense of humor had purchased an ice cream sundae in a local fast-food restaurant and attempted to pay with a $200 bill depicting George W. Bush and the White House with lawn signs saying such things as WE LIKE BROCOLLI and NO MORE SCANDELS. The Dairy Queen cashier accepted the note and gave the woman $198 in change.*

With nothing of great interest at Danville's largest yard sale (except for a brilliant NASCAR play rug and toy cars that I bought for $15), we continued south toward the Tennessee border 90 miles away. Because every motel we passed had a NO VACANCY sign, we were desperate to get to Tennessee with plenty of time to secure ourselves a bed for the night. We put orange golf balls and presidential crockery on the temporary backburner, so we could increase our current average speed—which at 15 mph was an improvement on the previous day but would still leave us miles short of the border—and reach a new state in which to stay the night.

We passed 309 separate yard sales in just over 100 miles

---

*Apparently, the same happened in Roanoke Rapids, North Carolina, in 2003 when a man used one of the bills to pay for $150 of groceries, and then Deborah Trautwine, a fifty-one-year-old Pennsylvanian, was arrested after using a similar note in a clothes shop. (Just thought you might be interested.)

of travel, many of which were tiny things with just a table on the porch of a house. We stopped at only a handful of sales and left empty-handed, entering Tennessee and arriving in the small city of Jamestown, 50 miles south of a town of the same name in Kentucky.

With fewer than 2,000 residents, Jamestown wasn't one of the largest cities we had encountered while following 127 toward Alabama, but it was definitely the most significant. Because it lay approximately 234 miles from Covington, and was therefore more or less the halfway point of the event, the Fentress County Chamber of Commerce in Jamestown was considered to be the headquarters of the yard sale. We couldn't simply pass through without showing our faces, and as the chamber clerks would know of every accommodation within the entire county, we decided to kill two birds with one stone.

As we hopped up the rotten wooden steps toward the sandstone building in which the chamber is housed, deciding against using the even more precarious-looking ramp for wheelchair access, we entered by a sign welcoming us to Ye Ole Jail.

Bec and I stepped in and perused a brochure stand until a voice from a side room gained our attention: "Can I help you?"

The voice was that of Gale Reed, a woman in her fifties who was sitting behind a computer. She was the office administrator of the chamber and she sat opposite Walter Page, the director of tourism and membership.

"Yes," I replied. "We've been on the yard-sale route and were wondering if there's anywhere to stay. I'm sure we could find something by the interstate but that's about sixty miles away."

"I'll contact Julia," she replied, picking up her telephone.

Looking around the room, it didn't look much like the headquarters of Jamestown, let alone a 450-mile festival—it was small and quite cramped. However, one of the clerks of the chamber, a young man, sat at the side of the room with no desk, dressed in an expensive suit and looking like a mannequin in Bergdorf's. His name, Ruble Upchurch III, certainly did his punctilious appearance justice.

"Oh you do!" said Gale excitedly as she lowered the receiver from her ear, covering the mouthpiece. "Clare has a room at the Wildwood Bed and Breakfast. And she's English," she whispered.

That sealed the deal; not only would we not have to travel 60 miles to the interstate and back, but with it being a B&B run by an English lady, continental breakfasts of cereal and a waffle iron were included and a good old-fashioned fry-up was on the cards.

"Excellent," I replied. "We'll check in now and have a drink. Especially after the last few days we've had."

"That might be a problem," said Ruble. "It's a dry county."

"For Christ's sake," I snapped. "Not again." Ruble moved quickly toward a cupboard as if I had scared him. But then he returned with a bottle of table wine in his hand.

"Here, take this," he said. "They make it at a winery just out of town."

We thanked the chamber clerks for the wine and for managing to do the almost impossible of finding accommodation so close to 127 at a bed and breakfast that, according to the woman, people normally had to book over a month in advance during the busy season. Before we left, they invited us to take a walk upstairs and see why the building is billed as Ye Ole Jail.

On the top floor of the chamber—in a hot and stuffy room, which felt and looked like a badly converted attic—stood a solid steel cage, separated in the middle to form two formidable and incommodious cells into which a small mattress and toilet had been squeezed. Remaining intact and untouched from the final day of their use, the damp and repugnant cells conjure torturous visions more in common with a dungeon of the Tower of London, and it's hard to believe that the jail saw its last inmate as recently as 1979.

We checked into our room at the Wildwood Lodge at five in the evening, just before one of the two rather eccentric sisters who run the charming establishment took her dog for a walk, leading him across the side of the road instead of through the accommodation's seventeen acres of woodland, due to a bear warning. With wild animals roaming casually outside our very door, we sat on the lodge's upper deck and enjoyed the bottle of wine and the magnificent views as the sun descended behind the Cumberland plateau.

I would imagine that a cup of tea and a fry-up is the best way to start a day of golf ball searching, and although Julia apologized for having to cook bacon the American way (so it's like plastic), no breakfasts come better than the ones that are dished up at the Wildwood Lodge. We departed Jamestown at just after nine in the morning for the Saturday leg of the yard sale, gearing up for what we assumed would be the most popular day of the sale so far.

For being the headquarters and focal point of the yard sale, Jamestown was a bit of a letdown on the sale front, and we made good progress through it and also the small towns of Grimsley and Clarkrange before arriving in Crossville, 35 miles to the south of Jamestown. We had passed up 195 yard sales. In Crossville there was a sale of substantial size, one where we could rummage for purchases. As soon as we arrived, I dragged Bec toward a long wooden table covered in Nixon badges from his presidential campaign under which a tub of golf balls was sitting. There, among hundreds of white counterparts, glistening like a star on the top of Christmas tree, was one orange golf ball. I could hardly contain my excitement and quickly rescued him from his inferior bedfellows.

"How much for this?" I asked apathetically, trying to contain my joy.

"For what?"

"That!" I bellowed, indicating the luminous beacon of hope and all that is good in the world in my hand.

"One ball? Is that it?" he replied, not realizing what I was willing to pay for it—I had searched endlessly for it as if one orange golf ball were my Atlantis. "Just take it," he snapped.

Bonus.

As we strolled past other stands, including a Nazi-related stand that included a Swastika flag which could be ours for as little as $10, Bec was left having to think of another item for me to find. "Does that mean I'm a point down then?" she asked.

"I'm afraid so," I replied.

"I'm never gonna find some Washington or Lincoln crockery," she moaned.

"Actually, with the way some feel toward his presidency and the Civil War down here, there are probably some commemorative plates celebrating the day Lincoln was shot."

Crossville was the first city in which following a seemingly endless procession of yard sales began to feel a little uncomfortable. The sale of guns and other dangerous weapons had been prevalent since the outset, but in the middle of

Tennessee quirky John Deere coasters and baseball cards were displaced by articles such as regimental SS clothing and a COLORED WAITING ROOM sign, a vulgar memento from a shameful era in America's past.

Still, it was handy for presidential plates, and Bec managed to locate a French dish depicting the first U.S. president signing some sort of treaty or bill. With the scores now tied at one all, it was time to choose a second item for us each to find. I had to somehow locate something showing the English flag while Bec had the more straightforward task of hunting for a Superman mirror (the type where the character takes up more room on the mirror's surface than your reflection does, rendering it almost useless as a mirror).

Our friend Kerry Regan had instructed us to buy and bring her back the single most "gash" present we could find.* In Pikeville we found such an item. Just as I was thinking about purchasing her a trophy that she could use to pretend it was her who had been named St. Claire County Council Student of the Year, Bec was already parting with a dollar for a belt buckle featuring the insignia of the Whirlpool Corporation (the world's leading manufacturer of washing machines and other major home appliances).

As expected, Saturday was the busiest day we had experienced on the yard sale trail to date. We may have covered only just over a hundred miles, but we had passed an unprecedented 452 sales. We had the same amount of distance to cover on the final day of the event, but we were confident that with an early start and most sales being either canceled or put off until the afternoon due to religious commitments, we had more than enough time to reach Gadsden, set up our own stall, and make a profit. At six, we pulled into a Quality

---

*Gash means something inane, stupid, or rubbish.

Inn on the outskirts of the southern Tennessean border town of Chattanooga, a city made famous in a song by Glenn Miller (ask your grandma).

*L*ookout Mountain overlooks Chattanooga to the north and the Georgian border, just 2 miles to the south. Its main attraction, the Ruby Falls, is a 145-foot underground waterfall, which was formed more than 200 million years ago and is an ideal place to spend a morning off from laborious yard sales. Named after the wife of Leo Lambert, who discovered the natural phenomenon in 1928, the falls are now a staple of tourism in Chattanooga and nearby Rock City.

I don't normally visit tourist attractions or join tour groups while I'm abroad, because on the times I have done so, I more often than not have ended up less informed than I would have liked since I am quite easily annoyed by other group members. In 2005, Bateman and I toured Hearst Castle, the palatial mansion once owned by newspaper tycoon William Randolph Hearst, as a healthy escape from our frivolous law breaking (long story, about three hundred pages . . .). The 90,000-square-foot estate was magnificent and immaculate throughout. Roman baths with tiles inspired by Italian mausoleums and swimming pools surrounded by statues of Greek gods exuded a profound air of significant opulence and astronomic extravagance. The tour was ruined, however, by a group who found it necessary to yell such exclamations as "Wow!" and "Gee whiz!" after each and every fact about the house. Two years before that, I had taken a flight to the Grand Canyon and had the unfortunate fate of viewing the prodigious gorge while next to two guys from Alabama who, after boarding the plane and speaking at length about who they were and where they were from, continued to irritate the Native American pilot by asking him questions like whether he lived in a tepee and if the tour company offered night flights over the canyon. Night flights!

Entrance to the Ruby Falls looked busy. Very busy. Bec and I found a parking space in the second overflow lot and joined the back of a very long line of camera-wielding tourists. After twenty minutes and two short shuffles forward, word had reached our part of the queue that it could be anything up to two hours before we could see the falls and that it costs $15 to see them . . . each.

"Stuff this!" I said, rather too loudly. "I'm off."

"You can buy five Tic-Tac-Putts for that kind of money," Bec added.

We jumped into our car and continued up Lookout Mountain and across the border into Georgia, a state which hosted just a 40-mile segment of the route before the yard sales continued into Alabama. Here, the yard sales began to appear in places where there seemed to be no population at all and at road sides where it didn't look as if a house or building was anywhere in sight. Every few miles there would be a pickup truck beside a large table covered in all manner of "goods" on the side of roads that I hadn't seen quite as badly marked since the crockery episode in Oregon.

Finally, after losing our way on a couple of occasions, due to Highway 127 breaking up into a series of minor roads for the final segment of the yard sale, we made our way across the border and into Alabama, where the time had reached noon and we hoped the masses of departing congregations would now be swapping prayers and hymns for purchasing whims. Unfortunately, crossing the border meant we had entered a new time zone and the time was reset at 11 a.m., so many church services were just beginning. As our windows passed by more and more tiny, inadequate stalls, my attention was drawn away from what was outside, and focused more on what was happening on the radio. In all my time in America, the only interruptions you'd experience on music stations would be the hilarious local adverts with a tacky jingle and small print uttered at incomprehensible speed. As we crossed into Alabama, certain words during the broadcast of songs were being edited out. I wasn't even listening to a rap station—in which the only lyrics that could be broadcast at such an early hour would be *hoe* as long as it was the agricultural term. I was tuned into a popular and contemporary hits station. A simple line such as "Closing the goddamn door" taken from a song by Panic at the Disco left a sudden silence in the car between "the" and "damn"; and even the Sean Kingston song "Beautiful' Girls" had been totally rewritten so the word *suicidal* was suddenly replaced with *in denial* and *crime* was fazed out. It was all very surreal (didn't improve the song much, though).

At a cross section of two roads, just outside the last town of any significant size before Gadsden, we decided we would scour the stalls in a last-ditch attempt to buy some goods to sell farther down the road. It wasn't a large-scale sale, nor was it one with much variation in choice. It did, however, have a $10 Davy Crockett–style hat for me, and a $15 John Deere tractor assembly kit, which I'm sure Bec bought just because it was my money she was spending.

When we finally entered Gadsden, our sense of relief was palpable. Not only had we finally completed the yard sale route with enough time to spare, but we were again in a city of substance and civility, where people conversed on street corners and in shop doorways instead of while leaning on the side of a gate. Negotiating the final turn of the yard sale route, my eyes were drawn to Noccalula Falls, Gadsden's 250-acre public park. Instead of focusing on the botanical gardens or the 90-foot waterfall, my concentration was on its car park and the sign in it that informed me that Gadsden's yard sale, the FIRST AND LAST, was just 200 yards away and featured more than 150 vendors. Checking that I still had my NASCAR rug and Tic-Tac-Putt safely in the backseat, I pulled into the car park and we started discussing how to sell our goods. It wouldn't be easy. Although no one could resist the temptation of hitting golf balls into a molded-plastic base, we had no stall and had no idea of how we could obtain one, and it was already two in the afternoon. Our best hope was to ask a salesman nicely if we could use part of his/her table—he or she could keep whatever profit we'd make and everybody would be happy. Clutching the game and rug and wearing a coonskin cap with the tail hanging down my neck, I slammed my door shut and we prepared for action.

We needn't have bothered. An hour before our arrival, a storm had passed over Gadsden and all but five of the vendors had packed up and left, taking with them every potential customer and leaving nothing but a desolate and rain-sodden car park in their wake.

9. A BRITT ABROAD

Made by the Marshmallow Kid, the ceremonial fire is lit by Redbird Express while King Iowegian Rick and Queen Ms. Charlotte look on. . . . Perhaps I should explain.

When Bec and I arrived in Kansas City, Missouri, the last thing I wanted to do was drive. Because of the four days of constant yard sales, and the fact that I had to leave my beloved Tic-Tac-Putt in Alabama because I couldn't carry it on the plane, I wasn't in the best of moods. Bec was still finding varnish in my hair and tiny pieces of duct tape in places you wouldn't imagine, and I had somehow managed to flood one of Birmingham airport's departure gates with burning hot coffee when I accidentally pushed the wrong button on the industrial-sized coffee machine (which looked more like the control panel of a submarine). As we boarded our plane ten minutes later, we could see the coffee shop assistant still combating the uncontrollable flow of brown liquid armed with just a mop, sporadically placing WET FLOOR signs on the tiled floor, and shrugging his shoulders in exasperation. Nothing was going to cheer me up in Kansas City.

Not even watching (on television) Barry Bonds hit a record 756th home run of his career, causing a frantic melee within the stands as hundreds of people leapt across one another in a desperate attempt to grab a million-dollar ball, could lighten the mood. Because it was cheaper to fly to Missouri than any other nearby airport, I was left with no choice but to drive the 300 miles north to Mason City, Iowa, in another horrid Chrysler PT Cruiser, the only car the rental company had remaining, and that meant an American-made car—something that could handle straight roads pretty well but steered appallingly when introduced to any sort of curve or turn. Larger cars are even worse to control, and the entire operation of turning the wheel and waiting for the vehicle to shift in the desired direction like an eighteenth-century sloop is long and drawn out. Still, roads in states such as Iowa and Missouri are flat and straight, and so there wouldn't be a great need for starboard or port.

WELCOME TO IOWA—FIELDS OF OPPORTUNITY reads the sign on the border, although after traveling for an hour deeper into the state and witnessing not a single undulation or diminutive change in the contours of our featureless surroundings, just the word *Fields* would be a more accurate and appropriate slogan.

After a drive lasting over four hours, it was with great relief that we arrived at our motel in Mason City, Iowa—a city near our next festival, and two hours south of the Minneapolis airport (where, extra expense be damned, we should have flown to in the first place). Stepping out of the motel's pool following a refreshing postdrive swim, we made our way to the nearby farming town of Britt.

Like all of its surrounding settlements, Britt isn't anything special. Its tiny population of 2,000 residents is in slow decline, the town stands on the junction of two highways perpendicular to each other (conforming to the patchwork quilt-like design of Iowa) and, according to city-data.com, Britt is home to two registered sex offenders (just thought I'd mention it). With almost a third of the town's economy generated by the revenue created by the transportation industry and farming (like much of the rest of the state), it came as no surprise that the local landmark is two huge farming silos, situated by the side of the main train line on which the town was founded. And it's because of the antiquated train tracks that I was in Britt in the first place.

There may not be a station as such, but Britt stands on

one of the few train lines still in use in America today and the town witnesses freight trains pass daily on their way to Chicago, Nebraska, and many other destinations to which the famous Union Pacific and Santa Fe lines would run. After the introduction of the railroad, towns situated near the tracks attracted vagrant workers to their streets who used the freight carriages as free transportation. These people became known as hoboes, and the town of Britt celebrates their rich heritage annually at the National Hobo Convention.

In 1899, three of Britt's energetic men, Thos. A. Way, T. A. Potter, and W. E. Bradford, proposed to do something different to show the world that their sleepy farming town was capable of doing anything the larger cities could. The National Hobo Convention had been held in Chicago's Market Street annually for some time, but the three men succeeded in bringing it to Britt the following year, at the turn of the century. By all accounts, the festivities received mixed reviews; Britt had wanted attention, and with hundreds of young residents dressed in torn clothes and fake blackened eyes, ragtime music, horse races, and journalists descending upon the town from as far away as St. Louis and Philadelphia, that's exactly what it got. Tensions existed, however, as the "real" hoboes who attended the turn-of-the-century event were reportedly disillusioned with the festivities and saw the choice of attire by the spectators as blatant exploitation of their brethren.

Although Britt had gained a notable reputation as being a hobo town, the convention wasn't held for more than thirty years, and it was only due to the demise of its county fair that Britt decided to observe Hobo Days again. In 1933, at the peak of the Great Depression, the first annual convention began, and when the annual festival day was moved to

Saturday in 1971, a total of 25,000 people took to the streets of Britt in celebration.

According to research that I had conducted into the Hobo Convention, Britt had claimed that 2007 would see the 107th annual event. And that's where I have a bit of a problem. I don't wish to seem picky or fastidious, but *107* isn't even accurate to within a reasonable margin of error. For starters (as you will be well aware if you have been paying attention), the convention didn't really begin to be celebrated annually in Britt until 1933 and the town saw just one hobo celebration before that. Since then, it has been held every year with the exception of 1941–1945, when America was at war. By my calculations, that made 2007 the 71st annual Hobo Days. Not bad, but not *107*.

As I explained my findings to Bec and she showed no interest whatsoever, we pulled into one of the dozens of available parking spaces on the side of what looked like abandoned streets to visit the chamber of commerce for more information about the convention. I was sure the people at the chamber would be very excited by my findings.

The chamber was unlike any I'd ever been in before. For starters, no chamber people were even there and, what's more, it was situated in the far corner of a shoe shop. A large, mild-mannered gentleman, who with a beard would make an exceptional Santa look-alike, stood behind the counter and must have noticed our loitering.

"Can I help you?" he asked.

"We were just after some information about the Hobo Convention," Bec replied.

"I can tell you all you need to know."

Bill Eckels was the owner of The Cobbler Shoppe, a small main-street business specializing in footwear and clothing. I had never met a cobbler in my life before venturing to the States, and Bill was now the second in under a month. He noticed we were from the U.K. almost immediately and began to tell us of his family's Scottish roots, before informing us that his grandfather staked everything he owned in a bet that he could outrun a horse and cart in a 200-yard race. His grandfather won and the Eckels family have remained in the area ever since. After ten minutes or so, we realized that although Bill had spoken at great length about the history of his family and of the town, not a single word of it related to the Hobo Convention.

"The Hobo Convention?" he asked, after I had mentioned it to him again. "I'm not quite sure. I've never been." We thanked him and left.

Hobo Days wouldn't officially begin until the lighting of the Jungle Fire at 7 p.m. With several hours to spare, Bec and I visited the Hobo Museum just a block away from the Cobbler Shoppe to garner some information about life as a hobo, as I was pretty sure that not all freight-train riders looked like my idea of them: adorable German shepherds that could cleverly foil an assassination plot before boarding a conveniently placed boxcar without a word of thanks from their temporary master (all to the tune of "Maybe Tomorrow" by Terry Bush).*

The Hobo Museum is located in the Britt's disused movie theater, and although it is no bigger than a village hall, it contains the most extensive range of hobo artifacts in the world. In the foyer, above a Christmas tree and a list of people who were hoboes—including folk singer Burl Ives, Winthrop Rockefeller, and Clark Gable—an important mes-

---

*I apologize to people who have never seen a single episode of *The Littlest Hobo* and didn't get the reference.

sage adorns the entrance to the main display room and serves as a constant admonition to all who fail to distinguish between the homeless. "A hobo is someone who travels for work, a tramp travels but will not work, a bum neither travels or works"—a poignant, if grammatically incorrect, definition.

Because of the building's previous use, the entire display area stood on a gentle slope so that each table was propped up by several books and one wall was a good 6 feet taller than its opposite partition. The theater hasn't shown a film since 1975, except for the hour-long documentary that plays on a loop on a small television screen at the back. As the titles rolled, Bec and I settled down and watched with interest.

There isn't a definite explanation as to why the workers became known as hobes, but the most common explanation is that they began work as farmhands and the term derived from the words *hoe boys*. At the height of the Great Depression, and with no work or prospects at home, many decided to leave in the hope that there would be work for them elsewhere— embarking on a freight train was an illegal but free and direct route to elsewhere.

Life as a hobo was a bitter struggle. The danger of boarding and alighting from moving carriages was a continual threat to their lives and when done safely, the men and women would still need to evade capture by the railroad companies' security staff whose members were notoriously heavy-handed. For safety, the hoboes banded together, forming a sense of brotherhood among travelers, and camps began to spring up by the sides of the railroad. These were called jungles and were a safe haven where a weary hobo could stop for something to eat or to wash his/her clothes before catching a train to a new destination.

The documentary *Riding the Rails* was as touching as it

was informative and not only focused on the facts surrounding hoboes, but became concentrated on the stories of half a dozen Americans who had lived such a life. When asked to think back on their experiences and if they would ride a boxcar today, Clarence Lee gazed forlornly as if in a trance, and then tears started falling from his eyes. "No, I don't want to ride one today. That was days though, good gracious."

Life as a hobo was tough but their true identity stemmed from an unlikely combination of a maltreated existence and an unquestionable sense of camaraderie, and where torn clothes and a life of immeasurable hardship was their fare to feel the cool and liberating wind in their faces.

Just before seven, we made our way to Britt's own Hobo Jungle, an area to the side of the tracks that was complete with boxcar, picnic tables, and kitchen area. It was used by the hoboes and open to the public for the duration of the weekend to give festival-goers a chance to meet and talk with them about riding the rails and to listen to some of the best storytellers in the country. Upon our arrival, it was obvious that the 2007 Hobo Convention was to be an event of great significance, reflection, and mourning.

Maurice W. Graham rode the freight trains at the tender age of fourteen during the Great Depression and first came to Britt in 1971. Due to his fondness for the older engines, Graham became known as Steam Train Maury and quickly became a favorite among the hobo community. Maury had been crowned Hobo King five times and was honored with the title of Grand Patriarch of the Hoboes at the 2004 convention. Just three months after Britt's 2006 Hobo Days, Maury "caught the westbound" after suffering a stroke at his home in Ohio, leaving behind two daughters and his wife of sixty-nine years. To Britt and the hobo community, Maury's death was a considerable loss and was why the 2007 event was dedicated to the memory of the hobo to whom the rest looked for guidance and wisdom. The town certainly won't forget him—the road on which Bec and I parked adjacent to the jungle has been renamed Steam Train Way.

At seven, a small crowd was sitting on two three-row bleachers that overlooked a specially constructed pyre, which looked more like a half-completed game of Jenga. Karl Teller, known as Redbird Express and dressed in a cap and a garage-attendant shirt, looking more like a truck driver than a traditional hobo, began proceedings by welcoming everybody to the 2007 Hobo Convention. Following salutes of the four winds (a sign of appreciation for what the separate breezes bring with them, involving a gesture resembling something between a one-armed zombie impression and a Nazi salute), the ceremonial fire was ablaze and ashes from other hobo conventions held in the past year were asked to be added to the flames. A dozen or so people approached the fire, tipping the contents of their specially made urns (ranging from jewelry boxes and miniature vases to a metal flask and a Sour Cream and Onion Pringles tube) into the fire as a symbolic gesture of fellowship.

As a tribute to his memory, Steam Train's widow, Wanda, paid homage to his brethren and handed out several awards, announcing that Slo Freight Ben, a three-time former queen and just four years shy of her hundredth birthday, was to be honored as Hobo Queen for Life. As she was pushed in her wheelchair by her daughter Carol, Slo Freight (real name Benita Sankey) embraced her friend, and jokes were made of the time when with no ride and an eagerness to attend the convention, Slo Freight, an octogenarian at the time, began to cycle to Britt from her home 126 miles away.

Soon it was time for the hoboes to entertain the crowd and at first it seemed as if participants were allowed to enter only if they had some sort of gimmick or novelty or were just young and therefore "adorable." First up was a girl by the name of Angie Dirtyfeet, who was spurred on encouragingly by her mother, Minneapolis Jewel, a candidate for the 2007 Hobo Queen and who it seemed was attempting to gain some early plaudits and kudos by parading her daughter as a future Barbra Streisand by demanding such tunes as "Twinkle Twinkle Little Star" and "Jesus Loves Me." Liberty Justice finished the evening's proceedings and serenaded the audience with some traditional hobo folk tunes. With a guitar on his lap, a hobo with a strikingly close resemblance to ZZ Top's Billy Gibbons plucked a string bass to form a two-piece orchestra, his niche being the constant gusts of air from an oxygen tank sitting at his feet and making a strange musical accompaniment.

On Friday afternoon, Britt's town center was bursting with life, a completely different scene from the one the previous day. Adults were inspecting a multitude of sidewalk stands selling anything from hobo gifts to candy floss, while children took to the streets and enjoyed the dozen or so attractions. An inflatable bungee-run stood just yards from the Cobbler Shoppe's front door and so we made our way inside to talk with a representative of the chamber. As usual, no chamber member was there and so we talked to Bill once again about the weekend's crowning ceremony.

"The crowning ceremony?" he said. "I don't know. I've never been."

The list of past convention kings and queens acts as a useful who's who of Britt's dynasty. With past royalty including names such as The Pennsylvania Kid, Ramblin'

Rudy, and Luther the Jet Gett, the roll of honor reads more like a card from an evening of amateur wrestling. In Britt's municipal center, just across the street from an attraction in which students were attempting to soak classmates by hitting a target and triggering a mechanism that would drop them into the water, local artist Leanne Castillo had her art on display.

Sixty-five people have been hobo royalty since Charles Noe was crowned in 1900, and the art on display featured every single one on fifty-seven paintings. Placed in chronological order from the first or only time they were bestowed with the title, it was a fascinating insight into the look and appearance of a hobo. As I expected, images of the late Steamtrain Maury dominated the gallery—miniature pictures of the patriarch were available for $3. Although there is no set dress code for a hobo, with a long, white, and wise-looking beard and tired face, Maury seemed to typify the look. Facial hair is almost a permanent fixture on a hobo, and some sort of headwear appears to be obligatory attire as it's said to mean something about the wearer. Denim or dungarees appear in nearly every picture and some would proudly flaunt a staff—not only to be used as a walking aid but also as a personal symbol of an experienced traveler.

With a few hours to spare before a hobo poetry reading, we visited one of the local bars on the main street. Despite the quirky name, J & D's Hob Nob is just like any small-town bar in America (with the exception of their Christmas decorations being up in August). It was dark, there were neon signs advertising different brands of "Lite" beer, and country music was blasting out of the speakers. What was first noticeable about the bar was that there were just as many hoboes in the bar during that afternoon as there were in the jungle during the lighting of the ceremonial fire the previous day. Some were talking of old times and laughing with fellow travelers they hadn't seen since the 2006 convention, while others sat quietly reading a paper or just simply sleeping, their heads dropping to their chests before they repositioned themselves and nodded off again.

At four, we made our way toward Steam Train Way and the Hobo Jungle for an afternoon of poetry reading. Joining the small crowd that had assembled to listen to the poignant words, it became obvious to us that the most important item required for a poetry reading was a milk crate. Upturned, the plastic box helped whoever recited the text into adopting the official poetry reading pose, a position in which every reader soon became comfortable. Slamming his right leg onto the base of the crate, resting the book on his thigh, and leaning toward the crowd, Redbird Express began the event by reading some poems from a book of hobo poetry. Many other feet took to the crate, including those of the chairperson of the Hobo Foundation who organizes the event and a man who attempted to recite an entire lengthy poem from memory, resulting in the piece taking much longer than it should have due to constant, "No, hang on"s and backtracking.

After the hour of poetry, Bec and I had the chance to meet some hobo royalty. Dressed in a pair of brown shorts, a blue Hawaiian shirt, and a baseball cap worn backward, the medallion-wielding 2006 Hobo King approached us and shook our hands.

"Hi, I'm the king," he said.

His name was Iowegian Rick and if anyone had traveled to the convention by way of freight train that year, it was him. With a graying goatee, long, greasy hair, and not a great deal of teeth, it wasn't hard to believe him when he said that he had spent the last year traveling the country—in most part by freight train.

"We've traveled all the way from England," said Bec.

"And you, my dear, are an English rose," he replied, kissing Bec on the hand.

No wonder he won the title last year; maybe he should change his name to Slick Rick.

"You gonna run for king again?" I asked.

"Oh, no," he laughed. "Being king is too much responsibility, and I'm not into that."

After asking Bec if she would dance with him at the post-coronation ceremony the next night, he returned to the Hobo Jungle slowly, limping.

Saturday was the final and most important day of the weekend's festivities. Not only would there be a parade through the streets of Britt in the morning, but a new king and queen would be crowned in a ceremony in the afternoon. The cavalcade of floats began in the west of the city at the local high school and made its way past us. Like the parade I'd seen before in Elko, where local businesses and organizations would throw candy to the audience, Britt's was nothing special and the only notable difference was that although just as many horses were used in the hour-long procession, somehow the roads didn't end up resembling an urban cesspool.

For lunch we made our way to Mary Jo's Hobo House, a café opposite the museum which prides itself, as the name suggests, as a great supporter of the hobo culture. Once inside, the strain placed on the café that day had resulted in the menu containing just two items: sloppy joe and a salad. Minneapolis

Jewel and her husband, Tuck, sat on a table close to us and were parading through the bar with placards and sandwich boards in a last-ditch attempt to gain a few additional votes for their claim to become the 2007 Hobo King and Queen. For me, their rudimentary campaign was wasted—it had the opposite effect on me. As far as I was concerned, his sign, VOTE TUCK FOR KING OF HOBO'S, which included an incorrect use of an apostrophe, was more than enough reason not to offer him any support when it came to the all-important voting.

By noon, many of the audience members for the ceremony had gathered in the city park for the handing out of free mulligan stew, a dish which was prepared by hoboes in camps and jungles since as early as the turn of the twentieth century. According to the local newspaper, the *Britt News Tribune*, this year's free mulligan stew's ingredients included 450 pounds of beef, 900 pounds of potatoes, 250 pounds of carrots, 300 pounds of cabbage, 35 pounds of peppers, 100 pounds of turnips, 150 pounds of tomatoes, and 24 gallons of mixed vegetables, and would serve approximately five thousand people. It came in a little handy tub and was pleasant to the mouth, similar in taste to a beef casserole.

As the microphone bellowed into action, Bec and I (armed with cushions we had bought from a nearby Dollar General) climbed onto the backseat of a stand with a direct view of the bandstand where the crowning would take place. We were sitting next to Come On Pat, the 1996 Hobo Queen and a lady whom Dexy's Midnight Runners had come remarkably close to naming a song after. Her king that year was Liberty Justice, and hush descended on the city park when he placed his oxygen tank by his feet and began to sing the national anthem. Although it was the umpteenth occasion during the summer that I had to endure the song, it was the first time that I enjoyed every second. With the constant jets of air entering his nostrils and acting as an interesting musical instrumental, resounding through all four of the city park's speakers, it sounded as if "The Star Spangled Banner" was being performed by a duet of Johnny Cash and Darth Vader.

Dozens of hoboes sat patiently in the bandstand while arrangements were made for the opening speeches, and it felt as if Bec and I were commentators with the former queen as our expert guest. I asked Come On Pat who her money was on.

"Oh, Minneapolis Jewel will be queen," she answered confidently.

An update on the fund-raising for the new Hobo Museum was being announced by the founder of the Hobo Foundation, and I opened a notebook and attempted, to the best of my abilities, to make a note of what happened next.

The 1997 king, Frog, whose name stands for Friends Rely on God (and was not named that only because he had one leg and presumably had to hop everywhere), approached the microphone and recited a poem about how industrial America was both founded on and built by the hoboes of the country. Then Adman, the 2004 king, recognized Slo Freight Ben and her presence at yet another Hobo Convention. Minneapolis Jewel, who you could tell wasn't the quiet type, took to the stage and awarded the 1994 king, Iowa Blackie, with a whoopee cushion, before Roadhog U.S.A., dressed in American flag suspenders, praised Britt as being "the friendliest place on Earth." Another past king, "Luther the Jet Gett" made some speech which involved Disney's *High School Musical* and a 1937 Johnny Lomax song that had something to do with a canal. Finally the present queen, Ms. Charlotte, spoke at length about her time as hobo royalty and said that now that she had worn the crown after years of failed bids, there was good reason to step down.

It was only then that I realized that the speeches, poem reciting, and general time-wasting antics had nothing to do with the naming of a king and queen. Then Britt mayor James Nelson announced the rules and regulations on how a hobo can claim candidature for the prize.

To become king, a man has or had to be a legitimate rail rider, either currently or in the past. This is decided by a committee who screen each entrant and ask him a series of questions. To win the crown of Hobo Queen, a woman doesn't necessarily have had to have ridden a freight train but must be familiar to the hobo community and recognized as a worthy contender by the screening panel. Goodness knows who this screening panel was, but it appeared as if seven contenders had qualified for the final stage (or simply were the only people who had thrown their names into the ring). Much like the Film Festival in Corvallis, where judging was based on the very fair and simplistic voting system of the power of the clap, each potential royal had two minutes to wow the crowd before the applause separated the very regal from mere peasants.

A hobo who went by the name of Green Card George was first up. His chief selling point was that he had been sober and clean for over two years. He finished his couple of minutes with a song and yelled "God bless Britt."

Inkman, otherwise known as Tommy from the Railroad (Tommy Maras to his postman), decided on using his two minutes by reciting a poem he had written. I'm not sure what it was called but it began as a poignant reminder of how Uncle Sam had treated hoboes, and appeared to be a definite crowd-pleaser. "A hobo is someone who builds palaces and lives in shacks," he said. "Built America but is denied the vote, builds factories and is then denied work in them." The poem continued into some pretty terrible comparative analogies including something to do with building cars and pushing wheel-barrows.

Next on the stage was Tuck, the husband of Minneapolis Jewel, who was nervous when put in front of a microphone. He simply spoke about the pride he would feel about becoming king and told us that he would celebrate the victory with all of his fellow hoboes (sorry, "hobo's").

The only hobo who stood in their way was Liberty Justice, the only entrant who had won the title before, and who opted for the American way of doing speeches: praising troops and saying things like "God Bless America." He ended with the line "You can all be hoboes; you don't have to ride the tracks."

For me, the winner was Inkman, and the crowd's applause seemed to indicate it would be a close call between him and Liberty Justice. The judges appeared from their vantage points and convened in front of the bandstand. It was obvious they had chosen the winner. But we wouldn't find out who it was until after the queens had had their say.

As far as I was concerned, a hobo called Lady Sonshine had the crown in the bag. According to her speech, 2007 was the fourth straight year she had entered the competition, and if her emotional words of "I am already a queen in the hearts of the hoboes and that's good enough for me" wasn't going to gain her the crown, the rendition of a folk song based on the life and memory of Steam Train Maury that she had performed earlier in the day was going to do the trick. Apart from Crash, a girl who looked about fifteen years old, the only person who stood between Lady Sonshine and her date with destiny was the charismatic and (literally) larger-than-life presence of Minneapolis Jewel. She had already won the title in 1986, 1991, and 1997 and was once again throwing her hat into the ring . . . she actually did throw her hat into the crowd at one point. Thankfully, her speech was as short and unimpressive as her husband's. "I do believe in hoboes. I do, I do, I do," she shouted before placing the microphone back in its stand. The audience applauded the three entrants and the judges made their decision.

I'm not a betting man, but as a similar test in Corvallis proved, the democratic voting process of applause is not an accurate way of measuring someone's moral judgment with which to elevate someone to a position of power. Instead, I studied the statistics. The separate applauses that followed Inkman and Liberty Justice were far more prolonged than the ovation Tuck received. But because a previous winner of Hobo King hadn't won the title again since 1982, my mind was firmly set that Inkman would leave Britt with the crown. As for the queens, Lady Sonshine had it in the bag—I'm sure that even Steam Train was staring down at her from a giant boxcar in the sky. Only an idiot would have voted against her.

"And the 2007 King of the Hoboes is . . ."

What the Tuck!?

Tuck had won the crown. Now anything was possible and it became clear that these "sporadically placed judges" had probably been positioned in Chicago, at our motel, and on Tuck's lap.

Thankfully, the judges were proved to have been paying attention when during the ladies' round Lady Sonshine was named as Tuck's queen, defeating Minneapolis Jewel in two run-offs for the title. Both Tuck and Lady Sonshine were crowned in the Britt sunshine—an upturned tin cut into two crowns adorned their newly regal domes.

That evening, we made our way into the Hobo Jungle for the postcoronation party, the final time that the hoboes would be together in Britt that year. A storm to the north of the town had buried the Jungle beneath a continual swathe of dark and menacing cloud cover, and the lightning illuminated the night sky as often as a different chord was struck during the evening's entertainment, created a scintillating natural ambience. As king, it was Tuck's duty to place the first log on the ceremonial fire. In doing so, he managed to create a plume of smoke that covered half of the public in attendance, causing many positioned near the fire to quickly jump up and brush any burning cinders off their clothes.

The evening played to a similar tune to when the convention first opened. Liberty Justice entertained with a series of hobo folk songs and many other guests appeared to add their own tone to the closing of the convention. By popular demand, Lady Sonshine, accompanied by Serenity, repeated the Steam Train Maury song that had won her the title of queen, and followed it with a stirring and melodically sublime version of "Where Have All the Flowers Gone?"

By Monday morning, Britt had returned to its sleepy and normal existence, and the only remnant of what the town had just experienced was the discarded signage, which had welcomed visitors to the 107th Hobo Convention. Thinking we wouldn't see Bill again, Bec and I had the night before posted a card through the back door of the Cobbler Shoppe to thank him for all his help during our stay. But then, stalling for time before we had to make the four-hour journey to Kansas City, we decided to say our good-byes in person.

"I was wondering who sent the card," he said, pleased to see us. "I was guessing it was from you guys."

Bill allowed me to use his computer so I could print an insurance document to give the rental company due to a crack in the windshield, and then he showed us to his workshop, where he was busy mending a customer's boot. Using glue that had nasal potency equal to chloroform, Bill demonstrated the steps taken in his line of work. I asked questions and was generally interested in the repair of a heel, but with the fumes from the glue racing through my sinuses, I most probably looked like a kid who was feigning enthusiasm.

On the return drive to Kansas City, I had plenty of time to evaluate the weekend's events and the oddities Bec and I had experienced. To be honest, I wasn't sure what to think. Since then, I've read many accounts of other hobo conventions held around the country, and it seems that the opinion of Britt is divided. For years there have been conflicts between the town leaders and the Hobo Foundation, and many hoboes had been driven away by not wanting to get mixed up in politics. Still, the large Hobo Cemetery in the town is proof that it is a common wish of many of the brethren for Britt to be their final stop.

Although the true hobo is now a rarity, that is no reason to forget them and the economic change they made to the country.

Following the recent deaths of Steam Train and Slo Freight Ben (who, sadly, "caught the westbound" a month following the convention), the true hobo, one who rides the rails in search of work, is in faster and faster decline—a fact no one at the convention tries to deny. Instead, it seems as if the emphasis has shifted; it now acts as a window through which audiences can view a past American culture of unique spirit and kinship that is far too absent in the world today. Perhaps my only previous knowledge of such a life, through watching countless episodes of *The Littlest Hobo* as a child, wasn't that far from the truth after all.

Maybe Britt should take a new approach and hold a Cobbler Convention every year. I already know two who would attend—although I'm not sure which of the two would have to be crowned Cobbler Queen. The only thing about which I was sure was that during the entire four days of stories, songs, poems, and general revelry, neither of us saw a single freight train passing by.

10. CAPTIVE

AUDIENCE

The angelic "Rangerettes" perform on the arena floor—before the rapists, murderers, and other criminal scumbags take center stage.

I love the British Broadcasting Corporation. Not only do we receive countless hours of broadcasting (for which certain programs alone are worthy of the fee we pay to get the channels), but the discerning Brit is treated to an overwhelming choice of eight television stations, ten national and many local radio networks, a constantly updated Internet site, and an interactive television service. Best of all, there are no adverts. And that in itself is worth paying 37p a day for. Programs aren't constantly interrupted by someone trying to interest you in a loan, no one is asking if I've had an accident at work, and there are no jingles or cheesy melodies affixing a telephone number into my brain subconsciously. As a public service broadcaster, its role has always been to "educate, inform, and entertain," and as a result, its weekly schedule remains impartial to a particular company or brand, and broadcasts a wide range of programming to cater to the needs of a nation.

American television has always tended to annoy me, and on the final leg of our journey, in Oklahoma City, where we had checked in early at our motel and had nothing to do but watch hours of what it had to offer, it had peaked. The major networks (with the exception of PBS, which broadcasts intellectual programs and British sitcoms from the 1970s) tend to have a similar lineup each and every night: a couple of terrible sitcoms (based in a big house with a moral dilemma to achieve every night) followed by a reality show, the news, and then a chat show. I'm not saying some good hasn't come out of American television in the past, but with daily lineups like this, it's no wonder that the majority of people I have spoken to in America don't even realize that basketball is actually crap.

I don't know why I've ranted on this for so long, apart from the fact that American television tends to show the end of a program, adverts, the start of the next, and then *more* commercials just half a minute later, the only thing that tipped me over the edge in Oklahoma City were the references to Asian automobile companies mentioned during radio and television commercials. *Hyundai* was suddenly pronounced "Hon-day" instead of "Hi-un-day," *Mazda* was "Moz-da," and *Nissan (Ni-san)* was somehow replaced by "Nee-son." Goodness knows what they'd do with Mitsubishi.

I'd now spent exactly two months on American soil and yet our arrival in Oklahoma seemed for the first time that we were in a foreign country—nothing seemed quite right. The restaurant at which we ate an afternoon meal appeared to be a cross between a diner and a motorway service station gift shop. Sitting behind us was a guy who looked as if he had followed us here from the Hobo Convention, and our lazy-eyed waitress was shocked to discover that we weren't Russian. Following the meal, as Bec and I awaited the bill, our waitress returned and began some lighthearted small talk.

"So, how long you guys here for?" she asked.

"Oh, we're only here for tonight and Thursday," I replied. "What's there to do here?"

"Frontier City down the road is pretty cool. It's only open on weekends, though," she said. "I'm free on Thursday."

I wasn't sure if she was making a pass at Bec or me, but we quickly paid the bill, leaving a healthy tip for the waitress whose hopes of spending a day with us had been dashed suddenly.

In the hope of finding somewhere we could feel at ease, Bec and I headed for downtown, and in particular Oklahoma City's entertainment district. Once an area of abandoned warehouses, Bricktown is now the social heart of the city, an area where vibrant bars, sporting facilities, and theaters are set in a restored district where even a canal runs through. The modern-day structures blend beautifully with the style of the city's past.

Just a few blocks north of Bricktown stands the Oklahoma City National Memorial, a vivid reminder that a murderous act of terrorism is unfortunately what the city is most famous for. At the time, the 1995 bombing of the Alfred P. Murrah Federal Building was the deadliest terrorist attack on American soil, injuring more than 800 people and claiming the lives of 168 others; and today, a three-acre memorial commemorating the fateful day is on the site where the federal building once stood. Twin bronze archways stand at either end of a thin layer of water, known as the Reflecting Pool, and are each inscribed with a time: 9:01, representing the final minute of peace, on the east gate, while 9:03 stands opposite, signifying the time at which recovery began. On the banks of the memorial, the pool is overlooked by the Empty Chairs, 168 glass-and-bronze chairs set out in nine rows signifying the loss of life. Each seat is meant to symbolize the empty chair at the deceased's families' dinner table and each is engraved with the name of the victim, with unborn babies featuring on the seat of their mother and nineteen smaller chairs representing the children who died in the blast.

Returning to Bricktown, we visited a few bars and struggled to find anything exciting or eventful that would be happening on an arbitrary weekday evening. In the end, we stood in line to buy a ticket to watch the minor league Oklahoma

Redhawks play at the 13,000-seat AT&T Brickyard Ballpark. Bec didn't want to sit through an entire game, though, so instead we decided to watch a couple of innings from possibly the best seats in the house, which had a commanding view overlooking the entire stadium—the front seats of our rental car on the eighth level of a multistory car park.

The 100-mile drive from Oklahoma City to the strangely named town of Okmulgee is a pretty dull but necessary one, as although it lies an hour north of the town of McAlester (our destination), it was the home of the closest motel with a vacancy.

The historic city of McAlester, population of just under 20,000, is the largest city in the Native American Choctaw community and is home, according to the WELCOME TO MCALESTER sign, to COWBOYS AND ITALIANS. Through coal mining in the nineteenth century, the city gained popularity with Italians who came to work in the mines, and an act in 1907 joined McAlester with South McAlester to form one municipality. More recently, the city was the location for the trial of Terry Nichols for his role in the Oklahoma City bombing, and just seven months before our arrival, McAlester experienced a major ice storm, which left many parts of the city without water and electricity for a week—damage in rural areas was described in the local newspaper as "looking like 1,400 tornadoes came through."

In the summer, the temperature pushes the mercury to 100 degrees, and to take its mind off the sweltering heat, the city is proud to host the Oklahoma State Prison Rodeo—an event entered not only by regular professional cowboys but also by inmates from the local and statewide penitentiaries. It's the largest rodeo in the world to be held behind the walls of a jail. The sixty-seventh annual Prison Rodeo was set to be one of the biggest yet—there was a record number of entrants for the three-day spectacle, and it coincided with Oklahoma's centennial (it'a actually an event which is only thirty-three years younger than the state itself). To learn more about the event and the history of McAlester, Bec and I went in search of the building which had become our first port of call in any town—the chamber of commerce.

Set in an old nursing home, the McAlester Chamber of Commerce not only had our tickets for the two shows, but the clerks there were more than informed on the event and the town. Along with hundreds of IPRA (International Professional Rodeo Association) riders, inmates from eleven correctional centers across Oklahoma would compete over the three days. For only the second year, two of the jails in contention were all female and would be competing by the same rules and ride on the same crazed animals as their male counterparts. I picked up a few pamphlets and browsed posters and newspaper clippings about the event.

"If watching a bull skewer a pedophile isn't reason enough to vacation in Oklahoma, then nothing is," quoted one article. But I had seen many earlier reports on the Internet that the event badly mistreated animals, and many have declared that the Prison Rodeo is simply "state-sponsored cruelty." Personally, I couldn't possibly comment on something which I hadn't witnessed myself, and I was only hoping the event wouldn't be anything like the three-hour rodeo I once watched with my dad in Cheyenne in 1997. I was bored to tears.

The Oklahoma State Penitentiary is a formidable place. Its solid, towering beige edifice shows no evidence of its age, and rifle-bearing wardens overlook the jail's perimeter from the dozen turrets 50 feet above the ground. Prior to Oklahoma's statehood in 1907, all its felons sentenced to jail were sent to Kansas and kept at a cost of 25¢ per day, but following the state's admission to the Union, McAlester was decided upon as the site for the state's penitentiary. When $850,000 had been approved, construction began in 1908; inmates who had been originally sent to Kansas returned to Oklahoma and set about building their own future cells and jail blocks.

All the buildings first built, with the exception of the New Cellhouse, still stand today and by the looks of the outside, they haven't seen a lick of paint since they were erected. The New Cellhouse was destroyed three years after $30 million worth of damage was caused to the building following the most costly riot in American history on July 27, 1973. Five years after the riot, a federal court found that the conditions within the penitentiary were unconstitutional, and additional buildings were built. Today, the prison is home to medium-security prisoners as well as hardened criminals in the jail's newest addition, H Unit. Here murderers, rapists, kidnappers, and armed robbers live alongside one another in a maximum-security unit whose features include disciplinary segregation cells, death row, and the lethal injection chamber, where since 1976, eighty-three men have drawn their final breath. Between 1915 and 1972 (when the death penalty was briefly outlawed in America) according to the Oklahoma Department of Corrections' website, a further eighty-three prisoners have died while incarcerated in McAlester: eighty-two as a result of electrocution and one by hanging. Currently, eighty-two prisoners await death in the penitentiary, one of whom is named Richard Smith.

Surrounded by the rather prosaically named Perimeter Road, the west side of the correctional center is slightly more inviting—color is used on the walls. Between two turrets

painted in red, white, and blue (and looking more like giant
Lego bricks forcibly prised together) stood a giant gateway,
below which a drawbridge and moat wouldn't have looked
out of place. Because a simple walk through the gateway
would lead us behind the walls of a maximum-security prison,
a mere matter of yards away from convicted felons, two wardens armed with shotguns and rifles were poised atop each of
the turrets, and several uniformed men and women were positioned in front of the entrance. We approached the gateway
to begin what we knew would be a rigmarole of questions and
body searches, and immediately discovered just how stringent and incredibly tight the security was.

"Any tobacco or knives?" asked one young woman.

"No," I replied.

"OK. In ya go."

Once inside, the rodeo area is an impressive sight. Built
specifically to stage the annual event, the 14,000-capacity
arena is made up of proper seating at the very front and concrete blue-and-red–painted terraces overlooking the rows of
seats. At the far eastern end, huddled behind the chutes in
two caged areas of the seating, stood the male and female inmates who would be riding the animals later in the evening.

As we sat in our front-row seats and awaited the beginning of the rodeo, country and western music filled the arena
in preparation for the start of the rodeo. I don't know about
you, but I find country and western music to be pretty repet-
itive. I have nothing against it, but due to the similarity, both
melodically and lyrically between songs of the same ilk, it is
incredibly difficult to recognize when one song ends and another begins, as I noted earlier. I did notice that a great way
to start such a song would be with the line "I was heading
down to [insert Tulsa, Memphis, Nashville, Austin, or a similar city name here]." Subsequent verses can be filled quite

effortlessly by using words such as *whiskey, jukebox, beer*, or *pickup truck*, and with a guitar or banjo as a stringed instrument accompaniment, you'll be onto a winner.

As preparations were still being made by the event's organizers, many in the arena were already on horseback and parading around the perimeter, throwing objects into the crowd. Believing it to be free food or a gift of some sort, I stood up and raised my arms to suggest I wanted whatever they were handing out. Unfortunately, the riders turned out to be members of God's P.O.S.S.E., an evangelical organization whose members work within the Criminal Justice System, and what they were handing out were free copies of the Bible.

Finally, the MC flicked on the microphone and welcomed the seven thousand-strong crowd to McAlester and Oklahoma and the world's biggest behind-the-walls rodeo. A group of people known as the Canadian Valley Rangerettes, an all-female equestrian drill team, stormed into the ring clad in red, white, and blue and wielding American flags as they raced through the arena, throwing dirt into the air as they weaved and slalomed their way through one another with brilliantly timed equine choreography to the tune of "America the Beautiful." Following this, a quick invocation to Jim Shoulders, a rodeo legend who had passed away two months before, was announced. We were almost thinking that we had escaped a national anthem since they started playing "America the Beautiful," but then country and western performer Jarrod Birmingham took to the microphone and did the inevitable.

I was one of the lucky ones. Being seated on a chair next to some railings, I could place my hands in my pockets and lean against the iron bars until we could sit back down again. Three seats to my left, a teenager had noticed my lax posture and had adopted a similar stance. Upon noticing this, his mother quickly took her hand away from her heart and clipped him around the ear for insubordination before returning to her reverential pose. By now it was eight-thirty, so at least we knew what time we could arrive for the following day's show to skip the preliminary patriotism.

The whole event was split into fourteen separate events. Only four would be contested by the professional rodeo and there were three unique events you wouldn't see anywhere else. The first was the Mad Scramble, where all of the chutes are opened and the arena explodes with wild bulls, broncos, and inmates determined to stay mounted—a perfect show starter guaranteed to get the audience excited.

And it certainly did.

No sooner had the chutes opened than Soson Anderson, a female inmate from the Mabel Bassett Correctional Center (and in for four separate counts of shooting with the intent to kill), was thrown into the air like a rag doll.* During the ensuing melee, a team of medics entered the fray and rushed to her aid while trying to avoid a similar fate themselves. As the frantic spectacle came to an end and the beasts returned to their pens, Soson was strapped to a stretcher and became the first of many people to leave the arena supinely.

As the pros showed the crowd how to wrestle steers to the ground, tie their legs together, and leave the ox to loosen the double knots himself, the crowd were introduced to one of the events for which the Oklahoma Prison Rodeo is famous.

Bull Poker, as it's known, has little to do with royal flushes or straight faces, and has more in common with musical chairs, albeit a more brutal version of the game. Basically, a

---

*The program doesn't state what the inmates were in for, but the Oklahoma Department of Corrections' online offender search is most useful.

garden table is placed 20 feet from the door of a chute and while music plays, five men circle the table until it stops. At that point, each participant sits in the closest seat and a 2,000-pound angry bull is released from the adjacent pen. The final inmate to remain in his chair wins a cash prize and leaves with his limbs intact (and presumably excrement in his pants).

The crowd rises from their seats at the announcement of Bull Poker—they are excited by the prospect of an inmate or two leaving the arena on a stretcher or a bull's horns.

It was certainly a spectacle when the music stopped and the inmates took their positions, the MC's voice shrieked in anticipation as the chute door swung open and a bovine tank on steroids emerged. Immediately, the man positioned closest to the bull, whose back was facing the mammal, darted out of the way as the beast charged straight for the table. It lowered its head and for a nanosecond, the belligerent beast seemed to have disappeared beneath several feet of garden furniture. When it came back up, the white table had been destroyed, snapped clean in half by the beast's upward head thrust, which sent fragments of plastic and inmates into the night sky. After only a matter of seconds, a "winner" was declared. On the ground was a chair holding a nervous wreck of a man, cowering and witnessing the desolation around him, grabbing hold of his seat in fearful determination and looking like a victim of a hostage crisis. Bull Poker is definitely one of the crowd's favorites, so much, in fact, that as I consulted the program, I saw that another round of inmate goring was due later in the evening.

If an inmate being impaled by a ton of aggressive bull isn't your cup of tea, your evening might be brightened by a gentleman dressed as a clown who hides in barrels to protect him from the animals. If at any point in the proceedings, the crowd seemed unimpressed or bored, Ron Hunter, with painted face and extravagant clothing, was on hand to drum up support and interest from the audience by cracking a joke instead of a rib. The high school principal's career as rodeo clown began in 1985 after he commented that the current clown was horrible. Dared to try it himself, he took over the role and has been at the Oklahoma State Penitentiary Prison Rodeo ever since. For the most part, he completes his duties very well, and although a great deal of his material is rehearsed with the MC, you can tell he is pretty quick witted. At one point, he left his microphone on between events, and the audience got to listen in to a conversation between Ron and one of the inmates.

"Can I run to the far end of the arena?" the inmate asked.

"Sure you can," he replied. "Just make sure you stop at the gate!"

Following a severe round of bareback riding, in which inmates attempt to remain on the back of a wild horse for eight seconds while being bounced fiercely by the animal's constant bucking to remove his unwanted passenger, the animals are put to use again in the Inmate Wild Horse Race.

For my money, this is the best event. Six broncs (one for each of the three-person teams) are released from different chutes. As each one kicks and storms off in any direction it so chooses, the team must not only catch and place a saddle on the beast, but also one member must mount the horse and ride it across the finish line located at the halfway point of the arena, 100 feet from the pens. Because six teams competed at the same time, a sudden skirmish enveloped the arena, and the action was almost impossible to catch with just one set of eyes. As one team was busy shooing its horse into a corner in order to saddle it, another gang of inmates raced by, chasing its horse in an attempt to save one of their clan who was being dragged unceremoniosly across the arena floor. Back at the chutes, the Lexington Correctional Center team called for medical assistance after witnessing one of its members fall to the ground following a flurry of kicking from one of the animals. Finally, after ten minutes of nonstop cowboy action in the face of frenzied equine calcitrations, the crowd cheered as the home team brought their horse across the line. The audience returned to their seats, short of breath and still reeling from what they had witnessed. They didn't have a great deal of time with which to recuperate, though; once all of the horses had been captured and sent to the back, it started all over again, with teams from the remaining five correctional centers.

Another round of Bull Poker was announced and the crowd rose from their seats, cameras at the ready. This time, the bull ran straight past the table, saving the lives and limbs of the participants and making every single one of the inmates an instant winner.

The crowd was becoming impatient and baying for blood following an unimpressive inmate bull ride and a bloodless IRPA event involving cowgirls riding their horses around three upturned barrels in a cloverleaf pattern. But then the audience was finally introduced to the event the majority saw as being worth the entrance fee on its own.

It's called Money the Hard Way, and the premise couldn't be simpler. Every inmate enters the arena, each with the same task in mind: to rescue a pouch in which a hundred dollars is found. That sum of money may not sound like a great deal, but when you realize that it's the equivalent of four month's pay to an imprisoned criminal, it's certainly "big money" to them. The catch is that the elusive pouch is tied between the horns of a 3,000-pound Brahma bull.

As they took to the sandy arena floor, the hundred or so

inmates waited patiently for the chute to open, the brave prisoners edging nearer to the door but the majority hanging back, wanting no part of the action. The pen opened, a raging, angered bull flew out into the arena, and the song "I Fought the Law" blared out of the penitentiary's public address system. A dozen inmates surrounded the bull, and among the fracas of arms and legs reaching across the beast, bodies were tossed into the air or forcibly thrown to the ground as the bull made his way through the remainder of the convicts. As several stepped aside, a group of opportunists ambushed the creature, and one managed to dislodge the pouch. Other prisoners trailed the bull or were dragged before realizing that the pouch had already been removed and the money won. The crowd cheered to congratulate the victor on a job well done, but through the noise, an undercurrent of disappointment was detectable due to the brevity of the event.

The crowd flooded to the exits after Money the Hard Way, and the convicts who still had a round of bull riding did so to a depleted audience. As Bec and I reached our car, the show was still continuing on the inside, and the organizers were more than likely kicking themselves for not scheduling Money the Hard Way last.

Bec and I discussed the event while attempting to leave the penitentiary with the procession of other vehicles, already anticipating Saturday's rodeo and another chance to see the classic battle between wild ranch animal and convicted felon. We were so engrossed in our conversation that we accidentally took a road that went under, but did not join, the main highway, before coming to an end after a mile and a half. It wasn't a completely wasted detour, however. Because of the serene conditions of the road and the lack of other vehicles, we witnessed our first ever armadillo in the wild—a nine-banded armadillo, to be precise, whose pale taupe, bony armored shell and long tail were illuminated beautifully by my rental car's headlights just moments before I ran over it.*

*T*he next day, we arrived in McAlester having passed dozens of signs informing us that Jesus would be returning (one of which stated that HE WAS COMING HERE AND YOU'D BETTER BE READY). Now, this may be true, but if the Lord had chosen Oklahoma as a setting for the second coming, he had surely selected McAlester as a joke. Maybe I'm wrong and he did have a sense of humor after all.

We arrived in the main street just in time for the start of yet another town parade, the final time we would witness one of these spectacles. And of course, this time, the town people were out in masses to attend a parade honoring a Prison Rodeo.

In a clothes shop, just off the main parade route, Bec and I got talking to two of the assistants about the rodeo and its unsavory participants.

"Are you going tonight?" asked one.

"Yes," Bec replied. "We went last night, too."

"I do like the Prison Rodeo. My favorite participant is in it again this year," stated the other.

"What's he in for?" I asked.

"Murder," she replied breezily. "He stabbed his girlfriend seventeen times."

Bec and I stared at each other in disbelief and the assistant noticed the looks on our faces. "Oh! That was a long time ago," she continued. "He's a lovely guy really."

Outside, the parade passed without a single hitch and

---

*Don't worry—it's probably still alive. Surely all of that armor can protect itself from a four-wheel drive vehicle traveling at 50 mph.

with only a minor amount of horse shit littering the street. My personal Prison Rodeo parade highlights were the arrival of the terribly named Little Miss District 12, and the appearance of the McAlester Scottish Rite Freemasonry members, who took to the streets donned in fraternal caps behind the wheels of miniature cars, weaving in and out of each other's path and generally looking like a bunch of secret-handshake weirdos.

Following the parade, the day's prerodeo schedule of events was to be kicked off by Jarrod Birmingham, the same country and western singer who had earlier ruined my hope of attending a national anthem–free event. As he took to the stage, welcomed to McAlester by the local mayor, rainfall as I've never experienced hit the city in dramatic fashion. Quickly, people rushed beneath shop awnings or ran into buildings, darting through fast-forming puddles in an effort to stay dry as Jarrod and his entourage fled the stage. The heavens didn't just open that day, they appeared to have been severely ram raided.

Bec and I rushed to a nearby coffee shop for shelter, where we bought a single coffee and kept spitting swigs we had taken back into the mug so we wouldn't have to buy another as we waited for the torrential downpour to subside. After thirty minutes, we ventured back onto the soggy, vacant streets and beheld the scene. Drainage covers gargled under the gallons of water, which rushed uncontrollably down the sidewalk curbs. In the main street, from pipes and loose guttering, water spewed onto the already sodden and saturated ground. The entire place was devoid of revelers and stands, and neither the organizing team nor Jarrod Birmingham were anywhere in sight. So much for the post-parade celebration.

At eight-fifteen, we made our way to the penitentiary for

the second and final rodeo of the weekend. The first thing I noticed as we stepped into a field that served as a parking lot for the rodeo was that a helicopter was circling the penitentiary, shining a bright light down upon the grounds of the building. Either this was for dramatic effect during the early stages of the rodeo, or someone had escaped.

Realizing it would take a quarter of an hour to walk from our car, make our way through the rigorous security checks, and locate our seats, we believed we had timed it perfectly to miss what would have been my ten thousandth time hearing the national anthem. Just as we entered, some young girls approached me and asked if we would like to purchase a program. As I quickly displayed the copy I had bought the previous day, the arena was suddenly hushed as the words "O say, can you see . . ." echoed through the stands. Oh well.

Everyone around us stood as if anchored in position by the words of a song, and even the guards on their prospective lookouts had put down their guns to adopt the motionless position. If the prisoners had any sense, they would abandon their fifteen-year tunneling plans or rudimentary schemes of absconding, and simply use the time during the anthem to make their escape. From what I could make out, as long as the lyrics are being blurted out, any American within its audible proximity is seemingly immobilized and rooted to the spot as if suddenly paralyzed from the hair down. With one arm permanently affixed to their chests, the guards wouldn't be much of a great shot, either.

The final show promised to be a messy affair—due to the downpour earlier in the day, the arena's sandy surface had turned into a treacherous quagmire. Sadly, the majority of rounds passed without highlight. The Mad Scramble was injury-free and Bull Poker followed a similar path to the unsuccessful round in Friday's show. Such was the drought of death-defying action and lack of inmate injuries that the guy sitting behind us dozed off and was slowly dripping his soft drink onto the floor.

Suddenly, without warning, the crowd burst into life with the introduction of Daniel Liles, an inmate of the Oklahoma State Penitentiary and, in the crowd's eyes, therefore a hometown hero.

"He's a veteran," shouts the MC. "Give it up for Daniel Liles. It's his fourteenth straight year at the Prison Rodeo!"

In response, the crowd gave Liles a standing ovation for his years of service to the event. At the same time, I sat down and thought that if he was able to attend a prison rodeo for so many consecutive years, what on earth was he in for?*

His bareback riding attempt came to a disappointing end as he didn't last the eight seconds required for an official score. As a result, he jumped up and slammed his fist to the ground. I can't imagine he was a fraction as inconsolable as the family of his victim, however.

A further round of the Wild Horse Race was followed by the final Bull Poker—a dull affair where the table remained intact and the bull plowed mercilessly through only half of the contestants. The gentleman who had nodded off woke just in time to save the last sip of his drink and to see the IRPA Barrel Racing, though the earlier downpour had dampened the ground to such a degree that the riders couldn't come close to the times of those who had taken to the course during Friday's dry conditions.

Not learning from their mistakes, the organizers decided to stick with their plan to stage Money the Hard Way as the

---

*First-degree murder and "injury to a public building" (whatever that means). Liles and his brother murdered Joe Yarborough in a motel room in Oklahoma City before disposing of the body by the South Canadian River in August 1982. Standing ovation, anyone?

penultimate event, and as it started, the crowd began rattling their car keys in anticipation of a quick win and an immediate mass exodus. As the surviving masses took to the arena floor, the bull was released and was quickly surrounded by some enthusiastic inmates. Luckily for the members of the audience and the longevity of the event, the Brahma broke free from the pack and evaded the early attempt on its $100 pouch. The beast ran to the opposite end of the arena, more than 50 yards from the nearest felon, and I could sense overwhelming trepidation among the crowd and the anxious contestants. It turned and faced the 100-strong pack and as a dozen inmates stepped away from the main bulk of the mob toward a now foot-scuffing bull ready to charge, suddenly everyone's keys were placed firmly back in their pockets. Fueled by adrenaline and stupidity, a convict made a dash for the animal and quickly changed his mind midway through his assault. As a timely reminder to the other felons, the man was skewered by the behemoth's right horn and sent hurtling 12 feet into the night sky before returning in a heap to the muddy arena floor. Immediately, half a dozen inmates rushed past their fellow inmate without any concern for his well-being, their concentration fixed firmly on the prize. As they set upon the bull, two were sent to the ground immediately and violently. One of the remaining contestants escaped a viperous lunge as another made a last-ditch attempt at the pouch as he fell to the ground. Incredibly, he managed to recover it from the beast's possession, and he sprinted to safety, raising the pouch aloft and bringing the crowd to a standing ovation. Applause continued while members of the audience recovered their car keys and made a swift move toward the gate.

And that, in the unbefitting conditions of a muddy field surrounding a maximum-security penitentiary, was it. The

end of a memorable journey of American oddities and delights. Only minutes before, Bec and I had been witnessing
the seldom-seen sight of murderers and rapists being shoved,
shunted, lanced, and launched by a feverous array of bovine.
And in two months I had jumped in a pit of mud, won a film
festival, bared my bottom to hundreds of commuters, and
been "killed" by a Native American on five separate occasions.
Now all that was awaiting me was the prospect of home.

Once again, I'd had to compete against the summer temperatures that hit the United States, and as I boarded my
plane at Oklahoma Airport, I promised myself that if I ever
returned to America, it would be in the spring or autumn,
when heat wasn't something that needed to be battled con-
sistently.

I just didn't realize how soon it would be.

After returning home, I realized that the only event on
which I missed out, the World's Largest Machine Gun Shoot
in Kentucky, is held biannually. It was to be staged next in
mid-October, and pushing my credit card to breaking point,
I booked two seats on a flight to Cincinnati, with one specific
traveling partner in mind.

11. GOING OUT
WITH A BANG

After the Ford Mustang in Oregon, the rental car company's upgrades just got silly.

Shit. I've lost my passport."

"What do you mean, you've lost your passport?"

"I mean, I've lost my passport."

We hadn't even stepped foot outside my front door and Bateman was already reminding me why he is such a joy and nuisance with whom to travel.

"Where did you last see it?" I asked.

"In the pub last night. Do you reckon they're open?"

"At half five in the morning? Probably not."

Fortunately, my local pub also acts as a bed and breakfast and so someone was available to unlock the front door and allow Bateman to retrieve his passport so we could begin the five-hour drive to Gatwick Airport.

It had been cheaper to book a flight to Cincinnati than to Louisville, and we took a flight that traveled via Detroit, where we found a sparkling new airport that had tried rather too convincingly to impress. A giant fountain stands at the entrance, and beneath the numerous check-in desks and luggage carousels lies a concourse that not only links one terminal to the remainder of the airport but must be an epileptic's nightmare. At the bottom of a long escalator, a hallway approximately 100 meters long with pedestrian conveyor belts at either side uses elaborate colorful lights and a soundtrack similar to the shower scene in *Psycho* to brighten the travelers' commutes, creating an atmosphere similar to a hospital's multisensory room used for children with severe mental disabilities. Reaching the end of the psychedelic corridor, we made our way past a lady who had fainted to customs. This meant having to complete another Visa Waiver Departure/Arrival form, which would have to be presented during another meeting with whatever insolent megalomaniac was working as immigration officer at border patrol.

In light of Bateman's outstanding speeding fine, I decided to be completely truthful on my form and so ticked the box marked "Business" under "Reason for travel." Bateman opted for "Vacation" and hoped an American criminal record wasn't revealed during his light interrogation. As we made our way through the terminal, we joked that if worse came to the worst, he could spend a few days at the airport while I went and shot some guns. We soon found, however, that it was I who was destined for trouble.

I was chaperoned to booth 26, where I met Mike, a severe-looking chap with a haircut which suggested that, much to his displeasure, he had just been drafted into immigration after completing his spell of frontline fighting in Iraq.

Mike had already dispensed with one senior citizen and after having spent twenty minutes questioning a Brazilian before calling for a colleague and his Alsatian to take him to a nearby room for further interrogation, Mike called me to approach the booth.

"Good afternoon," I said with an overwhelming sense of merriment.

"Hey."

"How are you?" I asked.

"What brings you to America"—he consulted my form—"Mr. Smith?" From here on in, every question he asked managed to make my presence seem dubious and illicit, even to me.

"Well, it may sound strange," I replied, "but I'm going to a Machine Gun Shoot in Louisville."

"A Machine Gun Shoot, hey?" pointing at his own hand-gun in its holster. "Why?"

"Well, I'm writing a book about strange events in America, and seeing as we don't have them readily available in England, I thought it was ideal."

"There a company paying you to do this?" he asked.

"Well, sort of. I wrote a book for them a couple of years ago and they stupidly asked me to write another."

He looked up at me clutching my passport in his hands. "What was your first book about?"

Shit. The worst question he could have possibly asked. It was time to not lie, necessarily, but withhold certain aspects of the truth.

"Oh, I just traveled around America—a bit like this one actually."

"Oh yeah?"

"Yeah."

"Doing what?"

"Oh, nothing special."

"What though?"

"I kind of went around America breaking strange laws."

Mike stopped, looked up at me, and placed the rubber stamp at arm's length. "Breaking laws?" he asked. "You didn't evoke any interest from the police, did you?"

"Only in Chicago," I replied. "We were almost held at gunpoint. Funny story actually."

What on earth was I doing? The simple answer was "No." Instead, I was regaling Mike with the story of the time Bateman and I were mistaken for bad-assed gangsters following the slowest and least exciting police chase in history.

"Right sir, you're going to have to go to booth thirty-two," he uttered, completely interrupting me at the best bit of the story when one of the Chicago cops, upon hearing that we were from England, leant his head through the window and shouted "G'day!"

"What for?" I asked. "There's nothing wrong, is there?"

"You're a Smith. We get a lot of them, so we have to check you are who you say you are."

At this point, I was a bit nervous. Further interrogation followed, but this time I simply kept my mouth shut and luckily was allowed passage into America. I joined a queue of people waiting to hand over their Customs Declaration forms. Bateman and I were discussing my lengthy immigration process and its favorable end with relief . . . when suddenly, Mike halted his queue of tourists, departed his booth, and walked purposefully in my direction.

"Mr. Smith!" he shouted. "You said you came over here for some sort of crime spree a couple of years ago? You weren't actually arrested or cautioned for any violation, were you?"

"No," I replied. "But Bateman was stopped for speeding and didn't pay his fine in Wyoming." (Of course I didn't say that—I'd learned my lesson as soon as Mike's eyes viewed the tick next to the word *Business*).

"Oh, OK then. Enjoy your holiday," Mike replied, eyeing me with suspicion. Finally, he made his slow retreat to his booth to await unsuspecting arrivals from an Air France flight from Paris.

Upon our late arrival into Cincinnati, we checked into one of the nearest motels to the airport, remembering to stay well clear of the infamous Budget Host. When we arose, we were to make the most of our short time in the States, driving 100 miles south to Louisville to attend the opening day of the World's Largest Machine Gun Shoot.

Our rental car, a silver Dodge Charger, was the first convertible I'd ever been given by a rental company—

perfect for summer travel (if you ignore its steering ineffi-
ciencies) but not so great if you happen to be in Kentucky in
October. We found that lowering the top to be subjected to
the subsequent wind chill wasn't advisable. When we finally
arrived at our motel in Louisville, top firmly up on the car,
we realized it was too early to check in and so I approached
the desk merely to ask two questions. One I was sure they
could answer with considerable ease, while the other, I knew,
would be rather more taxing. The helpful clerks knew almost
straightaway the location of the nearest and best place where
Bateman and I could buy breakfast, but, as I predicted, struggled when asked if there was anywhere in the city that would
be showing the Rugby World Cup. The Rugby World Cup is
an international rugby tournament, similar to the World Series in a way, but with the major exception that nations from
all over the planet are invited to take part, which therefore
actually justifies the inclusion of the word *world* in its title.

When I had first booked my flight to Louisville, England's
national rugby team had been in a terrible state. They had
underachieved at the Six Nations tournament and had lost
all three of their World Cup warm-ups; even the Welsh had
beaten us. A 36–0 thrashing in an earlier group game at the
hands of South Africa left me assured that by the time I flew
to America, on the weekend that coincided with the semi-
finals of the tournament, England would have already been
eliminated.

Trust England. A scintillating display of rugby brilliance
against the Australians a week before our departure had
earned them a semi-final meeting with the French, and we
realized that we would somehow just have to fit watching the
match into our hectic three-day schedule.

Besides having a rather amusing name, the Knob Creek
Gun Range is well-known because it was once a military mu-

nitions test range and is conveniently located on the very edge of the Fort Knox Military Reservation, a major United States Army post, and the home of the U.S. Fort Knox Bullion Depository. The fortified vault holds more than 140 million ounces of gold, and the public isn't allowed inside. However, if you have witnessed the opening title sequence to *Disney's Duck Tales* in which Scrooge McDuck dives into a huge pile of gold coins, I imagine the vault to be similar if not exactly the same as that.

The biannual event is open to members of the gun range as well as the general public and as a result, the range, set in a region surrounded by nothing but forests, has a great deal of space devoted to areas in which attendees can park their cars. Such is the popularity of the event that in the lower parking lot (or field, as it is commonly known), dozens of people carrying an array of different firearms and clad in all manner of attire including bomber jackets, body warmers, and protective goggles gathered and waited patiently at the far end of the field for a yellow school bus to transport them the 800 yards to the main entrance.

Access to the event is a paltry $10 per person per day and only $5 for shooters below the age of twelve. Yes, you read correctly, *shooters younger than age of twelve.* While queuing to purchase an entrance wristband, I was offered a Rudy Giuliani campaign badge, before noticing a poster mocking the politics of Hillary Clinton. With Kentucky being such a deeply Republican area, the NRA-endorsed notice warned that "her" in the White House meant a return to a Bill Clinton–style administration, in which he lobbied for both the Brady Bill and the Assault Weapons Ban, two major pieces of gun control legislation meant to make America a safer society. How dare he do such a thing!

Once in, it becomes abundantly clear that the Machine

Gun Shoot is an eclectic mix of all my past experiences. The presence of so many gun-loving people evoked memories of the Custer's Last Stand Reenactment I had spent with Rod and Bob in Montana. The buying of weaponry and assorted paraphernalia was reminiscent of the World's Longest Yard Sale, and the politics, views, and opinions on display definitely reminded me of the Redneck Games.

We were positioned by the main range, where shooters had booked firing lanes months in advance to guarantee themselves a spot. But the events hadn't started up here yet, and the only shots that could be heard came from the two lower ranges. Before shooting started, Bateman and I decided to head for a nearby stand in search of some cheap ear protection.

"Where you from?" asked the gentleman, from behind his little counter.

"England," we replied.

"What you after?"

"Some ear defenders, please."

"They're all there," he said, pointing. We found a heap of varying designs ranging from plugs on string to the standard building-site ear muffs that wrap around the top of your head.

"It always this busy here at the shoot?" I asked, as he proffered a stuffed monkey wearing a cape with the words *Knob Creek 2008* written on it in my direction.

"Oh, no," he replied. "By tomorrow, you won't be able to move."

In the end we each opted for a set similar in size and shape to little Walkman headphones stylish in the late 1980s. Before we could even rip them from the packet, though, the warning that a ten-minute shoot was about to begin was sounded, and then all hell broke loose. No sooner had one bullet broken free of its chamber than a horde of ammunition was unleashed into the range, sending tremors through the ground as a barrage of deafening crashes, bangs, and explosions created a wall of sound that thundered toward me in an unrelenting onslaught. As the shooting area became little more than a haze, the blast created by the firing of a monolithic cannon positioned at the far side of the field reverberated through my legs and engulfed the crowd in a plume of smoke. As more armaments caused untold damage to the refrigerators, old cars, and metal drums placed by the organizers for use as targets, the hundreds of detonations created such an overwhelmingly loud noise that I could no longer hear the sound of the helicopter that had been hovering above my head ever since the seemingly eternal racket began. Next, an M4 assault rifle added to the din and as it dismissed its cartridges in blisteringly quick succession, its empty shells flew out, streaming down the back of the gentleman to its left in a continual waterfall of lead. With no break in the din since the beginning, the firing reached its conclusion, with a cacophonic crescendo of blasts, eruptions, and ear-splitting shots. The throng of exhausted spectators and I began to remove our protective headwear (or fingers) from our ears and surveyed a torn and battered field, leaving almost perfect silence and a distinct smell of gunpowder lingering in the air.

Because it was only the opening afternoon of the three-day festivities, we decided to use Friday as a time for exploring the wonders of the Machine Gun Shoot, and would not be parting with our money to participate until later on in the event. On the lower range, a field which was perhaps half the size of the main range, people waited patiently in line to try their hand at a plethora of intimidating firearms that could be hired and shot for as little as $20. It was also the location of the Jungle Walk, a competition in which each entrant was handed a semiautomatic submachine gun and had to shoot a series of targets in the quickest time possible. Since the Jungle Walk was fully booked until the following day, Bateman and I decided it was best if we left the Knob Creek Gun Range and used the remainder of the day to grab something to eat and find a bar that would definitely be showing Saturday's all-important rugby game.

Due to Bateman's job as a person who beats up unruly people (otherwise known as a doorman at one of Newquay's nightclubs), he was in constant need of protein. If he wasn't drinking one of those obscene milk shakes, then he demanded chicken; and for a person of Bateman's stature, his poultry requirements added up to an entire farm. Forgetting the fact that Wal-Mart is a huge conglomerate with the wealth of a small European nation, it's a good thing that we found one with a delicatessen equal to the task of fulfilling Bateman's dietary desires. Upon returning to our motel, the meal had almost satisfied his appetite, and his early whining for yet another meal came to an end when he thankfully fell asleep at only six in the evening.

I crept out of the room and jumped into the Dodge to make my way down from our accommodation on Bardstown Road in search of Molly Malone's Irish Pub, in the heart of Louisville's entertainment district, which, I was told by the clerk at the motel's front desk, would be the best possible chance to watch the game.

My journey on Bardstown Road, in the direction of Louisville's downtown area, was going well—with each of the many bars that passed my window, the possibility of the match being broadcast somewhere in the vicinity increased. Suddenly, my progress was abruptly halted by the obstruction of a police barricade, dozens of cops, and several squad cars surrounding a man in a blood-stained jumpsuit holding a large kitchen knife in his right hand. As ordered by one of the officers, I dutifully took an alternative route . . . and then found a place to park on a side street several blocks away and walked back up to see what was going on.

Upon leaving the car, I heard an explosion similar to a gunshot that resonated through the narrow alleys. Running back toward the barricades through the commotion of sirens and whistles, I passed a child who had seemingly suffered a bullet wound to the stomach and had slumped onto his mother's lap as she cradled his tiny limbs. No one seemed to care. Pedestrians would simply walk by not batting an eyelid.

And they were right to do so.

As a hearse approached at the top of the hill, followed by a group of teenagers in the long, mournful ghost masks made famous by the series of *Scream* films, it soon became apparent that no crime had been committed and there wasn't a knife-wielding maniac on the loose. In actual fact, the streets had been closed off for Caulfield's Halloween Parade. And why not? After all, it was October the 12.

In my search for Molly Malone's, I made my way through numerous Freddy Kruegers, Jason Voorhees, and more demonic and gruesome characters including the chainsaw-wielding Leatherface from *The Texas Chainsaw Massacre* and Richard Simmons (just kidding—mass murderers are one thing, but that's just taking it too far. Children were at this event!). Eventually, I made it to the Irish bar, which, bolstering my hopes of them showing the match, was directly next door to The Celtic Center, a gift shop selling Irish merchandise advertising the international rugby tournament. Fortunately, Molly Malone's would be broadcasting the match. Unfortunately, it wouldn't be shown live and was instead to be broadcast twenty-four hours following the game, at exactly the same time Bateman and I would be at the Cincinnati airport awaiting our flight home.

A live sporting event shown a day after it took place? Is there any sense in the idea?

The owners of The Celtic Center were sitting outside their business awaiting the remainder of the Halloween parade, but they didn't know of anywhere in the entire city that would be showing the titanic clash. Defeated, I made my way back to the car trying first not to stomp my feet in rage, and then not to dance like the animated Ghostbusters did, as Ray Parker Jr.'s 1984 hit blared out the speakers of a passing 1959 Cadillac Ambulance decorated perfectly to match the vehicle used in the film.

After returning to the Quality Inn, Bateman was still fast asleep in a now pitch-black motel room and so I made my way to the front desk. With the help of Terence in reception, a copy of the local Yellow Pages, a Louisville entertainment tourist guide, and Terence's laptop, we spent over an hour contacting sports bars, restaurants, nightclubs, and even out-of-state gambling establishments in a bid to find somewhere that would be showing the World Cup Rugby. Sadly, the match happened to kick off at exactly the same time as a game between the Universities of Kentucky and Louisiana in American football (a sport similar to rugby but much softer owing to the players' helmets, padding, and protective clothing).

After numerous phone calls and Google searches, we finally found a drinking establishment that would be showing the game live: Molly Malone's. And not the one on Bardstown Road, either. In fact it was Molly Malone's Irish Pub of Covington, 100 miles northeast of Louisville, who stated proudly that they were the only pub in the entire state of Kentucky that would be showing the game live.

As Bateman awoke, I told him about the location of the bar and we planned the following day with military precision, covering every minute in detail. We would have breakfast at eight and arrive at the Machine Gun Shoot an hour later to ensure ourselves of an early slot on the Jungle Walk. At one in the afternoon, we would begin the drive to Covington, watch the rugby from three until five, and return to Knob Creek a little before seven so as not to miss the highlight of the weekend: the Night Shoot. Barring extra time or a mechanical breakdown, it was a foolproof plan.

Or it would have been if I'd asked Terence for a wakeup call. Bateman and I woke at nine-thirty and arrived at the Machine Gun Shoot ninety minutes later than planned. Thinking this may have ruined our chances of taking part in the Jungle Walk, Bateman and I ran past the cannon and machine guns on the main field and made our way down to the lower range. A huge queue, snaking its way up the path, waited in line to hire random firearms from vendors on the range, and there were several people skulking around the sign-up desk for the Jungle Walk. Kevin, dressed in a camouflage jacket, a cap, and jeans looked up at me as I approached him.

"Hiya," I said. "I was just wondering when the next available time is for the Jungle Walk."

"Well, next slot is gonna be around two-thirty," he replied.

"Ah. That's a bit of a problem for us, you see. We're going to leave to watch a rugby match at one. Neither of us are going to win, either, so can you possibly sort something out?"

Kevin ran his hand across his clipboard while stroking his beard with the other. "I'll tell you what I'll do," he said. "You sign up and pay now, and when you get back from your game, we'll sort something out. To save more time, my buddy's doing a safety talk and taking questions on the course right now, if you wanna listen."

I signed mine and Bateman's names onto the bottom of the list and heard the strangest response I had ever heard from someone after discovering my name. I'm used to someone calling me Dick or commenting on how common a surname such as Smith is, but Kevin's response was certainly unique. "Richard Smith, huh?" he said in bewilderment. "Sounds more like a disease."

I've never been very good at paying close attention or following orders—perhaps that's the reason why during a charity parachute jump once, after having spent two weekends training in how to perform the perfect departure and descent, I ended up bungling out of the plane in a downward spiral before pulling on the wrong toggles and landing in a heap almost half a mile away from the airfield. The Jungle Walk briefing was the same. I would try to listen intently to the man, but even though I knew I would be handling a dangerous weapon, my mind began to drift onto trivial matters involving the power cables behind the man and the wart on the left side of his neck. As a result, all I could remember was that they wouldn't tell us where the targets were and there was a certain time when we were prohibited from shooting. I think. Or it may have been a time when we had to shoot nonstop.

As to not join any queue for firearms that could result in us missing the match, we decided it was best if we simply browsed the aisles of Knob Creek's military gun show. In all honesty, the sale wasn't too dissimilar to some of the gun stands I had seen on U.S. Highway 127 at the World's Longest Yard Sale. With the exception of the occasional night-vision scopes and grenades, which both had price tags attached, we found that the SS uniforms and Nazi accoutrements had made an unwelcome return to tabletops, as well as a T-shirt Bateman wanted to buy with the words GIVE WAR A CHANCE! HAPPINESS IS A MUSHROOM CLOUD emblazoned atop a smiling face and nuclear explosion. I searched in vain for a souvenir, but either the objects were too expensive or I didn't actually know what they were. Anyway, there was almost nothing I could have bought which customs probably wouldn't question me about the moment I returned home.

At one exactly, we left the range amid a torrent of gunfire from another ten-minute blitzkrieg from the automatic weapons, the occasional cannon fire, and the introduction of a Gatling gun, which alone caused a wild and unrelenting surge of gunfire that showered the range in a turf-uplifting barrage. Hopping back into the Dodge, we set off for Covington.

Just a mile from the Ohio border, overlooking both the Cincinnati skyline and the beautiful John A. Roebling Suspension Bridge, was Molly Malone's. Downstairs, the bar was well lit and the place exuded a gentile ambience as friends settled down to watch the American football game. As rugby fans, we were shown to the staircase to the upper-most extremities of the pub's three stories. A musky smell greeted us along with a mix of Australian, French, and English supporters (as well as a small number of Americans who had probably wandered in by mistake). We approached the bar, ordered a couple of drinks, and paid $20 each for the privilege of watching the match.

In the end, the 200-mile journey, the overpriced drinks, and the extortionate fee for viewing didn't matter an iota, when a last-minute drop goal 4,000 miles away in Paris saw half of the room on its feet and England's progression to the final.

"Right, you drive. I'm gonna carry on drinking," demanded Bateman. He headed into a nearby gas station's shop as I filled the tank.

Over a hundred miles and six cans for Bateman later, we arrived back at Knob Creek. By now, the day had entered the twilight hour and neither of us was overly keen on taking part in the Jungle Walk. Bateman simply wanted to continue his celebrations and I was only too happy to join in. We approached Kevin and told him that we believed the conditions were too dark and that we would like our money back.

"Are you sure?" he asked. "We can do it in this light, you know."

"Are you sure?" I asked, hoping he would reconsider or stall enough so the light faded even further.

"Yeah. We'll give it a go," he quipped.

"Thing is," I replied, "England won, and my friend is pretty drunk." Bateman wasn't drunk at all, but I imagined that if I said he'd only had a few, Kevin would still hand us an Uzi.

"Oh, here's your money back then," he groaned in disappointment.

With my money securely in my wallet, Bateman and I made our way back up to the main range for the Night Shoot, Knob Creek's weekend highlight. There was no set time the Night Shoot was to take place—the brochure I was handed on arrival stated simply that it would be staged at some point between five and ten. But I figured we hadn't missed it. I'm no genius but I worked that something called a Night Shoot would more than likely have to occur after it gets dark.

A crowd of maybe a thousand people had gathered behind the range and on the roof of a building that overlooked it. As Bateman and I took to the roof, we jostled for position among a throng of people who must have drawn a similar Night Shoot–must–happen-at-night conclusion. Several pickup trucks appeared on the range to arrange metal drums and pyrotechnical equipment on the field. Twenty minutes of general fannying about followed, the audience grew impatient, and rumors that "it would start any minute now" circulated a number of times.

As a helicopter circled overhead, I was reminded as to why the Night Shoot hadn't already begun. All weekend, raffle tickets had been sold to visitors of the Machine Gun Shoot, with the first prize being a trip in a helicopter to fire the opening few shots of the Night Shoot. As the chopper hovered above the range, short, infrequent gunshots could be heard. Compared to the earlier rumbles from the range, they sounded as if someone was aiming at the targets with a potato gun. After a couple of minutes, the helicopter banked to its left, pointed its nose to the ground, and disappeared over the trees. At that moment, I could hear tons of camera and video equipment quickly being turned on and focused on the darkness in front.

A quick crackle from the right of the range was followed shortly by a bombardment of bullets. Being the Night Shoot, tracers (special bullets that burn brightly to enable the shooter to follow the bullets' trajectories) were allowed to be used and so the range quickly became an arena of explosions and beautiful technicolor as if a firework factory had suffered a terrorist attack. A series of the pyrotechnics were struck and half a dozen plumes of flame filled the night sky from the metal drums on the ground, illuminating the entire range.

As further explosions filled the air, tracers stormed the field like a belligerent rainbow, along with an unyielding din that made the Siege of Stalingrad seem like Sunday school. Ten minutes later, the final shots were fired, like a solitary clap following a round of applause, and the crowd around me stood in awe and disbelief, as Bateman and I quickly headed for the gate.

* * *

*A*n early shower the following morning helped a great deal to clear the hangover that had enveloped every sensory part of my body. Even after I had eaten breakfast and restored lost fluids to myself, something didn't seem quite right . . . I felt as if I were missing something. I looked around. My wallet and phone were both on top of the television, and the car keys were on the floor. It was Bateman's bed that was what was wrong—it remained empty and certainly hadn't been slept in.

I knew I needn't worry. Bateman had done this to me once before in a strange town named Grand Island in Nebraska, which was neither grand nor an island. That night he had disappeared after some libations and had arrived back at the motel a little after noon the next day. I imagined he would do the same this time round.

I tried to cast my memory back to the hazy details of the night before. I distinctly remembered visiting several bars on the road where the Halloween parade was held, and when I was offered a free lift home when the final bar on our post-victory celebration bar crawl closed its doors, I didn't think returning to the motel at 3:30 a.m. was too much to ask. Bateman disagreed and the last I saw of him, he was getting into a car with four complete strangers.

Phew! At least that meant he was going to be fine. Right?

An hour passed and there was no sign of him. At noon, I visited the local Wal-Mart and bought a sandwich for lunch, before returning to the motel to check out and to ask if any of the staff had seen or heard from him. They hadn't, and so I did what any good friend in a similar situation would have done: I looked for him somewhere he definitely wouldn't be and I made my way to the Knob Creek Gun Range for the final day of the Machine Gun Shoot.

Either the majority of people had already had their fix of gunfire earlier in the weekend or they'd found themselves in the anonymous vortex into which Bateman had slipped, because compared to Saturday, Sunday at Knob Creek was like a ghost town. The main range was still unleashing hell and fury, but few people were perusing the aisles of the gun sales, and, more important, the queue that made its way up the bank away from the rental range a day before was totally nonexistent today. Two days of witnessing constant gunfire and the Jungle Walk reimbursement money burning a hole in my pocket told me that the lack of line was a sign: It was about time that I added to the noise and tried my own hand at pulling one of the triggers.

Above the sign-up desk was a large list of weapons and how much the use of the gun and a certain number of rounds would cost. As a person who thought an M4 magazine was a publication for motorway enthusiasts, the display may as well have been written in Arabic or hieroglyphics for all I understood about semiautomatic firearms. I tried to make sense of the "BAR—20 rnd mag," "M249 Minimi—50 rnd belt," and other nonsensical abbreviations, but finally opted for the only weapon of which I had heard.

"I'll have a go with the Grenade Launcher," I said.

"You do know it only shoots fake grenades with paint inside, don't you?" replied Brad, who stood in front of the armory of weapons.

"Does it?" I replied. "In that case, I'll go for the AK-47."

In actual fact it was an AK Valmet, the Finnish version of the terrorists' favorite, and a gun that made Brad attempt a quote from the Quentin Tarantino movie *Jackie Brown*.

"AK-47," he chuckled. "The very best there is for when you absolutely, positively got to kill every motherfucker in the room."

I nestled the butt of the assault rifle into my right shoulder, and Brad positioned my legs so I held most of the pressure on my back leg. Then he asked me if I wanted the gun to fire single shots or to place the AK into automatic mode.

"I'll start off with singles, please," I replied.

As I squeezed the trigger gently with my finger, the tip of the rifle rose swiftly into the air, as a bang echoed through the range. It sent a slight twinge into my shoulder and left a rather impressive-looking hole in a car door over 50 yards away. Another shot into the car door followed before I repositioned myself and aimed at a refrigerator. Gaining confidence after a couple of shots into the ground, I asked Brad to switch the beast into automatic mode and I let loose with the remainder of the magazine. I tightened my grip as the rifle reacted like a wild animal in my arms and began to shoot whatever it chose. The magazine came to a sudden end after just a couple of seconds of shooting into the air. I wasn't surprised at the brevity of its automatic display—the Valmet can discharge an impressive seven hundred bullets a minute.

Suddenly I needed further unnecessary destruction of appliances and old vehicle parts, and I threw another $40 in Brad's direction and selected another gun from the rack. I chose one that reminded me of the A-Team. The old green hunk of metal was a Heckler and Koch G3, an automatic battle rifle first built by the West Germans a decade after the conclusion of the Second World War. It was about the same length as the AK, but was a bulkier and firmer piece of weaponry, weighing at least 10 pounds. It felt cumbersome in my hands and as I once again opted to begin with just single shots, my legs had fallen completely out of position. If Saturday's queue suddenly reappeared, filling the alleys with tens of dozens of marksmen, it would have been pretty obvious to any passerby just which one of us was English.

I took suggestions as to what I should shoot at from some spectators, and Brad advised that I should finish off the round in automatic mode. With just a twenty-round magazine placed into the gun in the first place, the remainder of the bullets took what seemed like a little squeeze's worth in order to use up. Goodness knows how much the Night Shoot and regular bursts of artillery were costing the owners of the guns. The seconds I'd spent with the G3 and the AK were not only one of the most exhilarating experiences in my life, but also the quickest $80 I'd ever spent.

I was enjoying my time with Brad and the other gun-obsessed entourage, but I was reminded that I was doing so on my own. Bateman was still missing. So I returned to the motel, where I expected he would be waiting for our trip to the airport.

He wasn't.

Now it was serious. It was half two in the afternoon, and our flight left Cincinnati airport, a good hour and a half's drive away, in just over four hours' time. Goodness knows what had happened to him.

Unfortunately, I have a transatlantic touch of death about me—whenever I travel to America, someone very well known seems to die. When I first visited the States in 1997, Gianni Versace was murdered the very day I arrived. In 1999 Jill Dando (a British television presenter), Oliver Reed, and Alf Ramsey (England's triumphant 1966 World Cup winning coach) completed a hat trick of heaven-bounds in just the space of a week; and during the time I spent just four days in Las Vegas for my twenty-first birthday, both the famed 1966 World Cup final commentator Kenneth Wolstenholme and

Dudley Moore passed on. The death of CBS anchor Peter Jennings occurred when Bateman and I were touring the nation on a frivolous crime spree in 2005, and Mike "Frank Butcher" Reid had kicked the bucket a day after our hopes had been sunk in Heber Springs' Cardboard Boat Race just three months before I had boarded the plane for the Machine Gun Shoot.

Perhaps I should just stay at home in future and not jeopardize the lives of countless celebrities by clearing customs at American airports.

The only reason I point out this strange peculiarity is that as far as I knew no one famous had died since my arrival in Cincinnati three days before. What if, in a cruel twist of fate, the Grim Reaper had Bateman in his sights this time round? What's worse was that if he really was dead, I'd probably be the investigating detectives' prime suspect.

At three, I had waited as long as I could and with the risk of missing the flight and the money I had spent on the tickets, I packed both of our bags into the trunk of the Dodge and made my way to Cincinnati, hoping that Bateman had somehow sponged a lift to the terminal from whoever he had spent the previous night with.

At a little before five, I had checked in, proceeded through the relevant security checks, and settled down in the departure lounge in front of an NFL game between the Dallas Cowboys and the New England Patriots. Following one of my occasional glances over my shoulder in a hope that Bateman would appear behind me, my name was announced on the airport's public address system—I was advised to contact my nearest airline operative.

As I searched the various gates and corridors for a member of staff, I was reminded of the only other time my name had been announced at an airport. It was at Alicante Airport in Spain, after I had just finished watching England play Switzerland in the 2004 Football European Championships in a bar with my friend Max Dennis. I was a little worse for wear and after the announcement was made that I was the only passenger to have not boarded the craft, I reached the gate with seconds to spare and eventually fell asleep in the toilet. I don't care what you say about airplane lavatories, I sat on the toilet with my head in the conveniently placed sink, and I could have lost any bodily fluid from any orifice during the flight home, and it would have been collected safely with little mess or fuss.

Eventually, I found an appropriate representative and following a lengthy telephone conversation between him and some other Cincinnati airport staff member, I was handed a number which I was asked to call.

It was the number of the Emergency Room at Louisville's University Hospital, and as I rushed to the nearest pay phone to check on my friend, my hand was shaking badly.

As it turned out, Bateman's life wasn't in any sort of danger at all. In the late morning, he had been found asleep on the grounds of one of Louisville's universities by several members of an American football team who needed his body moved in order to begin their practice. They called a police officer to wake him. It seemed that after spending the early hours at a basketball player's party in the suburbs of the city, Bateman had been dropped off at the motel by the same people who had offered him a lift when I last saw him. Unfortunately, it turned out to be one of the other two Quality Inns in Louisville, and so after walking a bit to try to find the right motel, Bateman gave in and collapsed. Because the motel's room key was his only possession after losing both his passport and wallet during the night, the policeman had no other choice but to take him to the hospital, where the nurses rang the

only number on the card . . . which put them through to the
local branch of Domino's Pizza. With Bateman finally coher-
ent and making sense, he informed the nurse that he and I
had a flight to catch that day and that I could probably be
contacted at the airport.

Whatever thoughts I had of returning to Louisville to
pick him up were soon dismissed when it turned out that he
didn't know where his passport was and that according to
the nurses, all he was suffering from was a severe hangover.
He didn't need me to hold his hand. And anyway, Bateman
had always complained about the short length of our stay.
Now he had the chance to experience Louisville for a little
bit longer . . . albeit from a hospital bed, on his own with no
money. Still, a holiday's a holiday.

Stepping aboard Northwest Airlines flight 32 from Detroit to London, I breathed in what was to be my final gulp of
American air. There would be no more late additions to the
plan, and the concrete runway beneath me would be the final
piece of U.S. soil I would see. I had visited America almost
half a dozen times before, and if this was the last time I
would see the country, I was glad that this was how it was
done—an eighty-day journey of wonder, bewilderment, and
sometimes shameful scenes, through the heart of both the
country and its people. After visiting almost a dozen events
and festivals, meeting an array of different characters and
making many new friends, it suddenly dawned on me that
after being in the company of so many people for so long, I
was suddenly on my own. Still, maybe this final experience
wasn't one worth sharing. The movies on the plane weren't
exactly Oscar winners, and the screaming child sitting three
rows behind me made me wish that I had somehow smug-
gled the Valmet into my hand luggage.

EPILOGUE

*B*ateman made it back to the U.K. two days later wearing the very same clothes he had on when he was found, after finding his passport and booking a flight home.

When I returned home from the summer, I found that the Reenactment committee Antony and I "acted" for had sent us checks for $70, even though we had no Social Security numbers.

Unfortunately, Antony's grandmother, Elizabeth Luke, passed away peacefully on the third of November, at age sixty-four, after a brave battle with her illness.

Acknowledgments

There are several people who I'd like to thank and without whom the book would have been drab, mundane, and prosaic (okay then, even more so). With the exception of immigration officers and people who steal global positioning systems from police officers in Massachusetts, I seem to have an uncanny knack for meeting the kindest and most generous Americans each and every time I step foot onto their fair land. In every instance, I am in need of some sort of assistance or aid, and, without a prompt or gentle hinting, they react in unrelenting benevolence, like a flock of natives to a beached whale. Not least deserved of a mention are the Beatties, whose skills in cooking and open-arm Montanan welcoming made Camp Wishah-Kudah-WunWun a home away from home when Antony and I were starting out on our journey. June and Rod were the perfect hosts, and with the exception of bruising my shoulder, the pair made living in a field in the middle of the Montanan wilderness as comfortable as it could possibly be. Also a big thank you to Bob Port and his lovely wife, Jill, who along with Rick Williams and his wife, Pam, made our entire visit to the camp a lively and enjoyable one.

Also, a lot of appreciation goes to Mark Braconi and his wife, Aleks, who not only kept Antony and me sane at the Mooning of Amtrak, but who can now categorize themselves with such locations as Long Beach and the Pacific Ocean as being the only positive aspects of Los Angeles.

The kind deeds of Jeremy of the Yamaha and Honda dealership in Little Rock shouldn't go unnoticed and nor should the helpful staff of Riverside Box Supply, who provided us with cardboard, which in no part attributed to our dramatic boat building disaster. That was completely our fault. I would also like to thank Betty Seder, Ruble Upchurch, Walter Page, Gale Reed, and all of the other clerks and managers of the chambers of commerce I visited, whose names I didn't manage to learn but whose assistance and information was equally of great help.

The week Antony and I spent in Corvallis was one of the most comfortable and fulfilling of the entire journey, and this was in no small part because of the hospitality of Mary Jeanne Reynales and her husband, Dave. Thanks also to Andy Foster, Bill and Michele Powell, Peter Platt, the rest of the "Fall from Grace" crew; and thanks to the Turd for being such a worthy adversary. We really appreciated all of the gang's generosity to a couple of useless Brits who, it was quickly discovered, were useless both in front of and behind the camera.

A big thank you to Bill Eckels of the Cobbler Shoppe who acted as Britt's replacement chamber of commerce clerk, but whose knowledge of the National Hobo Convention was vastly inferior to his proficiency at cobbling.

Finally, a special thanks to Antony, Bec, and Bateman for their companionship, to my agent, Rebecca Winfield, and to my British and American editors, Katie Espiner and Lindsey Moore, for allowing me to do something I enjoy so very much, and for ensuring that the book was delivered on time.

Thanks once again to everyone, and I apologize in advance to anyone whom I may have accidentally forgotten. And I'm sure Antony would like to echo my sentiments and would do so if he was still with us. But he's back in Cheltenham.

11/08
11.09

ALSO BY RICH SMITH

Two Englishmen on a crime spree break American laws!

YOU CAN GET ARRESTED FOR THAT
2 Guys, 25 Dumb Laws, 1 Absurd American Crime Spree
$13.95 paper (Canada: $18.95) • 978-0-307-33942-3

Did you know that it's illegal to fish while wearing pajamas in Chicago, Illinois, to enter a theater within three hours of eating garlic in Indianapolis, and to offer cigarettes or whiskey to zoo animals in New Jersey?

How did these "only in America" laws come to be, do the police know they exist, and would they care if anyone broke them? In *You Can Get Arrested for That,* Englishman Rich Smith—along with his best mate, Bateman—aim to find out in this not quite Bonnie and Clyde adventure.

THREE RIVERS PRESS • NEW YORK

Available from Three Rivers Press wherever books are sold.